Teacher Diagnosis
of
Educational Difficulties

Merrill's
International Education Series

under the editorship of the late

Kimball Wiles

Dean of the College of Education

University of Florida

Teacher Diagnosis
of
Educational Difficulties

Robert M. Smith
editor

Charles E. Merrill Publishing Co.
Columbus, Ohio
A Bell & Howell Company

Copyright © 1969 by Charles E. Merrill Publishing Company, Columbus, Ohio. All rights re-
served. No part of this book may be reproduced
in any form, by mimeograph or any other means,
without permission in writing from the publisher.

Library of Congress Catalog Card Number: 69–11433

1 2 3 4 5 6 7 8 9 10-73 72 71 70 69

Printed in the United States of America

Preface

Teachers cannot wait for the results of formal tests when they attempt to plan their teaching programs. The infrequent formal testing schedules of most school systems are inadequate to aid in planning daily lessons for the teacher who knows that a child's educational performance varies from one day to another and from one subject area to another. An alert and dedicated teacher wants to know today how she must approach a student tomorrow—how she can help him get the most from his school years. She knows that each day in those years must be used as effectively as possible.

This book is designed to help the teacher use those days effectively, by guiding her in the application of day-to-day and week-to-week evaluations of student progress. Specialists in all areas of early academic and personal development have contributed methods for diagnosing the individual student's strengths and weaknesses, and have suggested remedial procedures for helping the student overcome deficiencies. The emphasis in this book is on *informal* diagnosis—methods which the teacher can use in the classroom every day. With the development of informal diagnostic ability and techniques will come the opportunity to individualize instruction, to tailor the classroom program to each student's educational needs.

Regular as well as special class teachers will benefit from the techniques of informal educational diagnosis. And, this area of evaluation is equally relevant to administrators interested in responding to children's unique differences, to curriculum developers concerned about incorporating periodic checks into curricula, to psychometricians and school psychologists, and to today's students who will be tomorrow's teachers.

The infinite variety of personalities and skills present in every classroom demands that every teacher be able to identify and assess individual strengths and weaknesses so that she can design her program to give each student the full benefit of his educational years. The contributors to this volume sincerely hope that *Teacher Diagnosis of Educational Difficulties* will awaken educators to the realization that children's differences can be met with effective educational programs when teachers develop skill in assessing those differences.

It is with pleasure that I acknowledge the skillful assistance of Mrs. Donna Cone and Miss Linda Schmidt in typing this manuscript.

R. M. S.

Contributors

Dr. George Brabner, Jr.

Associate Professor and Chairman
Department of Special Education
University of Delaware

Dr. G. Phillip Cartwright

Assistant Professor of Special Education
The Pennsylvania State University

Dr. James J. Lister

Associate Professor of Education
Department of Pupil Personnel Services
University of Florida

Dr. Betty Jane McWilliams

Professor of Speech Pathology
Clinical Director, Cleft Palate Research Center
University of Pittsburgh

Dr. John T. Neisworth

Assistant Professor
Department of Special Education
Department of Educational Psychology
University of Delaware

Dr. Robert M. Smith

Associate Professor of Special Education
The Pennsylvania State University

Dr. Elizabeth Spencer

Associate Professor and Chairman
Department of Special Educational
Ball State University

Table of Contents

ix

Teacher Diagnosis
of
Educational Difficulties

Chapter I

FUNDAMENTALS OF INFORMAL EDUCATIONAL ASSESSMENT

Robert M. Smith
John T. Neisworth

Let us begin with some assertions. First, the desire and indeed the job of the effective educator is to help the student develop higher and higher levels of competency in a variety of domains. These domains include intellectual, social, emotional, and physical competencies demanded by society, and by the community, employer, parent, and the student himself.

Second, students differ markedly in terms of these educationally relevant competencies, no matter how homogeneously they are grouped. Homogeneous grouping has traditionally been based upon gross, superficial, and often instructionally irrelevant bases. For example, pupils are often clumped together because they have comparable I.Q. scores. But, are these children not different in their current proficiencies on a host of specific and more instructionally relevant dimensions? Some

1

have a greater command of the language, some are more proficient in mathematics or reading, others show greater social competence, while still others demonstrate a marked acceleration in their psychomotor development. Even if we chose to make our so-called homogeneous groupings on a finer basis, the problem of individual differences would still occur. Let us say that we decided to group children on the basis of similarity in reading achievement. Even this grouping is absurdly too gross. Children may attain identical scores on a reading achievement test but be quite heterogeneous in certain basic skills which in turn are subsumed under the general heading of "reading achievement." Some children read faster but with less comprehension; some students are poor auditory learners and would not optimally benefit from a phonics approach in reading. No matter how students are grouped, then, they will differ from each other in so many instructionally relevant ways that almost any criterion for grouping becomes a hindrance rather than an aid to optimal instruction.

Our third assertion is that teachers must have access to frequent and specific assessment data on their students. Educators must know where each student stands on a multitude of competency measures.

Fourth, we assert that teachers are able, and are in an ideal situation, to assess their students on dozens of specific, relevant dimensions. In an informal and unburdensome way, teachers should be able to collect specific assessment data within the classroom situation.

Finally, we contend that instructional environments, materials, and strategies must be designed to move a student from a lower to a higher level of competency on any particular dimension. Continual assessment is first necessary to discover a student's status on a certain dimension and later, after pedagogic help is given to move the student to a higher level, to find out if he has reached that level of performance.

This chapter, then, is concerned with the need for informal assessment; the instructional utility of such an approach, and the problems involved. We believe that frequent, informal, and specific educational assessment is feasible, and can assist the educator in practicing rather than wishing for, or paying lip-service to, the principle of individualization of instruction.

INEVITABLE INDIVIDUALITY

That no two people are identical cannot be disputed. This fact would be true even if it were possible to control the environment so rigidly that each person in our society would be exposed to an exact duplicate of every minute aspect of the environment experienced by every other member of society. Even with environmental influences controlled in this fashion, heredity alone would account for wide patterns of heterogeneity among people. Therefore, it is impossible to exactly duplicate individuals in any way. Dobzhansky (1964) has indicated the remoteness of possible replicability of an individual through inheritance by hypothesizing that the possible combinations of chromosomes between parents which could result in the development of a child exceeds a 32-place figure. It is true that identical twins closely duplicate each other since both organisms are formed by a single egg; however, even in this situation wide variation exists in the individual characteristics of each twin because of different environmental experiences.

If it were possible to control genetic transmission so completely that everyone in our society received the identical combination of genes, wide individual differences would still exist due to the great variation in environments characteristic of our society. Hunt (1961) has summarized much of the research concerning the possible environmental variables which influence behavior and development. It should be pointed out that influential environmental factors operate during the prenatal, perinatal, and postnatal periods. Variation in the environment begins at the time of conception, continues throughout the prenatal period, when each fetus is exposed to a unique maternal constitution, and extends throughout one's life. A child's postnatal environment is peculiar to the individual. Identical twins, therefore, differ from each other because of these varying environmental influences.

Each of us differs from every other person according to genetic endowment as well as in terms of our environment. These variations result in different patterns of development among individuals in physical, social, intellectual, and personal areas. The interaction of heredity and environment produces a unique organism which behaves in a certain way, has certain capabilities for learning concepts, and develops physically in a way that is peculiar to the organism. Those at the lower extreme of the continuum of individual differences are probably the result of poor genetic endowment and poor environment. At the other end of this continuum, individuals might be the result of superior genetic endowment and a highly favorable environment. The many nuances of the interaction between heredity and environment result in an infinite variety of individuals who, as a group, display wide differences in physique, emotion, social behavior, and, of course, learning.

Educational Implications of Individual Differences

Teachers must deal with the fruits of the heredity-environment interaction. Further, educators must provide special environments to modify the product that arrives in the classroom. Perhaps the most relevant aspects of this educational environment are the strategies and materials the educator chooses to employ. Which strategy and what materials, what special environment to provide for each child, are decisions that the teacher must make and put into practice. It would be just as ridiculous to provide each child with the same special instructional environment as it would be to fit all children with the same eyeglasses or pair of shoes. Just as a particular optical prescription permits each child to have optimal vision, so must an individualized pedagogic program be prescribed for each student's education. Earlier prevailing notions of using a single method of instruction and identifying "homogeneous classes" are no longer tenable. The extreme heterogeneity manifested by children of the same age, located in the same classroom, demands more than lip-service for educational programming, if the intent is to be responsive to variation within the classroom and to the individual needs of every schoolchild.

For an effective educational program, one must be aware of more than just the individual differences among children. The teacher must know each child's strengths and weaknesses. The degree to which a teacher chooses to accept and use a strategy of this type, based on data gathered from activities which check each child's progress, is dependent on the degree to which one views individual differences among and within children as being educationally relevant or significant.

Most teachers quickly realize that students in their classes, who are labeled for administrative purposes as being relatively equivalent in their ability and performance, are often very heterogeneous. This is true in almost all classrooms, whether designed for regular or special classes. The usual classroom contains students who:

1. Do well in all school subjects by performing at a level which is consistent with their "predicted ability;"
2. Exhibit unequal achievement in certain subject areas which require similar skills for an effective performance;
3. Have developed the basic technical skills for a subject but are deficient in applying these skills effectively;
4. Have not developed basic precursive or technical skills for a subject, or apply the processes involved in the subject inconsistently;
5. Are intellectually superior and do well in all subjects, or are intellectually superior but underachieve in all subjects;
6. Are mentally retarded and do not understand regular classroom instruction;
7. Have emotional problems which impede adequate performance in academic areas, or restrict effective interaction with classmates or authority figures;

8. Have other specific problems such as perceptual-motor difficulties, communication disorders, social difficulties, or physical disabilities which reduce their ability to perform effectively at a minimum level in all areas.

The effective teacher must be cognizant of the characteristics of all of these students, and must provide an environment that will allow them optimum development despite their differences. The teacher in a typical classroom must be prepared to offer special instruction to children with learning difficulties. The uniqueness of each child requires the teacher to adjust instructional methods quickly and effectively when relevant diagnostic observations from formal and informal assessment procedures indicate a need for change. For example, if a child is having difficulty grasping concepts of grouping in arithmetic, the teacher might continue using three-dimensional objects longer than would be necessary for other children in the class. Teachers tend to move children too quickly into skills requiring higher levels of conceptualization. One child's problem with arithmetic concepts would require deviation from the usual teaching procedures, even though the procedures might be successfully employed with many other youngsters in the class.

Competent and effective teaching demands constant evaluation of the curriculum, the individual characteristics of the children, and the impact of various instructional strategies. These data provide the necessary documentation for adjusting teaching techniques appropriately.

Teachers have used achievement test scores as the primary basis for making judgments about classroom grouping. This strategy is open to question. Two youngsters in the same classroom, both of whom are exactly the same age and score at approximately the same level on an intelligence test, could be low achievers in the same subject for entirely different reasons. One might have major problems in learning to read by a phonics approach because of a basic auditory difficulty which is unrelated to the child's hearing ability. The other youngster could be achieving poorly in reading because of difficulty in learning through a look-and-say approach, which depends on using visual clues. If both children are taught to read by a phonics approach, the first child will continue to have difficulty because of the basic auditory defect, while the reading problem of the second child will be more easily corrected because the phonics approach does not emphasize visualization. Grouping according to achievement would place both students in the same group, disregarding the teaching strategy which might be preferable for each student. Through knowledge of individual differences and the manner in which each child best learns, teachers can more precisely determine the appropriate candidates for various instructional tactics. Reading groups can thus be formed on the basis of multiple criteria, using, for example, both reading achievement level and preferred reading method.

In addition to these instructional considerations, the teacher must think about other requisites for excellence in teaching. The day-to-day demands involving organization and administration of the classroom and effective articulation with other segments of the school are all important components in the process of teaching and learning. The teacher must decide which instructional media will provide the clearest presentation of subject matter. It should be obvious at this point that a complete knowledge of individual differences within a classroom requires the teacher to consider these instructional alternatives before launching into teaching. Beginning instruction without this preparation is analogous to a surgeon's operating without any prior information or diagnostic clues about his patient. The implications of the teacher's being unprepared are not as obvious as those of the unprepared surgeon; nevertheless, children will be influenced in subtle ways, to different degrees, and with substantial long-term implications when a teacher fails to consider these important matters.

Status of Assessment in Schools

The commitment to optimize each child's education will occur only after necessary adjustments are made in instructional techniques, courses of study, and teaching materials. These adjustments are possible only after clear diagnostic documentation has been provided and a tentative direction charted for each student's future educational program.

Most school systems have available some type of professional diagnostic service, either on a permanent or a consulting basis. These services are frequently provided by state departments of public instruction, which allocate a certain portion of a psychologist's time to each school district or county. These specialists are often paid by the state. Affluent school districts or cities supplement these services by employing additional diagnostic personnel; the demand for diagnostic services always exceeds the supply of psychometricians. Rural school districts and city schools with overwhelming case loads cannot supply enough additional diagnostic assistance to teachers with students in actual or potential difficulty.

School psychologists and subject matter diagnosticians devote the greatest portion of their time to "hard core" cases, those children who are in extreme academic, social, intellectual, or physical difficulty. Children who are either located in, or are candidates for, special education placement take a great amount of professional time because their problems are complex. It is not strange, therefore, for regular class teachers never to have available the services of a qualified diagnostician. This unfortunate situation is typical, in spite of severe learning problems found in many youngsters in regular classrooms.

The attenuation of assessment services in the schools is a direct result of proportionately few college and university training programs oriented toward school psychology. The number of skilled diagnosticians is not adequate to the increasing need for them. One clear reason for this lack is the extensive academic and clinical experience required of certified diagnosticians. Moreover, school systems have difficulty competing with the higher salaries offered by agencies, publishers, colleges, universities, and industries.

In frustration, school systems often find it necessary to employ untrained or inexperienced clinicians to fill the void temporarily. These people offer advice to teachers about group testing, and individually administer those tests with which they have had some minimal training and experience. Consequently, teachers receive meager, often unreliable, and frequently invalid data on their students, with little or no translation or interpretation provided. These data are many times so vague as to be meaningless in providing direction for the effective modification of a child's educational program. Test scores, IQ numbers, and medical and psychological labels are frequently reported, but have little meaning for the teacher when they offer no guide for altering instructional procedures.

This paucity of diagnostic facilities is a fundamental weakness of many school programs. The extreme heterogeneity of students in a single classroom demands that teachers adjust their programs to focus on each child's unique needs, strengths, and weaknesses. Students' individual levels of competency and their many learning problems strongly suggest the need for an informed and comprehensive assessment of each student as a prelude to individualizing instruction.

Can the Teacher Conduct the Specific Assessment?

Every new and untested procedure has potential advantages and disadvantages for the practitioner as well as for the one to whom the procedure is applied. The successful transplant of a vital organ from one person to another enhances the reputation of the surgeon, and is of clear advantage to the recipient of the healthy, functioning kidney or heart. If the procedure is unsuccessful, both the surgeon and the recipient suffer. An important criterion for success is that the surgeon be knowledgeable, technically skilled, and experienced in conducting the procedure. This situation is somewhat analogous to effective teaching. If a teacher understands the advantages of educational diagnosis, develops the required skills for evaluating strengths and weaknesses in youngsters, and is able to translate the evaluation into meaningful experiences and activities, both the child and the teacher will benefit. If, on the other hand, the teacher sees no need to consider children's differences, or is unskilled in testing for educationally relevant characteristics, it will not be possible to develop an appropriate educational prescription for each child's abilities and disabilities. An effective teacher must constantly weigh the advantages and potential hazards involved in selecting among a variety of possible teaching approaches. The position taken in this book is that teaching and learning will be effective to the degree that teachers become aware of the importance of diagnostic clues. Some of the potential advantages and disadvantages of informal diagnosis by teachers need to be discussed. Each teacher can then judge the degree to which some alteration of existing teaching strategies is realistic and advantageous to students.

Advantages of Teacher Diagnosis.   The teacher is in the best position to assess educational problems of children. Rapport between the teacher and students is typically stronger than between the children and other adults; often, children and their parents are relative strangers to each other. As an intelligent observer outside the family structure, and with relatively minimal affective involvement, the teacher should be able to assess and evaluate objectively the total spectrum of behavior which characterizes each child. Teachers are in the most desirable situation for observing the entire range of typical student behavior. This comprehensive observation is crucial if valid samples of behavior are to be gathered. The proper focus should be on the usual characteristic patterns of behavior, rather than on the rare occurrences of extreme behavior that every child demonstrates. The need to sample *characteristic* behavior of each child and techniques for doing so will be discussed later on.

Most children in school are given intellectual assessment of some kind, and are tested on a variety of achievement tests to determine class placement, among other things. The results of these more formal measures are found in the child's cumulative folder, so that whenever necessary and appropriate, teachers can refer to the data either to support some theory they may have about a child's performance or to group children for instruction. Whatever the reason for using this information, the basic assumption is always that the child's performance on the tests is valid; and that the tests are a reliable indication of his real performance. Even under the most rigorously controlled testing situation, these assumptions are questionable. The inaccurate or erroneous administration of a test; the poor choice of an instrument by a diagnostician; any number of personal or social difficulties the child might have at the time the test is administered; insufficient time for a total evaluation; or a false representation of the data through an erroneous interpretation, can invalidate the test results. The teacher must assume that the tests were administered by a qualified person, and that errors which can easily creep into the evaluation have been minimized. By employing informal diagnostic procedures during the course of instruction, a skilled teacher can check on the correctness of the data reported from formal tests. If the psychometrician concludes from a child's performance that a significant weakness in auditory memory has been demonstrated, the teacher can check the validity of this conclusion by engaging the youngster in a series of sequenced activities which require him to repeat, verbally or through gestures, items which have been presented auditorially. Asking a child to repeat digits, determining how well words to a song are remembered, observing the ability of a youngster to follow commands which have been presented auditorially, or having a child remember a story sequence, are activities which can be used to check informally on the conclusions of the formal assessments. Realistically, then, the teacher can determine quickly and effectively how much credance to give to the data gathered through formal testing by using informal diagnostic strategies in the classroom.

The primary responsibilities of teachers include manipulating the students' environment, and providing appropriate rewards for correct and acceptable behavior. The type of manipulation the teacher chooses to use, and the manner and time for rewarding behavior, are determined by the objectives established for each student and by the characteristics each child demonstrates either in support or deterrence of the realization of the educational objectives. A close relationship between the diagnostic findings and their translation into a pragmatic school program is essential. Since the teacher is responsible for executing the program, it is important that he or she be an active participant in gathering, interpreting, and using information which may have practical classroom value. If the teacher is brought into the picture after evaluations of a child have been made, and is not encouraged to make use of informal procedures to check on the child's progress on a day-to-day or week-to-week basis, there is a high probability that data will be lost, an erroneous interpretation of the psychometric evaluations will be made, and there will be a general lack of communication and coordination of efforts.

For the teacher to become skilled in evaluating and diagnosing, there is need to divide each task into its component parts. By doing so, the teacher will be able to pinpoint quickly the specific factors which hinder a child's progress in a much larger area, such as learning a sight vocabulary, learning to group objects, interacting with authority figures, or being able to tolerate the taunts and ridicule of others. Each of these large areas contains a number of specific components; if one of these parts malfunctions for some reason, the child will be unable to achieve effectively in the broader behavioral area. The teacher is in the ideal spot to pinpoint these weaknesses and to intervene with the appropriate teaching strategy at the most desirable moment.

Disadvantages of Teacher Diagnosis.   Employing the teacher as an informal diagnostician has certain potential disadvantages, many of which are obvious. Teachers may not have enough time for informal progress checks, particularly where classes are large, and where teachers and children are required to cover a certain amount of material during a prescribed time period. This instructional inflexibility does not allow the teacher to pace the program according to the children's important educational and psychological characteristics. It is unfortunate indeed that a number of teachers find themselves obligated to meet such restricting demands that adjusting instruction according to individual differences of students is completely forgotten. Succumbing to pressure of society, the community, or a strong lobby group, results in an attempt to force uniform material on children without considering their individuality. This philosophy of uniform teaching violates the cardinal requirement for effective teaching—individualization of instruction.

It is difficult to stimulate teachers to become skilled in the use of informal diagnostic procedures because most university and college teacher-training programs do not provide opportunities for learning informal classroom evaluation. Many colleges and universities require prospective teachers to complete a course in measurement and evaluation; however, this course typically focuses on formal techniques of measurement, some of which may require administration and interpretation by trained clinicians. Less attention is given to observing the behavior of children within the ongoing class. Thus, many teachers do not develop a sensitivity to techniques which might be used for evaluating behavior in a dynamic setting. They are not trained to see relationships between certain behavior and other events, or to separate a simple relationship from a clear case of cause and effect. A child might have a reading problem and do poorly in spelling because of reversals caused by visualization difficulty. Here the reading problem does not necessarily cause the spelling difficulty, or vice versa; both problems occur as the result of a third variable, which in this case is an inability to make use of visual stimuli. An unalert teacher could erroneously interpret poor achievement in reading and spelling in some cause and effect fashion, and remain unaware of the influence of this third active variable.

As teachers become skillful in diagnosing the patterns of strengths and weaknesses in children, there is some danger in their beginning to view themselves as competent school psychologists or clinicians. It is important that teachers understand the limits of their ability to diagnose educational difficulties. There are many hazards involved in administering formal clinical instruments and interpreting results without the necessary training and clinical experience. Never should teachers attempt to use tests with which they have not had experience under competent and strict supervision. To do otherwise violates ethical principles of psychology and education, and could deleteriously influence a child's educational, psychological, or social life in a very dramatic way. Teachers should always assume a conservative posture in this regard; when comprehensive, in-depth testing and assessment seems warranted, the child should be referred to a qualified professional. The teacher, however, can become an expert in the construction, administration, and interpretation of informal and specific educational assessment measures.

One must weigh the advantages and disadvantages of teachers' becoming informal diagnosticians of educational difficulties. A certain minimum amount of diagnostic effort exists in almost every classroom. Teachers informally, naively, or unconsciously diagnose anyway—everyone does. The plea here is for conscious, systematic, objective evaluation, and for recording and using these observations.

TESTING AND ASSESSMENT

Specialists in the measurement and evaluation of human behavior are asked to estimate children's behavioral capabilities and achievement in a variety of dimensions and for a number of purposes. It is alarmingly clear that the accuracy of these estimates is critical since these data are used to make significant decisions. The results of behavioral assessments are being used to "do things to people;" therefore, those using this information must know the meaning, limitations, and appropriateness of every evaluative procedure employed with youngsters. This section will review certain uses of psychological and educational evaluations; describe some of the problems involved in obtaining and interpreting data from the evaluations; and offer suggestions leading to a more complete understanding of the advantages and disadvantages in using information from formal evaluative procedures. Understanding *formal* evaluative procedures will be helpful to the teacher in conducting effectively her own informal assessment tactics.

Definitions

A sharp distinction should be made between the terms *testing* and *assessment*. Newland (1963, pp. 54-56) defines testing as ". . . the exposure of a client to any given device whether group or individual, essentially for the purpose of obtaining a quantitative characterization on one or more traits on that client." He elaborates by suggesting that ". . . testing is the controlled observation of the behavior of an individual to whom stimuli of known characteristics are applied in a known manner." Guilford (1954, p. 471) defines testing as ". . . the evaluation of individuals or individual performances on continua representing definable psychological traits and functions." Restrictions of a test can be appreciated by understanding that instruments which provide testing data are specific samples of the performance of an individual. The following statements illustrate this quantitative observation:

1. Susan is five feet two inches tall.
2. Charles scored with an IQ of 83 on the Weschler Intelligence Scale for Children.
3. Harry can run 100 yards in 10.8 seconds.
4. Gertrude scored at 3.6 years in reading on the Metropolitan Achievement Tests.
5. Morris achieved an SQ of 95 on the Vineland Social Maturity Scale.
6. Cindy scored a 92 on Mr. Jones' European history examination.

The concept of assessment is distinctly different from that of testing. Assessment involves obtaining a view of the individual as an organism interacting with its environment. Assessment also considers the myriad of variables within the individual which influence the behavior the observer is attempting to appraise. In assessment, the examiner should be concerned with the interplay of those significant variables. Although results from tests assign a deceptively precise score to a peron's performance on a given dimension, the assessment process views the individual's performance with respect to other variables, such as attitudes, interests, motivation, perceptual and conceptual performance, acculturation, rapport with others, and the significant social influences.

It is, therefore, the purpose of assessment to ". . . put test scores in their proper context and to relate them to the person tested rather than to the test used" (Gunzburg, 1958, p. 258). Assessment is more than simple quantification of an individual's behavior. It does not merely label an individual for statistical or research purposes, but instead attempts to explain why an individual obtains a certain score. The dangers of labeling have been indicated by Sarason (1953, p. 1): "The child . . . is automatically labeled . . . and then takes on, in the thinking of the clinician, all the characteristics that have been associated with the label . . . this seems to be subordinating observation to language instead of language to observations." Assessment embodies a qualitative characterization. By going beyond quantitative evaluation, assessment leads directly to the formulation of a diagnosis and appropriate remediation. Testing, then, is a molecular approach; assessment is more molar, since it considers the dynamic interplay of variables that determines an individual's behavior.

Illustrations of assessment include the following:

1. Gertrude is restless in class because she is unable to obliterate all of the peripheral stimuli around her.
2. Morris didn't seem to apply himself on the Stanford-Binet and missed more of the memory items dealing with auditory stimuli than those dealing with visual presentation.
3. Charles ran the 100 yard dash poorly because he got a poor start and did not run in a straight line.
4. Stanley reads poorly because of reversal difficulties which seem to be related to his poor discrimination between consonant sounds.
5. John has difficulty in simple addition and simple subtraction because he does not understand the concept of number.
6. Jane is disinterested in attending school because her parents want her to make all "A's" just as her sister did three years ago.

Functions of Testing and Assessment

Evaluation procedures should be used in an educational setting. Grouping for instruction, planning for guidance, identifying students in need of special diagnostic or remedial instruction, evaluating discrepancies between predicted and actual achievement, and promoting, all represent functions of psychological and educational evaluation. Traditional areas are also examined, such as intelligence, achievement, aptitude, interests, personality, social maturity, perceptual-motor development, and the performance of children in certain subject areas.

Dimensions of Evaluation

The evaluation process attempts to ascertain (1) what a person might be able to do; (2) what a person is presently doing; and (3) why and in what areas an individual is not performing.

Evaluating a person requires that some baseline be identified to determine if the individual's performance level is commensurate with a predicted possible level. The notion of potential capacity is an illusive concept, and a controversial subject in psychological and educational literature. Points of view range from the suggestion that it is possible to evaluate accurately an individual's capacity to perform on specific variables, to the belief that one's capacity can never be generally ascertained. Some psychologists and educators are averse to using the word "capacity" at all. Those between these extremes believe that it is possible to evaluate capacity in certain areas but not in all dimensions of functioning.

Assuming for the moment that students do have capacities for learning, we must differentiate between the individual's actual capacity for assimilating information or performing in a specific area, and the capacity which is apparent from an individual's performance on tests designed to predict his ability. Newland (1963, p. 78) has termed the former type of capacity as *basic* or *real*, and the latter type as *manifest* or *expressed*. In this context, basic capacity suggests an inborn, native ability which is not directly measurable by present day instrumentation. Manifest capacity describes an individual's level of performance which is readily apparent in the test situation, and which reflects the individual's basic capacity to some degree. The conceptual leap from an individual's manifest performance to what the individual "really could score" requires inferences of the highest order, and involves the assessment component of evaluation.

Achievement refers to the level at which a person is presently operating. Using appropriate achievement tests, an examiner can test a child's present levels of functioning and determine how well he is performing in a specific subject. Achievement test scores are usually presented in comparison with the child's chronological age peers. This performance is typically reported in terms of grade level.

To discover why a child is not performing at a higher level, the diagnostician must attempt to identify precisely specific areas of disability, such as speech, discrimination, memory, emotional development, and social interaction. Collecting data on these variables requires the expertise of a competent clinician who can determine which dimensions require further assessment, and which instruments will most adequately evaluate the dimensions under consideration. Effective teaching requires identifying the possible reasons for a child's not being able to perform as anticipated so that appropriate rehabilitative procedures can be initiated. In many instances, formal instrumentation is not available to specify these reasons. As we have emphasized, therefore, diagnosticians must use a variety of informal techniques to supplement the formal diagnostic procedures.

Assumptions Underlying Testing and Assessment

"Tests must be used for the purposes for which they were intended" (Delp, 1962, p. 49). Unfortunately, there is confusion among professionals as to the purposes tests serve. Some believe that no test is really useful. Others believe that a single test can reveal the intelligence, personality deviations, aptitudes, and social interaction capabilities of an individual. A third group of professionals complain about the problems inherent in testing and then willingly accept a test score at face value. The proper meaning of a test score comes only after the assumptions and the possible violation of assumptions of the test situation are clearly understood. The examiner as well as the consumer of test data should consider these assumptions, some of which will be discussed in depth.

Examiner Knowledge and Skill.   Factors such as examiner-examinee rapport, knowledge of proper test item administration, recording of responses, and the final scoring of the child's performance are all critical for effective testing and assessment. The examiner's personality and speech, the student's physical condition, and any family or personal problems of the examinee—all may have a direct influence on a child's testing performance. These influential variables warrant consideration by the examiner not only for judging the validation components of the testing process but also for identifying important qualitative factors in the assessment of behavior. It would be inappropriate for a child to be evaluated by someone lacking the necessary knowledge, background, and clinical experience. Too often, data from tests are used to decide the future educational placement and program for children regardless of the competence of the examiner.

Appropriateness of the Assessment Technique.   Although it is obvious that no one would evaluate a person's height in pounds, many unschooled examiners attempt to evaluate psychological and educational dimensions in ways which are equally inappropriate. The test that an examiner chooses for evaluating behavior should be one designed specifically to measure the behavior under consideration. For example, it is entirely inappropriate to use an intelligence test to diagnose creativity, brain damage, or personality. Tests designed for these specific purposes should be employed. Moreover, the examiner must know the adequacies and inadequacies of the instrument selected. The possible bias of certain items contained in the instrument; the dimensions the test purports to measure; the basal and ceiling levels of the instrument; and the directness with which the test scores can be interpreted into educationally meaningful experiences, must be considered before an instrument is selected. The issues of validity and reliability of the instrument are vitally important.

Errors of Measurement.   Measurement on any dimension involves some degree of error. Even in the direct evaluation of physical dimensions, slight but significant errors occur. Although specialists who develop psychological and educational instruments attempt to minimize errors of measurement, the complete obliteration of these weaknesses is impossible. Items may be inappropriate for certain groups, or they may measure behaviors inefficiently or ineffectively. These difficulties creep insidiously into the design of formal instrumentation and are exceedingly difficult to identify and control.

Comparable Acculturation.   It is assumed that the child being tested has been exposed to essentially the same type of environment as those on whom the test was standardized. (This consideration is, of course, not relevant to informal, unstandardized evaluative instruments.) The assumption is often difficult to accept, since we all are not reared in the same type of environment. Test developers attempt to standardize tests on various populations in order to control the potential influence of varying acculturation on the test performances of children. This issue is particularly relevant in the evaluation of youngsters with various types of disabilities. It cannot be assumed that a deaf child has been exposed to the same type of environment as a child with normal hearing, even if they are identical twins. Components of their environment could be quite similar in certain physical aspects but very dissimilar along psychological or social dimensions. Nevertheless, if the intent of the test is to predict how well a deaf child will do in the regular school setting, and if the test is composed of samples of regular school tasks, the test would be appropriate even though the deaf child's environment has differed from that of the standardization population.

Representative Samples of Behavior.   It should be understood that only the child's behavior during the testing time is being measured. Hopefully this behavior is representative of the past and future performance of the child, but the examiner must consider the degree of artificiality involved in the testing session. This weakness in formal testing supports the need for the teacher to supplement the formal measurement of behavior by using informal diagnostic activities to evaluate the full spectrum of a child's behavior within a dynamic setting.

If one were interested in learning how fast all sixth-grade children in the United States can run one hundred yards, precise accuracy requires that every child be asked to run this distance against the clock. Even if this were an important investigation, requiring every child to participate is a questionable procedure; it would be logistically impossible to get every subject to run the distance, and impractical because of the high financial expenditure necessary. Research methodologists have suggested a valid alternative procedure which provides as precise a measure as does the direct measurement of each sixth-grade child's performance. The alternative method involves selecting subjects randomly from the total population being studied, which in this case happens to be sixth-grade children. This smaller group, or sample, of children is representative of the entire population because the subjects were selected without knowledge of other, perhaps significant, variables. In true randomization, the achievement of the sample subjects will characterize the entire population from which the smaller group was chosen. Thus, the performance of all sixth-grade children could be generalized on the basis of the achievement of this representative sample of youngsters.

This same principle should be applied in studying the behavior of individual students. It is impossible to observe all of the behavior of an individual because of time limitations and the substantial financial expenditures involved. An individual's general behavior can be viewed as a population of behaviors which might include the student's feelings, attitudes, expressions, and actions. It is impossible to capture for study all of these manifestations by an individual; therefore, the technique of sampling representative incidents from this population of behaviors is useful. This sample of behavior, in turn, will characterize the total behavior of the person. Representative instances of behavior can be collected and evaluated, and used to attempt to alter or modify an individual's responses to problems.

Randomization in sampling instances of behavior is important when generalizations are needed. If a teacher is interested in determining a child's ability to discriminate among shapes, randomization would require that samples of the child's performance in visual discrimination (1) be taken at various times during the day, (2) in each of the subject areas which require use of this skill, and (3) on more than a single occasion. Behavior should be sampled frequently, with observation periods distributed throughout the day. Specific times for sampling behavior should be rotated during the day and week to control the influence of the time of day on behavior.

If information gathered from the observation of student behavior is intended to lead to an effective diagnosis and educational program, the observer must have a specific objective in mind. Broad observation of a child's behavior is much too imprecise a strategy to provide the specific information a teacher needs to modify or construct an appropriate educational program. The point to be emphasized, then, is that the observer must know which specific traits of behavior need to be observed through both formal and informal strategies. This specific goal will help to focus the thrust of the observation and reduce the possibility of unproductive "fishing expeditions."

Systematic sampling of the behavior of children is one of a number of components necessary to designing an effective educational program. Not only is it necessary for those youngsters having even a minor problem in school to be systematically observed, but it is equally desirable that the performance of all school children be systematically scrutinized. The data from these periodic observations should be recorded in such a way that the data will be useful to others. A continual, chronological record should be maintained in each child's folder explaining the implications of all evaluations; how they were translated into modifications in the child's program; and any recommendations for the child's future educational program. This dossier should follow each child throughout his school program.

Some Considerations in Observing and Recording Behavior

The term *observation* appears frequently in this chapter and others. The meaning intended here is a broad one, encompassing the "eyeball" inspection of a student's work by the teacher; data from standardized or informal tests administered to the student; and the collection of other information providing evidence relevant to the development of a more effective educational program for each student. The various processes and methods for collecting this information are all subsumed under the term observation.

On a pragmatic day-to-day basis, observation can take the form of a teacher's continuously checking a student's workbook productions, or other seat work selected to aid in understanding a concept or in developing a skill. These illustrations of independent work are often very revealing, and can provide important diagnostic clues to how well a child understands a concept and the degree to which this understanding is appropriately applied. In checking arithmetic workbook pages, it might be apparent to the teacher that a youngster is having difficulty in carrying; perhaps he doesn't understand the concept of zero, or perhaps he begins the process of addition in the wrong column. These weaknesses will show up in every item that requires an understanding of these two specific skills. Specific difficulties in spelling and reading can also be identified by inspecting seat work activities. It is important that prompt attention be given to these problems as soon as they are identified so that the youngster does not practice his errors.

Other informal observations which can be conducted on a day-to-day basis by the teacher include studying the performances of students during oral and silent reading periods, their written reactions to auditory or visual stimuli, and their explanations during show-and-tell periods. By carefully observing the behavior of each student, the teacher can develop tentative hypotheses about each student's performance. These hypotheses can be followed by administering either formal or informal tests which will point up each youngster's strengths and weaknesses under more controlled conditions. If, during a show-and-tell period, the child has difficulty in remembering a sequence of activities involved in some process, the teacher should note the nature of this difficulty and provide the child with ample opportunities to practice expression of ideas involving a logical sequence.

There are other less academic dimensions to which the teacher should be alert. For example, physical education activities provide an excellent opportunity for teachers to judge a child's reaction to competition; how well he tolerates losing; the degree to which youngsters have developed basic perceptual-motor skills; their eagerness to participate in group play; and how well children in the class share among themselves. This relatively unstructured environment provides a freedom not typical of most classrooms, and enables the alert teacher to judge each child's performance in many areas not directly related to academic work. Free play during physical education periods is a particularly good time to observe behavior because the children are exhibiting their individual wishes.

It is equally crucial for the teacher to make some judgment of conditions present at the time the child's behavior was under observation. Behavior is the result of an individual's interacting in a dynamic way with a multitude of environmental variables; it is not the result of a person or the environment alone. It is therefore obligatory that some estimate be made of the conditions or variables that were related to or influential in the observed behavior. To observe the behavior of a youngster is not enough; the goal of the diagnosis is to provide a clear means for removing any barriers causing a child's inadequate or atypical behavior, or preventing his maximum performance. If a youngster has a low tolerance for frustration, the teacher will want to know what circumstances might precipitate this problem. Atypical behavior may be the result of the child's inability to compete with other members of a group; his inability to handle the social dynamics of performing in the presence of certain members of the class; his having not developed all the necessary precursive skills required for satisfactory performance in some specific endeavor; or his lack of physical strength or other prerequisites for effecting a satisfactory performance. All of these factors could contribute to a child's inability to tolerate frustration. Each potential source of difficulty can and should be identified in the course of periodic informal student evaluations.

In general, the observation of children on any dimension should be conducted in as realistic a situation as possible. Evaluating the behavior of a child in a contrived setting is occasionally necessary, but it is clearly advantageous to capture the essence of all the important nuances of the real situation influencing a student's behavior. In addition, when children are unaware that they are being observed, they perform in a more typical way.

Other Strategies for Observation.   Other techniques are available that can be employed to focus on a specific behavioral dimension warranting more comprehensive study and to validate the day-to-day observations made without instrumentation. Teacher-made tests provide a method for precise student evaluation on a number of specific factors. These instruments are of dubious value unless we establish a clear objective for their use. In developing teacher-made instruments, one should focus on a specific behavioral entity, and attempt to evaluate a youngster's ability or performance through a variety of activities.

When a student has difficulty with visual memory, the teacher can develop a sequence of activities requiring the child to remember various visual stimuli which have been previously presented. Five or six objects of various sizes or shapes are placed in front of the child. The child is asked to close his eyes, and several objects are removed from the group. When he opens his eyes, he is asked to recall which objects are missing. The teacher can establish degrees of difficulty by requiring the child to remember progressively larger numbers of objects, asking that the objects be recalled in sequence, or that the student remember characteristics of a series of objects differing in several dimensions. From the child's performance the teacher can gain specific information for an appropriate remedial program. The alternative to evaluating a youngster's specific difficulties on the basis of a teacher-made test is to use a test designed to assess general reading ability. This strategy offers less precise data about a child's visual memory capabilities, for example, and therefore requires extrapolations and extensions of the information at hand. Such extensions are much too imprecise for accurately identifying specific disabilities.

Standardized instruments that sample behavior on a variety of dimensions can be used to assess performance informally. Achievement tests can be used to evaluate specific dimensions such as reading speed, tendency to make reversal errors, problems involving carrying or borrowing in arithmetic, and certain factors related to perceptual-motor development. Many achievement tests can be administered in individual or group situations; individual administration enables the teacher to observe a more complete spectrum of student behavior. There is some advantage in having certain normative data available against which each child's performance can be compared; thus, occasional use of formal instruments will help to validate the entire array of informal procedures the teacher uses more frequently. There is a potential hazard in using standardized tests for informal assessment if any variation from the suggested procedure of administration occurs. This can result in misinterpretation of the information. If any deviation occurs in the administration procedures, the deviation should be noted in the data so that it can be appropriately considered on subsequent occasions.

Check sheets and rating scales offer several advantages in the observation of human behavior. First and foremost, they help to focus the teacher's attention on specific behaviors, and encourage precise observation. If one wishes to observe a specific characteristic, rating scales will often define the spectrum of behaviors typifying individuals who have this characteristic. This procedure allows clear communication of information about a child among teachers and other professionals. Such precise communication is especially valuable to the new teacher and others without extensive classroom experience.

The use of check sheets and rating scales also alerts the school system to possible gaps in the educational program at various levels, and offers some indication of the appropriate sequencing for existing subject matter. If a group of children have common difficulties in a certain subject area, perhaps certain components of the subject matter are not being effectively taught. One flaw in the teaching method may be that the students are expected to make inordinate leaps from one concept to another without having understood those concepts which intervene. A well-developed rating scale or check sheet will provide the means for diagnosing strengths and weaknesses in curriculum at various levels, including daily lesson plans and even the structure of an entire subject area in K through 12.

In diagnosing educational difficulties, the teacher should gather data from as many sources as possible. There is always some danger in placing total dependence on observations from a single source, particularly those gathered by a teacher who might have strong opinions and feelings toward specific children in the class. The observations of others within and outside the school program are valuable in formulating the most efficacious educational program for individual students. The teacher, therefore, should provide each student with a chance to demonstrate his weaknesses and strengths, his concerns, his reactions to factors within the environment, his feelings toward others, and his aspirations. The employment of a simple sentence completion task, for example, will often allow the teacher to gain a clearer perspective of the child's feelings about important variables and issues which might affect his performance in other areas.

There is also an advantage in the teacher's surveying others' opinions, including a student's classmates, to ascertain their feelings toward other students in the classroom. Sociometric techniques can be employed to determine the degree to which a child is accepted or rejected by fellow classmates in various situations. Gronlund (1950) has reviewed the various strategies teachers can employ to determine sociometric position in a classroom.

At a more informal level, teachers can simply observe which children are consistently chosen as teammates in various activities. These observations can subsequently be validated by employing some variation of sociometric analyses. Standard teacher-designed interview schedules can be developed to provide structure and focus for those social variables relevant to classroom settings. A certain number of open-ended questions should be included in any interview schedule so that the reactions of the person being interviewed are not unduly restricted. Posing hypothetical situations to the person and asking how he would solve the problems, react to certain situations, or evaluate the performance of others, will reveal many of his opinions. This strategy can be employed in various subject areas and will lead to a precise indication of issues with which the individual is unduly concerned.

Related to the use of hypothetical situations is the technique which allows students to respond to problems in a contrived setting. Children can be asked to role-play, acting out solutions to various types of situations or problems. Observing the social interaction which takes place during an enactment, and the techniques by which children solve problems, enables the teacher to gain some understanding of students' strengths and weaknesses. Blackhurst (1966, pp. 136-142) and Smith (1968, pp. 214-220) have discussed the value of role-playing with mentally retarded adolescents. They emphasize the diagnostic and therapeutic advantages of using this technique in the classroom. Children can be deliberately placed in various situations requiring certain types of interaction. A tape recording can be made of the enactment and, at a later date, a more comprehensive evaluation made of each child's reactions to the problems and the techniques each used to solve the situation. Appropriate excerpts from various role-playing situations can be transcribed and included in a child's cumulative folder to illustrate his characteristic behavior.

Potential Problems in the Observation of Behavior

Accurate observation of human behavior necessitates that the observer be aware of certain potential problems in the collection of data, their interpretation, the diagnosis of a student's weaknesses, and the eventual development of a valid educational program for children. One major source of inaccuracy is the various biases of the subject and/or experimenter. Rosenthal (1966) has discussed influences of experimenter-behavior on an individual's performance. He notes that substantial errors in observation can result from factors such as not varying the time at which data are collected; using a single technique to evaluate performance; selecting an inappropriate technique which does not directly evaluate performance; inaccuracy in recording data; preconceived notions the evaluator may have of the individual; and lack of rapport between the observer and the observed. Other detrimental influences include possible experimenter hostility; dominance; status as viewed by the students; and the subject's perception of the observer. There is evidence to suggest that bias can be indirectly the result of the experimenter's age, race, sex, or need for approval. The observer must be aware of these potential sources of bias, and make every attempt to control them so that the observed behavior is a valid sample of the student's attitudes and competencies. The focus should be on the child's typical behavior, and not that which results from pressures and influences of an atypical environment.

There is always the possibility of distortion in the evaluative process. Distortion results from inaccurate interpretation of the data; a tendency of the observer to over-generalize the findings to other areas of perform-

ance; improper emphasis on irrelevant segments of a child's performance; and a desire by some professionals to label children, rather than to
focus on the manifest behavior of the particular student. It is vital that
the observer focus specifically on the behavior observed, and not suc-
cumb to the tendency to label or tag the "inner tendency" or "nature"
of the child.

To insure the accuracy of behavioral observations, the teacher should
check and recheck the activities and techniques employed. Informal
checking will help the teacher to refine the process of observation to eliminate those procedures which are providing an unreliable and imprecise
measure of performance. The teacher is wise to solicit the advice of
expert psychometricians in developing and using activities appropriate
for evaluative purposes. Procedures that are potentially promising
should be field-tested, at least in an informal way. Field testing can be
conducted by using students with already diagnosed weaknesses, such as
in visual discrimination problems, and administering the tasks to the
students to determine whether the new techniques will identify weaknesses.

Continual cross-check of data will validate the observations to some
degree. If a child appears from informal observations to have a weakness
in dimensions such as auditory memory, the teacher should check this
observation by inspecting the student's performance on other devices
which directly measure auditory memory skills. Cross-checking adds
credence to the observations and helps to justify continued use of certain
types of informal and formal instrumentation.

Collecting Behavioral Data from Informal Measures

Those teachers who see the advantage in frequently and systematically evaluating students in an informal way should consider factors
such as: (1) the assumptions underlying evaluation; (2) which educational dimensions when measured will provide the maximum amount of
relevant information; (3) the types of activities and experiences which
will best serve for informal evaluation of the factors under consideration;
and (4) the advantages in using formal rather than informal methods for
evaluating behavior. These factors must be considered to prevent launching into an ill-conceived and randomly-executed program of testing,
assessment, diagnosis, and personalized instruction.

Selecting Activities for Informal Evaluation. 1. Every activity selected for the purpose of evaluation should be part of the on-going
program. It would be inappropriate to select those activities which are
obviously foreign to the components of instruction which precede and

are subsequent to the evaluation process. Adhering to this criterion will provide a less contrived setting; the activity should reflect all the many nuances of the real classroom situation.

2. Activities should be interesting to the student being evaluated. If the activity is dull or boring, the teacher will not know whether a child's poor performance is due to a bonafide problem in the skills required by the task or to a disinterest in participating. It is important to elicit the student's best performance during periods of informal evaluation.

3. Activities for diagnosis should be selected to measure specific educational dimensions. This requires that the teacher have in mind which specific behaviors will be evaluated. It will be much more educationally informative to check on a child's performance in specific areas such as visual memory, auditory memory, discrimination between shapes, color discrimination, spatial to temporal translation, verbal fluency of ideas, and non-verbal flexibility, than to attempt an assessment of a large subject area such as reading or arithmetic. General subject areas embody a large number of very specific skills which children must master in order to achieve adequately. The teacher must divide a subject area into basic skill areas and then evaluate performance in each of these skills.

4. Activities should be developed to measure directly a child's performance in each of these specific skills. Indirect strategies require additional assumptions and extrapolations. For example, if the teacher wishes to determine the degree to which a child can interact socially with adult figures, evaluative experiences should offer the child a chance to interact socially with adults. It would be hazardous to assume that the child has difficulty in such interaction if the diagnostic activities required him to interact only with his peers or siblings, or worse, if a pencil and paper test were employed. A second illustration might help to emphasize this point. Assume that the teacher is interested in determining the degree to which a child is able to remember what is said. Activities designed to evaluate this skill directly include asking the child to repeat digits, recite poems, or to remember the basic theme of a story. To use visual stimuli or three-dimensional objects in evaluating a child's auditory memory skills attacks the problem much too indirectly. The probability of an erroneous diagnosis increases and can result in an imprecise and ineffective remedial program.

5. Every diagnostic activity should be chosen for objectivity. Teachers tend to be swayed by a child's performance in areas not directly related to those factors being evaluated. The teacher should be as objective as possible during the evaluation process and attempt to control any intervening effect which might bias the collection, interpretation, and

translation of the data. To this end, the teacher might enlist the services of other school people who might offer a more objective observation of a child's performance.

6. Activities should be varied enough that the youngsters do not become too familiar with the tasks. Such practice will result in the child's higher performance on similar tasks. To control this potential problem, the teacher might select several activities designed to assess the same competency, but which can be clarified in terms of degree of difficulty.

7. Activities selected to diagnose areas of educational relevance should provide valid measurement of the behavioral dimension. It may be difficult for teachers to judge the validity of the activities without help from other professional workers. In the absence of such counsel, the teacher will find it an advantage to compare a child's performance on informal activities to his performance in the same area on formal achievement tests. This comparison will provide some indication of the validity of those activities chosen for informal evaluation and, at the same time, provide a check on the validity of the formal instrument.

8. Children should be tested on more than one occasion to gain a reliable evaluation. A variety of activities should be used to determine the child's potential disability and the emphasis that should be given to establishing an extensive rehabilitation program.

Using Data from Informal Measures

The final objective of the observation and diagnosis of educational difficulties is that appropriate measures be taken to supplement and modify the school program for each child according to the individual diagnostic signs. This objective implies the need for informed interpretation of each student's profile in order to modify the instructional program in a way that will help the youngsters learn more effectively and efficiently. This adaptation can take the form of altering unsuccessful teaching tactics. For example, if the teacher has employed a phonics approach in reading, but has found this teaching technique to be relatively unproductive for certain youngsters, adjustments in teaching method might be in order. These adjustments might take the form of giving more emphasis to a visual procedure for teaching reading, or perhaps a combination of a visual, kinesthetic, and auditory strategy for those children with severe reading problems. If children have some difficulty in translating word problems into the appropriate algorithm, the teacher may want to provide them with activities in arithmetic which will make greater use of the manipulation of three-dimensional objects. Alterations in the teaching process and in procedures for helping the students understand certain concepts should be based on an interpretation and translation of data collected from informal and formal assessment devices.

Other adaptations in the instructional program made on the basis of data collected from informal assessments might include significant alterations in the curriculum for groups of children. If the teacher estimates that a group of children is not making conceptual leaps which some of their classmates can handle, the teacher might wish to give more attention to appropriate sequencing of subject matter, to enable the students to overlearn each of the major concepts contained in an instructional sequence. Because of the great heterogeneity in classrooms, teachers will find that certain children are unable to learn material incidentally; consequently, the instructional program and the curriculum will need to be directed toward intentional rather than incidental learning. Each important task and skill embodied in a concept must be identified. Instead of basing instructional groups according to levels of achievement alone, teachers should employ criteria which are of greater educational relevance for grouping.

Information gathered from the teacher's informal evaluations will help to decide whether a child or a child's family should be referred to another agency or specialist for further testing or remediation. The teacher more than anyone else within the school program is in a position to judge the advisability of seeking the advice of other professionals. It is often necessary to refer students to speech correctionists, clinical psychologists, pediatricians, and experts in other areas related to the child's performance in school. The teacher should make use of these professionals, and not attempt to provide evaluation and diagnostic services for the "hard core" cases whose difficulties exceed the experience and training of the teacher.

Finally, data from informal measures can be used by the teacher to evaluate specific classroom objectives. If a general weakness in a skill is manifested by most of the students in a class, the teacher may want to reconsider focusing on that skill at that period in the children's program. The inability of students to achieve at a certain level may indicate an inappropriately-sequenced program which has forced the students to move beyond their present level of readiness. It would be foolish to expect children to attack words and read at the second or third grade level without having been first exposed to a well-sequenced readiness program, which would include discrimination between shapes and sizes as well as activities leading to development of visual memory skills. The teacher must be cognizant of all these precursive skills required for successful performance in a higher level skill.

CONCLUSION

Hopefully, the contents of this chapter have alerted the reader to the general nature, problems, and pedagogic promise of informal specific educational assessment. The following chapters present discussions and informal strategies that may be employed to assess specific competencies within each of eight broad domains of competency: intelligent behavior, perceptual-motor skills, reading skills, written expression and spelling, speech and language, arithmetic skills, and emotional and social skills. Apprehension of the spirit and substance of the material that follows will perhaps provoke the teacher to adopt a new perception of the teaching-learning situation and to embark on a new course of dynamic instructional action.

REFERENCES

Blackhurst, A. E., "Sociodrama for the Adolescent Retarded," *The Training School Bulletin,* 63 (1966).

Delp, H. A., "Psychological Evaluation: Some Problems and Suggestions," in *Mental Retardation,* J. Rothstein, ed. New York: Holt, Rinehart & Winston, Inc., 1962.

Dobzhansky, T., *Heredity and the Nature of Man.* New York: Harcourt, Brace, & World, Inc., 1964.

Gronlund, N. E., *Sociometry in the Classroom.* New York: Harper & Row, Publishers, 1959.

Guilford, J. P., *Psychometric Methods.* New York: McGraw-Hill Book Co., 1954.

Gunzburg, H. C., "Psychological Assessment in Mental Deficiency," in *Mental Deficiency—the changing outlook,* A. A. Clarke and A. D. B. Clarke, eds. London: Methuen and Co., 1958.

Hunt, J. McV., *Intelligence and Experience.* New York: The Ronald Press Co., 1961.

Newland, T. E., "Psychological Assessment of Exceptional Children and Youth," in *Psychology of Exceptional Children and Youth* (2nd edition), W. M. Cruickshank, ed. Englewood Cliffs, N. J.: Prentice-Hall Inc., 1963.

Rosenthal, R., *Experimenter Effects in Behavioral Research.* New York: Appleton-Century-Crofts, 1966.

Sarason, S. B., *Psychological Problems in Mental Deficiency.* New York: Harper & Row, Publishers, 1953.

Smith, R. M., *Clinical Teaching: Methods of Instruction for the Retarded.* New York: McGraw-Hill Book Co., 1968.

Chapter 2

THE EDUCATIONAL IRRELEVANCE OF INTELLIGENCE

John T. Neisworth

Intelligence tests have been administered to virtually every school-age child in the nation. School administrators, guidance counselors, teachers, and parents have encouraged the extensive use of these tests. Intelligence testing has become perfunctory, almost ritualistic. Presumably, then, the administration and interpretation of these tests have great educational relevance. Supposedly, teachers and students are much benefited by the information yielded through intelligence testing.

There are psychologists and educators, however, who contend that the usual concept of intelligence, intelligence testing, and grouping on the basis of I. Q. are not only useless but are antagonistic to the educational enterprise. The New York City Board of Education has decided to abandon group intelligence testing. It has been suggested that the traditional concept of I. Q. and the use of group intelligence tests are of limited value, that they serve to destroy and impede the real business of education, and that alternatives to intelligence testing are needed. (Loretan, 1965, p. 171)

Since this book is concerned with informal assessment of educational difficulties, and intelligence testing traditionally has been a part of educational assessment, it was felt imperative that a chapter covering the topic be included. Nevertheless, the views expressed in this chapter are in accord with those who would abandon conventional intelligence testing and adopt a more productive and educationally relevant strategy. Hopefully, the arguments presented in this section will emphasize the importance of informal assessment of each of the seven competency dimensions discussed in the remaining chapters. The information gained through the informal and continual appraisal of these competencies could be an initial step toward a viable and educationally useful alternative to intelligence testing.

"INTELLIGENCE:" AN EXPLANATION OR DESCRIPTION?

The intelligence of students as revealed by intelligence tests is often used as an explanation for poor academic progress and inability to cope with the general classroom situation. Often a teacher will examine a student's recorded I.Q. to discover a reason for the student's trouble in class. If the I.Q. is low, the teacher may feel confident that the student's intelligence accounts for the difficulties. Furthermore, intelligence is most often regarded as an inborn, internally regulated, unchanging quality of the individual. Consequently, the teacher feels the problem "low I.Q." is not his problem as an educator but simply an unfortunate part of the student's destiny. To attribute failure in the classroom to low I.Q. and thus enhance the use of intelligence tests, and to assume that I.Q. is beyond our control, clearly reflect some definite presumptions regarding the definition, assessment, and determinants of intelligence. These presumptions will be examined in the following sections.

Defining Intelligence

Intelligence is often defined in terms of unobservable and unverifiable events or characteristics within the individual. Because stipulation of such characteristics varies according to one's theoretical frame of reference, there have been a myriad of definitions of intelligence. "There are almost as many definitions as there are psychologists to make them" (Kimble, 1956, p. 51). These imagined, fictitious conditions within the person are not only refractory to verification but are impossible to measure. Definitions of intelligence that involve hypothetical constructs such as cognitive structure, mental acuity, central nervous system integrity, intellectual potential, etc., do not permit the unequivocal identification or measurement of the thing being defined.

Another approach to defining intelligence, opposed to the use of fictitious inner processes, rests exclusively on observable, explicit behavior. For example, intelligence could be defined in terms of the behaviors required to cope with life's problems. (See Staats and Staats, 1963, p. 405.) Definitions of this sort specify the kinds of behaviors included under the concept of intelligence; the identification and assessment of explicit behavior becomes a relatively simple matter. Any intelligence test is, after all, a standard sample of behavior, and behavior only. No intelligence test ever measures mental capacity, thinking processes, or any other inner process.

All intelligence tests, then, are composed of items that assess behavioral competencies. The critical issue arises in the interpretation of the intelligence test results. If one subscribes to a definition of intelligence that implies inner processes, it is tempting to account for the test results on the basis of these alleged inner processes. For example, intelligence might be defined as "the mental capacity to deal with abstractions," or "the mental ability to learn." Tests comprised of numerical, verbal, and non-verbal problems might then be devised and standardized. Given the above definitions of intelligence, what is said of a child who performs poorly on the test? Not only is he described as a low-scorer (e.g., low I.Q.), but his performance is explained in terms of poor mental capacity, or weak mental ability, etc. Performance on an intelligence test, however, is only a reasonably accurate description of present competence in executing the kinds of behaviors required by the test. The intelligence of a child simply describes some current capabilities but in no way explains them.

To understand that intelligence is descriptive and not explanatory is critical, since on this issue hinges the interpretation and implications of intelligence test results.

What's in a Name? The Confusion between Description and Explanation

Assigning a verbal label, or name, to a collection or series of behaviors has had at least two uses. The first use, description, is highly desirable for convenience and communication. The second use, or misuse of naming, occurs when a definition is used as an explanation for the very events being defined or described. This use of naming as explanation has resulted in a most dangerous kind of circular reasoning and yields no explanation at all.

Naming as Description: Operationalism. It is often convenient and indeed necessary for us to be able to describe a collection of behaviors under one label or name. We develop concepts which include a number of more specific events. For example, assume that little Matilda displays the following behaviors in school: she doesn't play with the other children; blushes when spoken to; never raises her hand to volunteer an answer; refuses to speak in front of the class; and remains in a corner by herself during various social events. Now, how would you summarize Matilda's behavior? What single verbal label would you suggest that would communicate to others how Matilda behaves in school? One name we can use to describe her behavior collectively is "shy." Whenever we describe any person's behavior as shy, we mean to communicate quickly that the individual exhibits behaviors identical or similar to those above. So long as we are able to specify the behaviors that are included under a general term, naming for description or summarization is quite useful.

To clarify further, assume that a young boy, Malcomb, exhibits the following behaviors: his scores in reading and arithmetic achievement are only one-half the average achievement of other children in his grade; he has trouble in following simple verbal instructions; he is unable to walk the full distance on a wooden beam without falling, whereas others his age can; and he takes three times longer than his fellow students to learn the new locations of objects. In general, Malcomb's behavioral competencies on the tasks mentioned are markedly below that of his chronological age peers. Again, if we wish, we can group all these specific behaviors under one semantic roof: "retarded." If we can, on demand, specify behaviorally what we mean by retarded, the label is most useful in typifying Malcomb's behavior.

An operational definition of a term is one which specifies the operations or observations involved in arriving at the term. In the preceding two examples, "shy" and "retarded" are defined in terms of specified, observable behaviors. They mean nothing more than the behavioral events to which they are anchored. At no point have we explained "shy" or "retarded." That is, at no time have we attempted to specify the conditions antecedent to or causing shy or retarded behavior; we have merely labeled the behavior that may be assumed to be the consequence of some set of antecedent conditions.

Below is a diagrammatic representation of the example involving Matilda's behavior:

Figure 1

Naming as description; an operational definition of "shy."

Consequent
Behaviors

Antecedent
Conditions

Solitary Play

Blushes Often

Doesn't Volunteer answers

Won't speak
in front of
class

Isolates self
from social
events

Summarized as: SHY

Notice in the diagram the question mark in the antecedent-conditions box, to emphasize that no antecedent conditions have been specified to account for the consequent behaviors.

Naming as Explanation: A Tautology.   Earlier in the development of the physical sciences, and currently in the behavioral sciences, one often encounters a type of primitive and circular approach to explanation. A cluster of behaviors is observed and labeled; then, the label is used to "explain" the observed behaviors. Referring back to Figure 1, it is clear that while the label "shy" is descriptive of a cluster of behaviors, it by no means explains the behaviors. Yet we might hear a teacher say, "She just won't get involved with the other children because she is so shy." Or we may often hear a student's poor performance in school explained: "The poor child can't keep up with the other children in reading, writing, arithmetic, or social skills because he's retarded." The label that serves only to describe the behavior becomes the instrument of a very deceptive and fallacious explanation. This circular reasoning is by no means limited to teachers and parents. Work in the behavioral sciences has been generally cluttered and stymied by such pseudo-explanation. A person engages in physical violences *because* he is hostile, strives for continual promotion in his job *because* he is aggressive, or provides novel stories or gadgets *because* he is creative.

> Trait-names usually begin as adjectives—"intelligent," "aggressive," "disorganized," "angry," "introverted," "ravenous," and so on—but the almost inevitable linguistic result is that adjectives give birth to nouns. The things to which these nouns refer are then taken to be the active causes of the aspects. We begin with "intelligent behavior," pass first to "behavior which *shows* intelligence," and then to "behavior which is the *effect* of intelligence." . . . But at no point in such a series do we make contact with any event outside the behavior itself which justifies the claim of a causal connection (Skinner, 1953, p. 202).

The Non-Explanatory Value of Intelligence and I.Q.

Now let us examine in more detail the term "intelligence." As previously mentioned, intelligence tests are samples of behavior. Performance on these tests is usually compared with the performances of others who have taken the test, who form a standardization group. One can thus compare the performance of one child to that of others his age. This comparison is made by finding the difference between the student's score and the average performance; the difference, when divided by the standard deviation of the test score distribution, yields a value which describes the student's score with respect to the total distribution of scores obtained on the standardization group. Given an intelligence test with a mean of 100 and a standard deviation of 15, a child who scores 130 is two standard deviations above the mean; assuming a normal distribution of scores, this places him in approximately the upper two per cent of the score distribution. A child scoring thusly is often referred to as having outstanding mental capacity, accelerated mental development, and so on. The child's outstanding performance is by no means explained; it is simply described and indexed in relation to the performance of others.

Figure 2 again illustrates the use of naming for descriptive purposes. Performance on the test (i.e., execution of the specified behaviors) is summarized as intelligence, which has been defined as mental capacity. Obviously, the labels that summarily describe the cluster of behaviors (i.e., test performance) cannot also be used to explain the behaviors. Again note the question mark in the antecedent-conditions box in the following diagram. The cause or antecedents of the behaviors in question should appear in this box; the labels "mental capacity" or "intelligence" cannot be placed here since they do not come before the

Figure 2

Intelligence defined as mental capacity; Behavioral referents of "capacity."

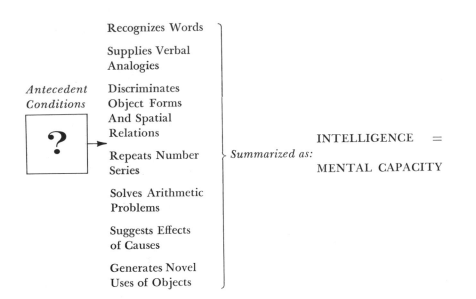

consequent behaviors, but are simply names attached to describe the collection of behaviors. To explain intelligence test performance in terms of capacity, when capacity has been defined in terms of performance, completes a perfect circle of reasoning. Performance does not explain performance!

What does explain intelligent behavior? What factors, what antecedent conditions, what determinants, are responsible for the origin, development, and nature of intelligent behavior? A lengthy discussion of research relating to the possible determinants of intelligent behavior is outside the scope of this chapter. A brief overview of some of the principal positions, however, is relevant; the position we take with respect to the cause of intelligent behavior is related to how and why we use intelligence tests.

POSITIONS ON THE DETERMINANTS
OF INTELLIGENT BEHAVIOR

For purposes of the following discussion, let us regard intelligence as a generalization that describes the level of competency a person manifests on a number of behavioral dimensions. Perceptual-motor capability; attainment level in reading, written expression, language, arithmetic; and social skills, may all be collectively described as intelligent behavior. The following four points of view are the major past and present positions on the causes of intelligent behavior. (See D. P. Ausubel, 1958, pp. 22-92 and J. M. Hunt, 1961, pp. 10-64.) The reader is urged to examine each position, decide which of them typifies his own thinking, and to deliberate the implications for education suggested by each position. The major positions invoke, in varying degrees, biological (hereditary) and environmental determinants to account for intelligent behavior, often referred to, respectively, as "nature" and "nurture."

Positions Emphasizing the Role of Heredity

Genetic Predestination.   Genetic predestination is also known as biological determinism, genetic determinism, and preformationism. This point of view completely denies the role of environment in directing, developing, or modifying intelligent behavior. Whatever degree of intellectual competence a person possesses is completely and directly the result of an ancestrally contributed heredity endowment.

Since the nature of intelligent behavior and its direction of growth are prestructured at conception, postnatal events make no contribution whatsoever to intellectual performances. Instead, acquisition of competence is controlled exclusively by relentless and immutable genetic determinants. Accordingly, good environment and education are desirable only because they permit the person to learn to use his inborn behavior potential. Differences in the quality of environments and educational experiences, however, have absolutely no effect in changing the course and eventual level of intellectual competency, since this is preordained at conception.

Genetic endowment as the exclusive determinant of intelligent behavior does not receive support from the scientific community. While there is little direct or explicit support of the position among the public, it is part of the naive psychology held by many people, reflected in expressions such as "blood will tell," "you can't make a silk purse out of a sow's ear," and "like father, like son." Use of concepts such as potential, capacity, native endowment, and natural ability, represents an acceptance of genetic predestination and unobservable, untestable inner traits of the individual. More subtly, and more gravely for education, formal or informal belief in the position produces an antagonistic predisposition toward human and social improvement endeavors. Many believe, for example, that education for the mentally retarded is admirable but futile, since retardation is generally predestined and hence incurable. As an outgrowth of this belief, sterilization of the retarded is advanced as a means of eliminating the problem. Many believe slum children will not benefit from early education or anti-poverty programs, since such children are born stupid. As final examples, one should be aware that much of the dogma and practice of Nazism were based on the unwarranted and thoroughly discredited theory of total genetic predestination of intellectual and ethnic superiority or inferiority. The racist contention that Negroes are genetically dull is also used as a rationale to defend a variety of inequities.

Try to imagine a school's administrative and instructional policies based on an assumption that the eventual level of behavioral competence is fixed at conception. Such a school would attempt to assess the genetic intelligence of pupils in order to assign them permanently to tracks or groupings appropriate to their potential. A school based on this philosophy would recognize, if not create, an intellectual caste system in which upward movement could occur only in spite of, rather than because of, instructional practice and expectations.

Predeterminism.   There is an obvious similarity between genetic predestination and predeterminism: both views stress the predominant role of genetic determinants. But unlike genetic predestination, predeterminism employs environmental factors to account for the facilitation, inhibition, or distortion of genetically-intended characteristics.

In regard to intelligent behavior, the predeterministic position is as follows: internal, genetic factors set the potential, rate, and stage sequence of intellectual development. An inherited "master plan" is said to exist, with respect to when and what intellectual competencies will emerge. There are stages, or phases, that may be expected to unfold in a natural process of maturation. The environment provides circumstances necessary only to triggering or releasing predetermined phases of the master plan. Environment is not regarded as operative in originating, directing, or modifying intelligent behavior. Intelligent behavior will undergo natural maturation if a favorable environment is available.

The word "maturation" has a familiar connotation with respect to physical development. Few would disagree that the development of the embryo, and most anatomical and physiological growth, are predominantly under the direction of biological determinants; indeed, there is much empirical evidence to support this view. It is quite another matter to generalize from the processes underlying embryological, anatomical, and physiological changes, to all aspects of development. Intellectual maturation implies that the development of intelligent behavior is under the same internal controls as embryological, skeletal, and general physical growth. Such a maturational model is merely a hypothetical framework for understanding psychological development and the acquisition of capabilities not directly dependent on biological factors. To assert that the development and content of intelligent behavior is predetermined because embryological development is predetermined leaves much to be desired with respect to logic, theoretical soundness, and empirical evidence.

The predeterministic viewpoint is usually traced to the philosopher Jean Jacques Rousseau (1712–1778). (See Ausubel, 1958, p. 27.) He believed that the environment must be free of restrictions to permit the unconstrained emergence of innately predetermined sequences of development. Accordingly, child-rearing practices, child guidance, and educational environments and methods must be free and unstructured to prevent the corruption or distortion of developmental processes. Environments and processes that influence children must be permissive and child-centered. The recommendations of such leaders in education as Pestalozzi (1746–1827) and Froebel (1782–1852), and much of the philosophy of progressive education, stem from Rousseau's doctrine.

The lingering impact of Rousseau, progressive education, and the over-generalized maturational model have given predeterminism wide acceptance, both outside education and with many teachers as well. Comments about student potential, pupil underachievement (implying an obstruction to full development of some innate ability), and a child's "going through a stage," reflect a predeterministic presumption. The use of intelligence test scores as indicative of unchangeable intellectual potential is certainly predeterministic.

An illuminating study has suggested that teacher expectation of student progress subtly influences the way teachers relate to students, with the result that students "live up" to expectations (Rosenthal and Jacobson, 1968, pp. 19-23). Teachers were deliberately misinformed that certain of their students showed great hidden potential for academic progress. Subsequently, the students with alleged potential showed remarkable gains in intelligence test performance. These results suggest that many teachers do indeed believe in intelligence tests as measures of potential, and in potential as an explanation and predictor of performances. Actually, the study demonstrates the operation of a self-fulfilling prophecy: when students are expected to do better, regardless of their supposed potential, they do better.

Entrenched as the predeterministic position has been, it is giving way to relatively new conceptions which emphasize the preeminence of the environment in directing the nature, course, and rate of intellectual competencies.

Positions Emphasizing the Role of Environments

Environmental Determinism. The fatalism of genetic predestination is not shared by environmental determinism; but absoluteness and exclusiveness of influence also characterize this position. Environmental determinism asserts that the nature, progression, and final level of intelligent behavior are exclusively the product of environmental impact. The view admits to no inherited abilities, potentials, or predispositions. This position is also known as situational determinism, and the *tabula rasa* approach. *Tabula rasa* is an apt term, since the person is viewed as a blank slate at birth and becomes only what his environment writes upon the slate. The individual is viewed as infinitely pliable, with no inherited predisposition to a quantity or quality of behavior thought of as intelligent. Philosophically, the view suggests no limits to the possible level of human capabilities since the level of the individual or species is set by the quality of the environment alone. Because environmental quality is quite susceptible to modification, it is argued, we may effect a continuous escalation of human competence.

Historically, John Locke (1632–1704) is known in philosophy as the chief exponent of environmental determinism. Itard (1774–1836), Seguin (1812–1880), Montessori (1870–1952), and other "sense empiricists" have championed the view in education. These educators have stressed multi-sensory stimulation as the tactic for building, modifying, and directing intelligent behavior. Itard is known for his attempts to educate Victor, the "wild boy of Aveyron." Found in the woods in the district of Aveyron, France, the boy was described as about twelve years old, lacking minimal standards of human capabilities, and behaving much like a wild animal. Itard employed multi-sensory stimulation and a variety of sensory training methods to build Victor's behavioral repertory. Although the boy did acquire a small vocabulary and a variety of simple but human behaviors, Itard considered his efforts with Victor a failure. While the project did not convincingly demonstrate the soundness of the environmental deterministic approach in educating intellectual behavior, Itard's limited success was sufficient to dampen the prevailing biological determinist point of view and to rally disciples who would carry on his new environmentalist approach.

The movement known in psychology as behaviorism has stressed environmental manipulation as the means for changing behavior, including behavior supposedly determined by innate factors. J. B. Watson (1878–1958), the father of behaviorism, and more recently B. F. Skinner and other behaviorists, have presented masses of empirical data and comprehensive analyses supporting the environmental deterministic approach.

Environmentalists direct much attention to the content and structure of the educational environment. They maintain that the level of intellectual competence manifested by a given student is a function not of any potential or native ability but of his experiences with the environment. Consequently, it has been urged that teachers become behavioral engineers, analyzing and modifying the environment to manipulate student behavior in socially desirable directions. To facilitate manipulation, it is urged that the teaching machine, programmed textbooks, token reinforcement, and other instructional strategies based on respondent and operant conditioning be incorporated into educational methodology.

Interactionism. This position rejects the *tabula rasa* notion that hereditary factors play no part in accounting for differences in intelligent behavior. While interactionism employs both heredity and environment as agents responsible for intellectual development, neither factor is given greater importance than the other. In an interactive process between two determinants, neither is more important; rather, each compounds and modifies the effect of the other. The interactionist position holds that heredity and environment are multiplicative rather than additive. Intelligence is viewed as the product of heredity *times* environment, rather than as the sum of the two.

At any moment in time the future course and nature of intellectual competence depends upon already established learnings. These previously established responses are the result of environmental experiences and the effect of these experiences on elaborating and modifying previously learned behavior. That is, what is learned becomes part of the nature of the person, and the learning is available to interact with future environmental events. The quantity and quality of a repertory of intelligent behaviors is the product of interactions between internal determinants and environmental conditions; the internal determinants are the result of previous similar interactions. Only at conception are the internal influences on development purely genetic. After the moment of conception, the environment elaborates and modifies genetic predispositions and becomes part of the complex of internal determinants. This complex is then available to interact with and be modified by future environmental events.

The interactionist view maintains that differences in the learning rates of newborns, while partially explained by differences in prenatal environments, are largely a consequence of hereditarily determined physiological differences. That is, some newborns are endowed with more responsive sensory and motor systems. These infants have a head start in interacting with and learning from the environment. After birth, however, the quality of the environment plays a greater and greater role in determining the upper limits of capabilities. A child with an inferior endowment could surpass in behavioral competence a child with an hereditary head start if given an advantageous environment. Environmental circumstances can be arranged to offset hereditary liabilities. In the interactionist view, the earliest antecedents of intelligent behavior are genetically determined, but intervention with compensatory environments can provide the necessary conditions for acquisition of intelligent behavior. Only the environment embodies antecedent conditions subject to manipulation.

Further Implications of the Environmentalist Positions. Only research can discover the conditions antecedent to intelligent behavior. We must determine what factors in the physical environment, what child-rearing procedures, and what educational strategies are conducive or detrimental to the acquisition of behavioral competence.

As pointed out in this section, both the environmental determinist and interactionist positions emphasize the nature of the environment. What we regard as intelligent behaviors are response repertories that have been acquired through interaction with the environment; that is, they are learned.

> More broadly, it may be suggested that intelligent behavior in general is learned behavior, largely of a verbal nature, which includes the following: tacts, reasoning sequences, and communication behaviors; reading, arithmetic, and mathematical repertories; attentional, observing, and discrimination behaviors; and various skills under verbal control. . . . This interpretation also suggests that many of the variables

which determine "intelligence" are accessible to manipulation. This, in turn, suggests not only that wide differences in intelligent behavior are a function of experience, but also that children could be trained to be "intelligent" (Staats and Staats, p. 411).

The implications of the foregoing are clear:

1. Success in the environment (in school, work, and social relations) requires the learning of complex and flexible response repertories.
2. Intelligence is defined and assessed in terms of these response patterns.
3. The quantity, quality, rate, and direction of response acquisition (learning) is highly susceptible to environmental manipulation.
4. Educators must be concerned with arranging the antecedent conditions of which intelligent behaviors are a function. Arrangement begins by identifying weak or inappropriate behavioral repertories, followed by employment of instructional strategies and materials to eliminate unintelligent responses and to strengthen and maintain intelligent behaviors.

WHAT INTELLIGENCE TESTS CAN AND CANNOT DO

We can probably agree that the major objective of educators is to assist their students in acquiring higher and higher levels of competency. We should now examine how and to what extent usual intelligence testing contributes to this objective.

As previously mentioned, all tests are samples of current performance; they describe present proficiency on the variables included in the test. More often, however, tests are used to predict. For decades, psychologists and educators have been demonstrating the relationships between performance on a test and later performance in some related or even unrelated activity. Tests have been devised that predict with moderate accuracy success in college or performance in a variety of employment situations. Once tests have established predictive capabilities, they may be used to make decisions about people. The decisions made from test results depend upon the requirements of the decision maker and the appropriateness of the test employed. In general, tests may not be used to make decisions not originally intended in their construction. Tests are often constructed for making selection or placement decisions (Cronbach and Gleser, 1957). Selection ordinarily involves choosing from among available applicants those who will be accepted or rejected. A company that wishes to hire a number of secretaries may administer a secretarial aptitude test to all applicants. The employer selects for the positions those whose scores forecast satisfactory performance on the job; the others are rejected. Many universities, for example, administer various examinations to applicants to help in the selection of students.

Placement refers to the differential assignments of persons to one of several jobs, treatments, or what have you. For example, men who pass the U. S. Army's selection test may thereafter be given placement tests. Ostensibly, these tests are helpful in placing the "right man on the right job." Tests designed to make selection decisions are not very useful in placement. "A test which predicts success within many jobs [selection] is a poor instrument for classification [placement] because it does not tell which job the person can do best. The ideal classification test is one which has a positive correlation with performance in one job and a zero—or better yet, negative—correlation with performance in other jobs (Cronbach, 1960, p. 356)." As Cronbach points out, entrance examinations given by colleges may be fair predictors of general academic success but are useless in placing students in the curriculum for which they are best suited. By the same token, tests which select from the population those who have adjustment problems are not helpful in assigning these persons to different therapeutic treatment programs.

Now, what do customary intelligence tests do and for what decisions may they appropriately be used? It is true that, typically, intelligence tests predict academic achievement (.50 correlation between intelligence test scores and school grades).

> A more fundamental point is that prediction per se does not change or improve anything. Of course, if it is possible to successfully predict achievement one can make decisions about selecting or rejecting students for certain courses or programs. This is done at the more advanced stages of schooling where schools act as a kind of screening station for society. At lower school levels and in fundamental school subjects, however, students are not selected and rejected. An effort is made to provide schooling for all and simple prediction does not help directly (Reynolds, 1965, p. 339).

Since intelligence tests predict general scholastic success, they could be used to exclude children from school. As educators, however, we do not wish to reject students from public schooling. We prefer not to use intelligence tests to make selection decisions. What we do wish as educators is to help each student achieve increasingly higher levels of mastery in areas thought to be important by society. We wish to assign students to appropriate instructional strategies and materials, thus implying a placement or classification decision. But intelligence tests, with their capability of predicting general success in school, cannot appropriately be used to place students differentially. Intelligence tests do not help us to individualize instruction. They do not tell us what teaching methods, what materials, or what curricula are best for what child. In summary, conventional intelligence tests:

1. CAN provide fair predictions of school success, assuming we do nothing exceptional to help or hinder certain students and thus destroy the prediction. Prediction per se is of little use since we do not use intelligence tests to make selection decisions.
2. CANNOT explain performance on the test or intelligent behavior sampled by the test.
3. CANNOT reveal the capacity or potential of a student.
4. CANNOT assist educators in matching students with educational treatments.

RECOMMENDATIONS

Educators must abandon the unfounded notion that children are born with immutable potentials to achieve. Such predeterministic conceptions of fixed capacity must give way to positions that stress the functional relationships between competency and environmental changes. After all, that is what education is, or should be, all about: arranging instructional circumstances in order to bring about desired changes in pupil achievement.

Second, educators must cease predicting that students will fail under static learning conditions. Certainly, the New York City Board of Education's decision to drop group intelligence testing is a dramatic step in the right direction. Further, New York City has implemented a program involving achievement testing, instructional strategies, and subsequent achievement testing to assess the effectiveness of instructional intervention (Loretan, 1965). We may agree with Joseph O. Loretan, spokesman for the Board of Education of New York City, when he proposes that "an alternative to intelligence testing is *teaching;* that we assess progress only of what we teach, after we teach it, and that this progress is not the result of something innate, but of 'external materials' of intervention through teaching." (Loretan, 1965, p. 30)

Finally, it is hoped that the contents of this book may serve as an aid to teachers in elaborating and amplifying intelligent behavior. Through the informal and continual assessment of each of the competencies discussed in subsequent chapters, teachers may begin to describe intelligent behavior, identify educational difficulties, effect instructional changes, and "do something about it." The emphasis in this book is on diagnosing educational difficulties, determining the specific problems students have in coping with school work. Rather than terminating in descriptions of immutable and academically fatal traits, the evaluation procedures suggest initiation or modification of instructional procedures to improve capabilities. Continued teacher assessment of student progress will reveal the effectiveness of instructional innovations. As educators, our description and diagnosis of intelligent behavior must lead to a prognosis of improvement.

REFERENCES

Ausubel, D. P., *Theory and Problems of Child Development.* New York: Grune & Stratton, Inc., 1958.

Cronbach, L. J., *Essentials of Psychological Testing.* New York: Harper & Row, Publishers, 1960.

Cronbach, L. J., and G. C. Gleser, *Psychological Tests and Personal Decisions.* Urbana: University of Illinois Press, 1957.

Hunt, J. M., *Intelligence and Experience.* New York: The Ronald Press Company, 1961.

Kimbel, G. A., *Principles of General Psychology.* New York: The Ronald Press Company, 1965.

Loretan, J. O., "Alternatives to Intelligence Testing," *Proceedings: 1965 Invitational Conference on Testing Problems.* Princeton: Educational Testing Services, 1965.

Loretan, J. O., "The Decline and Fall of Group Intelligence Testing," *Teachers College Record,* October, 1965.

Reynolds, M. C., "The Capacities of Children," *Exceptional Children,* 31, 1965.

Rosenthal, R., and L. Jacobson, "Teacher Expectations for the Disadvantaged," *Scientific American,* 218, 1968.

Staats, A. W., and C. K. Staats, *Complex Human Behavior.* New York: Holt, Rinehart & Winston, Inc., 1963.

Skinner, B. F., *Science and Human Behavior.* New York: The Macmillan Company, 1953.

Chapter   3

PERCEPTUAL-MOTOR SKILLS

Robert M. Smith

The concept of readiness for learning is a complex
topic, and one which we find to be highly controversial.
There is a manifest lack of clarity concerning the dimensions of readiness, and disagreement among behavioral scientists as to the significance of the concept.
Bruner (1960, p. 7) has suggested that the concept of
readiness is unnecessary, and that ". . . the foundations
of any subject may be taught to anyone at any age in
some form." At the other extreme, Hymes (1958, p. 28),
along with a number of other educators, believes that
learning can effectively take place only as the organism
matures in its own time. Tyler (1964, p. 210) has discussed the nature of this professional disagreement and
presented certain propositions about readiness which
he believes to have either theoretical or empirical
validity.

To a large degree the division of opinion in the
literature on the concept of readiness in education is
related to the age-old "nature—nurture" controversy.

Hunt (1961) has considered this topic in detail. Those who believe that development and behavior are fixed at birth, have taken the position that the ability to learn a concept or to execute some task in an appropriate way will automatically occur at a specified time as the organism matures. Most environmentalists believe that certain stimulation applied at any period of development will result in an elevation in the level of learning without dependence on any of the processes of growth. For a discussion of the environmentalist positions, see Chapter 2.

The most convenient position would seem to be one which suggests that learning is the result of a complex interaction between certain genetic components and the favorability of the environment with which an individual is associated. This intermediate position suggests that mental, physical, and emotional maturity result from this interaction and is highly unique for each youngster. The status of two children of the same age may be quite different on any of these dimensions according to the particular constitutional and environmental circumstance of each youngster.

There are certain obvious mental, physical, and emotional factors that dictate how ready an individual is to learn. Learning to read depends, among other things, on the degree to which a child can maintain certain postural adjustments; has ability in binocular fusion; is able to discriminate among various shapes; can interact with other people; is able to relate sounds to their appropriate symbols; and views the product of reading as desirable. There are many more precursors required to effective achievement in reading, just as there are numerous prerequisite skills required to perform satisfactorily in every other area of endeavor.

The position taken here is that the age-old academic problem which questions the source of these prerequisite skills is irrelevant to specialists such as educators, concerned with the modification of behavior. Scientists have demonstrated that various kinds of intervention have impact on a living organism, the limits of which are apparently dependent on certain individual constitutional predispositions. The mission of educators should be to identify the most significant factors of readiness, devise techniques for evaluating these variables, and suggest procedures for stimulating their development in youngsters. The various learning problems that characterize youngsters in regular and special education classes will be difficult to identify and remediate without a basic understanding of those skills prerequisite to subsequent learning.

FOCUS ON PERCEPTUAL-MOTOR DEVELOPMENT

Although there is disagreement among scientists on the factors of readiness required for future learning and the nature of the hierarchical arrangement of these skills, increased attention is being given to the vital role of the numerous skills subsumed under the term perceptual-motor development. The influence of this accelerated professional activity has resulted in the development of several evaluative techniques for assessing the performance of children in the various perceptual-motor areas, principally those involving: (1) the presentation of visual stimuli; and (2) the execution of some type of motor response. From his performance on these instruments, programs of remediation can be prescribed according to each child's profile of disabilities.

Functioning of the Perceptual-Motor System

The development of a stable perceptual-motor system is a highly complex process. It demands the effective interrelationship of various components, none of which is discrete enough to allow for the precise identification and characterization of its total mission. Although grossly over-simplified, the process might be said to encompass the following four major components which operate in a continually dynamic and integrated way:

1. Input, involving the extraction and reception of stimuli from the environment;
2. Integration, or the association of incoming information, with material which has already been incorporated in a person's repertoire;
3. Output, which involves the gestural and/or vocal expression of ideas; and
4. Feedback system, which constantly monitors the output of an individual and provides a means for adjusting any components of the system to effect a better match between problems and responses.

Assumptions.   Certain assumptions must be made before considering the function of each component of the perceptual-motor process. First, in order for the system to operate effectively, the individual must maintain a certain level of arousal. Specific parts of the brain have the primary responsibility for providing this stimulation. If the individual is at some degree of unwakefulness, because of a lack of available stimulation or because of an organic defect, information will not be received or processed. Studies in sensory deprivation (Solomon, 1961) attest to the deleterious influence of low arousal on information processing. When too much direct or indirect stimulation is available, the individual will experience similar problems in focusing on the most relevant stimuli, and information will not be processed efficiently. This situation will result in an over-responsive individual who is unable to select relevant stimuli.

The perceptual-motor system may be diagrammed as follows:

Figure 3

Perceptual-Motor System

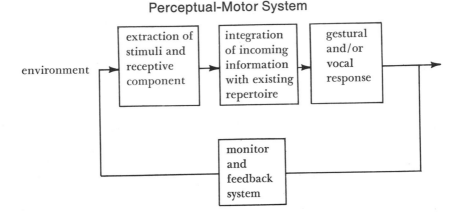

A second assumption is related to the stimulus-seeking characteristics typical of most individuals. Under normal circumstances an individual desires and actively seeks stimulation. Human beings who are within the range of normality will find many of their basic needs satisfied in environments which provide a variety of stimuli. Severely disabled individuals do not exhibit this typical need. Many seriously emotionally disturbed youngsters literally remove themselves from stimulus-complex environments. Youngsters with such severe problems, who are in need of comprehensive medical and psychological attention, are beyond the scope of this book. Excluding these youngsters, we can assume that individuals are stimulus-seeking organisms.

Third, there is little educational relevance in speculating on whether a child has a perceptual-motor problem because of brain injury. Although this question may be of academic interest to various specialists, including educators, and of practical importance to medical specialists, it does not help the classroom teacher in understanding, evaluating, analyzing, or properly redirecting the behavior of a child. The term "brain injury" does not describe a child's behavior, which is the area of proper concern to the educator. There is no unique behavior associated with the brain injured: one child might be hyperactive, another hypoactive or deaf, and a third youngster speech defective or cerebral palsied. Of what possible educational advantage is it for the teacher to know that a child's brain is damaged in a certain area? Does knowing this fact better define the limits of education appropriate for the child, the environmental intervention which is most efficacious, or the type of behavior that might predictably be exhibited by the child under various environmental circumstances? The assumption is that educators should not concern themselves with attempting to determine whether or not a child is brain injured; instead, the proper focus of the educator must be on manifest behavior of the child. It is this phenomenon that requires evaluation, analysis, and certain remedial procedures which, accordingly, are appropriate for each individual.

Reception of Stimuli.   The general model of the perceptual-motor process suggests that an individual has the ability and the need to extract stimuli from the environment. The environment should be viewed in a global sense, and include stimulation both internal and external to a person. Our sensory mechanisms are responsible for detecting stimulation and initiating the processing of this incoming information. This phenomenon occurs at a very early age; in fact, the greater the range of stimulation provided young children, the more actively they seek stimulation.

Learning cannot occur in a stimulus-free environment; that is, learning of the type that is meaningful for subsequent academic development. If an individual's receptive systems are inoperative, relevant stimulation from the environment which might have value for the solution of subsequent problems would not be received, processed, and available for future use. Studies in sensory deprivation have demonstrated the adverse effects of being placed in an environment devoid of stimulation (Solomon, 1961). In a critical review of the research on the effects of maternal deprivation, Casler (1961) suggests that the research strongly indicates detrimental effects of perceptual deprivation on future intellectual, physical, and social development. He cites evidence from psychological studies as well as neuroanatomical findings to justify this conclusion.

The effectiveness with which individuals extract stimulation from their environment varies according to the degree of intactness of their receptive systems, and according to the types of early experiences available to each person. Certain children have difficulty in efficiently and effectively receiving data from their environment because of an inability to mask-out peripheral and distracting stimuli. Their receptors receive any stimulation that happens to be present. This situation results in the processing of information that is imprecise and of questionable value in generating appropriate responses to problems. Children with this problem exhibit behavior that is vacillating, random, and unstable.

Other children may have more specific types of perceptual problems such as are illustrated by difficulties in distinguishing between foreground and background, discriminating among shapes, sizes, or colors, or spatial orientation. In many instances these problems can be traced to fundamental difficulties in the receptive component of the perceptual-motor process.

The accurate reception of appropriate stimuli is fundamental, then, for maintaining the integrity of other components of the perceptual-motor system, which is prerequisite for subsequent learning. Educationally, this means that stable and relevant stimuli must be presented to youngsters with receptive difficulties. This is particularly necessary during the stages of initial learning when stability among perceptual patterns is most desirable. If a child repeatedly receives unclear or different perceptions each time the same event is experienced, it is reasonable to anticipate that the entire perceptual-motor process will be adversely affected, and that learning will be minimal.

Association.   The integration of incoming information with the existing repertoire depends on the effective operation of the receptive component in the process. If an individual allows irrelevant stimuli to be introduced into the system, ambiguous associations will result. On the other hand, the exercise of a certain level of perceptual discrimination will provide a more stable, accurate, and meaningful associational network of information. This will increase the probability of giving appropriate responses to subsequent problems.

The establishment of association skills closely follows the development of an individual's receptive capabilities. Youngsters quickly learn, for example, that a certain type of environmental setting is related to comfort or discomfort. Stimuli received from various sensory modalities become associated and provide anchoring points for the further integration of subsequent sensory experiences. This introduction of additional sensory material serves to elaborate on existing patterns of integration and, by providing an individual with more comprehensive information concerning an event, ostensibly results in greater potential problem-solving ability. In short, the more elaborate the patterns of association and integration, the more varied the information an individual has concerning an event, and the greater the potential for effectively solving problems.

Expression. The output phase of the perceptual-motor process occurs after an individual realizes that a certain response is appropriate or necessary in a particular situation. The individual must then review his repertoire for any of the potentially appropriate responses to the problem. From these alternatives he must select the one response which he considers most appropriate to the immediate situation. Most teachers are aware of the wide differences among children in their ability to execute this operation. Some children have developed only a meager network of appropriate responses; other youngsters have developed an extensive repertoire of responses, but have difficulty in evaluating the possible responses and choosing the best one; still other children are able to select a response carefully from a wide range of alternatives. It should be clear, then, that the viability of an individual's expressive modality is based largely on the degree to which the receptive and associative components have been developed.

A response can be given verbally, non-verbally, or in combination. Dr. McWilliams discusses verbal expression in Chapter 6; the focus here will be on the non-verbal, gestural, or motoric output of a person.

A child's initial responses are motoric. Various muscles acting as systems develop patterns of operation to serve certain purposes. These systems become elaborated as an individual deals in various ways with his environment. This generalization results in the development of complex patterns of motor response, all of which depend on a satisfactory level of accomplishment in precursive skills. For example, an individual will not be able to jump or skip without first having accomplished the more basic skills of maintaining equilibrium, locomoting by walking, and running.

Gibson (1966, p. 57) has classified the various motor systems according to the primary function of each. He makes no assumption of an implicit hierarchy in this conceptualized system. The primary functions are:

1. Postural (preservation of equilibrium);
2. Orienting-investigating (orientation to special features of the earth);
3. Locomotion (moving about in space);
4. Appetitive (movements that take from or give to the earth);
5. Performatory (movements that alter the environment in a beneficial way);

6. Expressive (postural, facial, or vocal movements that convey emotional states); and
7. Semantic (signaling movements, especially coded speech).

As children learn to move about in space and deal more cautiously with the requirements of their world, in the sense of understanding the limits of their ability to maneuver their body, they gain greater freedom of response. This level of performance allows them to attend to the purpose of the movement without consciously considering how to execute the proper movement. Toddlers give full attention to the appropriate positioning of their legs in learning to walk. The more mature child is not as concerned with positioning and repositioning body components as he is with selecting the most appropriate type of locomotion available for achieving his wish.

Monitoring and Feedback.   It is important that the perceptual-motor process contain an accurate means for monitoring output, in order to determine whether an individual's response is congruent with the stimuli previously received. Components of the output are fed back to the receptive component of the system and are evaluated and modified accordingly. This monitoring results in any desired modification of the entire system; greater selectivity in the reception of subsequent stimuli; the need for making different associations; and alterations in the output phase. A match must occur between the individual's perception and the characteristics of his own movements. When this integration has taken place, perceptual-motor stability becomes established.

Interdependence of the Components.   At the beginning of this section it was mentioned that the system described above is an oversimplification of the perceptual-motor process. Any bifurcation of this entire process is artificial, since each component is interrelated so closely that relative malfunctioning in one or more of the components will seriously affect functioning of the other components. The following discussion attempts to rebuild these various entities into the total system so as to describe the nature of this dependent, dynamic relationship.

The literature reveals a great divergence of opinion among scientists concerning which of the perceptual-motor components is of greater relative importance. Watson (1919), Gesell (1954), and McGraw (1943) emphasized the central role of activity, and suggested that the motor rather than the sensory side is of primary importance in learning. Another advocate of this position was Dewey (1902), who emphasized the value of learning by doing. The most pervasive theoretical justification for this belief is the position of Piaget. He states that motor activity is transformed to perception and then to cognition as an individual proceeds through a series of complex stages in which experience is primary. These scientists, then, believe that motor activity precedes perception which in turn provides the basis for learning.

Hebb (1949) and Frantz (1965) have taken exception to this dominant theoretical position, and state that perception precedes action. Their belief is that early perceptual experience is required for the development and perfection of sensory-motor coordination, including the motor behavior that occurs during the early months of life. This school of thought has recently gained empirical support through the demonstration that infants are able to discriminate usefully among visual presentations at birth. Prior to this documentation the prevailing belief was that infants visually perceived only blobs, an assumption that was implicitly used to support the primacy of motor activity in the perceptual-motor process.

The theoretical attempts that have been made to separate the percepual-motor process and to speculate as to which of the components is more fundamental than the others, is in many respects comparable to the "chicken or egg" question. Issues of this type are interesting to consider and discuss, but irrelevant if one is responsible for formulating diagnostic and remedial strategies of instruction. The receptive mechanisms are not passive; we know that an individual actively seeks stimulation. This seeking takes the form of active and passive locomotion throughout the environment. As movement occurs, the perceptual experiences change, and the individual finds himself in a phenomenological environment which differs with every minute movement of the various muscle systems. A person can control sensory experiences through the manipulation of various groups of muscles. The extent of sensation present, whether too much or too little, will frequently dictate the type and extent of an individual's motor movement in accomplishing a goal.

If a child has an impairment in one or more of the perceptual-motor components, he will have difficulty executing certain activities that require the receipt of sensation, the internal processing of information, and the movement necessary for the achievement of a goal. The need for interaction among these factors, for the proper execution of a perceptual-motor task, can be illustrated by the behavior of an intoxicated person attempting to drink from a cup. In this situation information is misperceived; data about the spatial relationship that exists between the cup, hand, and mouth are erroneously or inadequately processed; communication between the various perceptual-motor components is impaired; and the execution of proper motor movements is impeded, resulting in both over- and under-compensation. The entire system is affected by disability in any or all of these components.

Another activity that illustrates the need for close harmony among the perceptual-motor components is the skill needed to kick a football. To execute this activity properly, the ball and foot must meet in a certain spatial location at a specific moment in time. Moreover, the football player must translate between temporal and spatial dimensions; that is, he must understand which of the movements precedes others and accurately perceive the location of his foot and the ball throughout the entire sequence of events. If the child misperceives among the various stimuli, his motor movements will lack appropriate timing and function inadequately. If his motor performance is faulty, he will not be able to maneuver his body into appropriate positions and thus not gain the necessary "up-dating" of information required for competent performance in a constantly changing perceptual field.

As individuals gain experience in interrelating the various components of the perceptual-motor process through the proper execution of activities, the process is no longer a conscious one. One doesn't have to think about the relation of input with output after having batted a baseball for a number of years. One's conscious attention, however, will have to be directed to these perceptual-motor components if one decides to learn to play golf without previous experience in a similar activity. Every part of the body must move in a specific sequence; perception of the ball in relation to other components of the activity is mandatory; and there is need to translate back and forth between sensation and activity if one's goal is to hit the ball in a straight line and to eventually break par.

Perceptual-Motor Development and Higher Mental Abilities

The position has been taken that higher mental abilities develop according to the degree that an environment is favorable to the individual. Intellectual development will be facilitated in direct relation to the type and variety of experiences an individual encounters throughout his life. It should be noted that maximum development of higher mental abilities occurs most dramatically when encounters between the environment and the child take place during the very early stages of development.

With respect to the broad parameters of experience basic to the development of higher mental abilities, the two factors that stand out in importance are: (1) the receipt and processing of information from the environment; and (2) the execution of certain behaviors in response to a problem. A justifiable hypothesis, then, is that perception and activity are fundamental components of experience. If either or both of these elements are impaired, one can expect the experience of an individual to be faulty to some degree; this situation results in reduction of efficiency and effectiveness in the development of higher mental abilities. The individual has less information to relate to the existing cognitive repertoire, and consequently is less able to respond properly. When a person has difficulty in responding to a problem, he will tend to withdraw from any area of development in which success has not been previously achieved. This psycho-social phenomenon of the individual's antagonism to activities in areas where he has previously failed only increases the magnitude of his experiential deprivation. In addition to bona fide problems in receiving and processing information, or in executing an appropriate response, there is always the possibility of precipitating a compounding psychological overlay. This psychological problem further reduces the individual's range of experience and his development in the higher mental abilities.

When a skilled diagnostician traces the origins of a child's learning problems, he will often find that some aspect of perceptual-motor development is the root of the problem. Reading, arithmetic, and social difficulties are symptomatic of more fundamental weaknesses. For example, a child may have difficulty in reading because of a basic defect in effectively distinguishing among shapes or sizes. This fundamental weakness could result in the child's inability to tell the difference between the letters p, q, d, and b. The genesis of this difficulty might well be the youngster's confusion between right and left. Another youngster may have a writing problem caused by an inability to translate an object from a spatial to a temporal orientation. A child with this type of disability may have problems in drawing a square or in writing his name because he doesn't know where to start, which component of the object should be done first, and where and when to stop. Such disability may be a manifestation of faulty development in certain perceptual-motor areas of functioning. A third child may have trouble in moving from left to right in reading and writing. His problem might be traced to an inability to coordinate both sides of his body, which results in weak body image and consequent difficulty in distinguishing between his own right and left and the right and left of objects in space. Until this problem is remediated, the child will continue to experience a reading and writing disability.

If an individual experiences difficulty in receiving information from the environment and in responding adequately to a situation, it is reasonable to assume that cognitive development will be adversely affected. The organism must have information coming into the system and a means for adequate response, in order for concepts to be formed. The development of an adequate perceptual-motor system is indeed basic to subsequent intellectual development. For this reason, attempts must be made to identify in which of these fundamental areas the child is experiencing difficulty, and design remedial procedures to alleviate his weaknesses.

DIAGNOSIS OF PERCEPTUAL-MOTOR ABILITIES

A number of formal and informal strategies have been used to assess various perceptual-motor areas. The recommended techniques reflect a great lack of unanimity among specialists concerning the factors on which focus should be directed. This variety of opinion emphasizes the philosophical and theoretical discrepancies existing among specialists of various disciplines. Certain diagnosticians are convinced that attention in assessment and remediation should be properly directed toward neurological reorganization. At the other extreme are those who feel that a complete optical examination with a prescription of appropriate exercises will provide the necessary remediation to establish basic perceptual-motor skills. The multitude of beliefs that lie between these extremes are described by the variety of evaluative procedures that have been developed to measure perceptual-motor competencies.

This section will review some of these formal and informal assessment techniques. Obviously, any examiner will select from the available strategies those that are applicable to the factors which he feels need study. He must consider the characteristics each instrument purports to measure; his competence to administer the instrument and interpret the data; the amount of time available; the setting under which the assessment is to occur; and the behavior of the child.

Formal Appraisal Techniques

Most of the formal evaluative techniques require the examiner to have specific training and supervised clinical experience for their administration. The teacher must always be sure that he or she has the proper background and experience for administering and interpreting the tests. Under no circumstances should the procedures be used by one who has not had this necessary training and experience. In every instance the test manual of instructions will outline these requirements. Data collected on children are often recorded in their folders, and decisions made about educational programming, without questioning the competence of the examiner. It is typically difficult to remove data from a child's folder once it had been recorded. With these cautions in mind, then, a brief review will be given of certain formal techniques to evaluate perceptual-motor competence.

Medical Evaluation. Physicians are often asked to judge the perceptual-motor abilities of children who experience chronic difficulties in and out of school. Their examination usually includes a general physical assessment of the youngster, record of the child's history, and a neurological examination, which can be either cursory or comprehensive according to the clinical signs. These examinations include the following:

1. Physical examination (complete check of the primary organs and the degree to which various body systems function normally);
2. History (collection of social history data with emphasis on environmental factors and particular attention to atypical circumstances possibly present during prenatal, perinatal, or postnatal periods);
3. Neurological examination (focuses on the extent of development of the central nervous system, with certain milestones in development recorded and compared to normative data from large groups of children of the same age); includes:

   a. Motor activity (raising the head, hand control, postural adjustment, movement, walking, climbing stairs, playing, writing);
   b. Reflex activity (the Moro reflex, tonic neck reflex, sucking, grasping, planter reflex, abdominal reflex, stepping reflex);
   c. Perception (use of the visual and auditory modalities);
   d. Social adaptation (smiling, feeding, crying, demanding, identifying); and
   e. Language (cooing, babbling, responding to name, using words to convey ideas).

Psycho-educational Evaluation. Of more tangible importance to the teacher in formulating a remedial program for youngsters who manifest perceptual-motor difficulties are the data that result from formal psycho-educational evaluations. With few exceptions the administration of these instruments requires specific training and experience. Several of the more popular techniques are:

1. *Marianne Frostig Developmental Test of Visual Perception* This test is appropriate for children between 3 and 8 years of age. It purports to measure six areas of visual perception including eye-motor coordination, figure-ground discrimination, form constancy, position in space, spatial relations, and a total perceptual quotient. The instrument can be administered to individuals or to groups; administration time ranges between 30 and 60 minutes. Although no statement indicating the level of training needed for scoring or interpretation is included in the manual, it is desirable for teachers to

have supervised experience with the instrument before using it independently.

2. *Perceptual Forms Test*   This instrument, appropriate for children between 6 and 8.5 years of age, was designed to identify those youngsters who do not have the eye-hand coordination considered necessary for beginning instruction in school. The children are asked to reproduce and complete certain geometric forms through drawing. Directions for administration, scoring, and interpretation are clearly given and the test is recommended to teachers as a means for evaluating visual perception and discrimination of youngsters below 8 years of age.

3. *Arthur Point Scale of Performance Tests*   This test requires administration, scoring, and interpretation by a qualified clinician. It assesses various perceptual-motor competencies in addition to general intelligence. It has been well standardized for subjects ranging from 4.5 years of age to adults.

4. *Bender Visual-Motor Gestalt Test*   This test of visual-motor coordination requires the subject to draw and copy nine complex geometric figures, some from memory and others by reproduction with the stimuli present. Various forms of the test have been developed for subjects between 4 and 10 years of age. Although the test was originally constructed to evaluate visual-motor coordination, it has also been used to determine incidence of brain damage and as a projective device to assess personality problems. A trained clinical psychologist is required for administration and interpretation.

5. *Porteus Maze Test*   This test is appropriate for subjects above the age of 3. It requires the youngsters to execute a series of mazes which increase in complexity. In certain respects it resembles several of the sub-tests from other instruments. Although the test requires a qualified examiner to interpret the more profound psychological implications of a child's performance, the visual-motor performance of a youngster can be readily ascertained by someone without formal training in interpretation.

6. *Lincoln–Oseretsky Tests of Motor Proficiency*   This instrument is designed to assess an individual's performance (ages 6 to 14 years) in gross motor skills, speed, coordination, dexterity, rhythm, balance, jumping, and manual ability. To a certain degree, sections of the instrument can be administered and interpreted by the classroom teacher.

7. *Rail-Walking Test*   This technique was developed to evaluate the locomotion abilities and general motor control of children above 5 years of age. It is a procedure which can be effectively used by

classroom and physical education teachers alike, and does not require a great expenditure for equipment.

8. *Cureton Physical Fitness Test*   This series of evaluative exercises will provide the examiner with data concerning the performance of adolescents in balance, body flexibility, agility, strength, endurance, and power. While normative data are not provided, ample justification is given for these areas being vital for physical fitness.

9. *Purdue Perceptual-Motor Survey*   This comprehensive technique for evaluating various perceptual-motor dimensions was developed by Kephart and his associates for use with children ranging in age from 6 to 9 years. Tasks embodied in the scale are easy to administer and interpret by teachers when the directions in the manual are followed. The perceptual-motor factors which are focused upon in this survey include balance, postural flexibility, laterality, body image, rhythm, translation of an auditory stimulus to motor response, symmetrical control of the body, directionality, eye-foot coordination, ocular control, form perception, figure-ground relationships, muscular fitness, and gross motor coordination. The primary focus of this scale is on motor performance in contrast to the receptive component of the perceptual-motor process. The survey is recommended to teachers for either formal or informal assessment of children.

Informal Appraisal Techniques

Most of the informal procedures that have been developed to evaluate perceptual-motor performance are not standardized, nor are there norms available for most of the activities in order to compare a youngster's performance with that of his peer group. This is not a great disadvantage, since most of the comparisons made in an informal diagnosis will be intra-individual and not between one child and another. A teacher may suspect that a youngster has a problem in eye-hand coordination. The child might be engaged in any task that requires various degrees of skill in eye-hand coordination, and his performance evaluated according to the manner in which he executes the task and his general level of performance. If a disability seems evident, the student might be given a specific remedial program and his performance assessed again following remediation. By using informal assessment techniques to compare his performance before and after remediation, a check can be made on the influence of the remedial program and a judgment made as to the advisability of referring the youngster for a more comprehensive diagnosis by an appropriate specialist.

Mention was made earlier of the wide range of possible observational opportunities available to the teacher. In perceptual-motor areas the teacher who is aware of the value of clinical educational diagnosis will be constantly alert to the behavior and performance of students in all activities. Important factors in perceptual motor performance that might be observed by the teacher include: (1) how the child holds his pencil and the manner in which he draws and writes; (2) how well he can copy and trace; (3) the technique which he uses to form numerals and letters; (4) whether a consistent pattern of reversals is evidenced; (5) how well he organizes materials for play and work; (6) how well he can move about the room without bumping into or tipping over objects; (7) how well he can identify and separate foreground objects from the background; (8) the degree to which discrimination among sizes, shapes, and colors is a problem; (9) how well the child can accomplish a task that requires a certain sequence of activities; and (10) whether objects in space appear confusing to him.

In most situations there is an ample source of data available in the classroom. Aside from the observation of behavior during the school day, the teacher will find it beneficial to hold periodic conferences with parents. These interviews should be semi-structured so that the vital information can be gathered in the most economical way, without too much delay, but still allow opportunities to explore in depth the areas that concern teacher and parent. To this end, it would be wise for the teacher to have certain key questions or hypothetical situations ready to present to the parents when they arrive. During this conference the parents will be seeking information about their child's performance in school and suggestions from the teacher about what they can do at home to supplement the school program.

The school records on a youngster are another source of information. A careful inspection of these records should be made by the teacher to determine any unique pattern of performance or behavior. The child's health records should be perused to see the nature of past illnesses, and whether there is a history of need for certain types of medication. Less attention should be given to an intelligence score or to an achievement score; instead, the importance of most school records lies in the possibility of gaining a more global or molar appreciation of a youngster's development, general performance, and limits of typical and atypical behavior. To use test scores or grades in isolation is hazardous; one can never be sure that they adequately represent the performance of the child or that the data were collected in an appropriate way by a competent person.

A survey of a child's performance in suspected areas of difficulty should include conscious observation of his performance in all of the subject areas. For example, the teacher's suspicion that a youngster has a problem in left-to-right progression should be established by systematically observing his performance in writing, reading, arithmetic, speaking, and so on.

As Dr. Brabner points out in Chapter 4, many activities the teacher selects for informal diagnosis can be chosen directly from existing standardized instruments. There is little merit in a teacher's spending time developing a range of activities for an informal assessment when highly appropriate tasks already exist in many formal tests. For example, if a teacher wished to check on a child's auditory memory abilities, the Digit Span or Memory for Digits test from the Revised Stanford-Binet Intelligence Test, Wechsler Intelligence Scale for Children, or Illinois Test of Psycholinguistic Abilities might be used.

In perceptual-motor areas there are a number of existing devices that are amenable to use in an informal setting. One of the most comprehensive instruments for ascertaining perceptual-motor weaknesses is the Purdue Perceptual-Motor Survey which was developed and standardized by Roach and Kephart (1966). The instrument was designed for children between 6 and 9 years of age, but it can be used with younger or older youngsters to gain some indication of perceptual-motor development. The tasks in this instrument are easy to administer, can be used in a group setting, and survey a rather complete spectrum of perceptual-motor dimensions. It is not necessary to use the survey in its entirety, but the teacher can choose tasks to evaluate those specific areas about which information is needed. Table 1 summarizes the dimensions which are evaluated in the Survey and the techniques that are used for assessment.

Other formal instruments from which a teacher can select tasks or activities for an informal assessment of perceptual-motor ability are: (1) Rail-Walking Test; (2) Lincoln-Oseretsky Tests of Motor Proficiency; (3) Marianne Frostig Developmental Test of Visual Perception; (4) Maze Tests; (5) Visual Forms Tests; (6) tests that require tracing, coding, or coloring; and (7) selected performance items from the Wechsler Intelligence Scale for Children. Many of the activities embodied in tests of these types are appropriate for informal appraisal of perceptual-motor performance.

A child may manifest perceptual-motor difficulties because of a problem in one or more of the components of this process. It is frequently impossible for even the most astute diagnostician to determine the exact reason for the location of the disability. Ideally, of course, one would wish to determine if the problem were primarily a receptive, association, expressive, or feedback weakness. In order to make a general determination of the site of the difficulty, any activity chosen for assessment should

Table 1

Relation Between Perceptual-Motor Functions and the Activities for their Evaluation in the Purdue Perceptual-Motor Survey

	Walking Board	Jumping, Skipping, and Hopping	Identifying Body Parts	Imitation of Movements	Obstacle Course	Angels in the Snow	Stepping Stones	Chalkboard Work	Ocular Pursuits	Visual Achievement Forms	Kraus-Weber Tests
Motor Coordination	X	X	X	X	X	X	X	X			X
Balance	X	X			X		X				X
Postural Adjustment & Flexibility	X	X			X	X	X				X
Body Control	X	X		X	X	X	X				X
Body Image		X	X	X	X	X	X				
Laterality		X	X			X	X	X	X		
Directionality				X		X	X	X	X		
Rhythm		X						X			
Auditory Motor Association			X							X	
Eye-Foot Coordination							X				
Ocular Control								X	X	X	
Muscular Fitness											X
Form Perception									X	X	
Figure-Ground Relationships										X	

emphasize only one of the process dimensions. For example, if you were interested in determining a child's level of performance in the association of visual stimuli, it would be advantageous to reduce to a minimum the need for reception and expression by the youngster in the performance of the task. Although this procedure is somewhat artificial, for diagnostic purposes the concept and its implementation have real merit.

Assessment of Receptive Abilities.   A discussion of auditory perception will be found in Chapter 6; this section will focus on the visual modality. In considering possible approaches to the informal assessment of visual receptive abilities, many of the activities suggested by Montessori (1965) are directly relevant. Table 2 summarizes some of her suggestions.

Table 2
Informal Procedures for Assessing Visual Receptive Abilities

DIMENSION ASSESSED	SUGGESTED EVALUATIVE ACTIVITY
1. Perception of Length	Provide the child with several rods or sticks (Cuisennaire Rods, for example) of varying lengths. Ask the child to tell which of two rods is longer, and which is shorter. Gradually increase the complexity of the task by requiring finer visual discriminations and by using objects other than rods. Have the child group rods according to similar lengths.
2. Perception of Size	Using objects of the same color and shape but varying in size, such as large blocks, ask the child to point to the smallest, the next largest, and so on, until the appropriate ordinal relationship has been shown among a set of objects. In this activity the child does not need to respond verbally or to move, just to point; thus minimizing the influence of the association and expressive components of the perceptual-motor process. As the child gains skill in this task, it can be complicated by adding other objects, or by varying shape and color as well as size.
3. Perception of Color	Display a series of plates in different colors. Ask the child to point to the appropriate color as you name it. Use widely different colors initially, gradually increasing the difficulty of the task by using more similar plates. Eventually the teacher might ask a child to point to all of the red objects in a picture. This task is more difficult than the former activity.
4. Perception of Shape	Using various geometric forms, have the youngster identify the one which is most round, square, or pointed. Later, have him pile the shapes so that those that are round are in one pile, square in another pile, and so on. This activity, as well as use of the simpler geometric forms which can be inserted into appropriate slots, will be helpful in analyzing a child's perception of differences in shape.

The proper reception of visual stimuli and the ability to discriminate length, size, color, and shape are basic skills required for even moderate success in subsequent academic areas. Other activities that might be used to assess general receptive abilities include:

a. Having a youngster look at and interpret a picture according to criteria such as color, movement, function, shapes, details, or relative size of objects. The task can be arranged so that it is not necessary for the child to respond verbally; the teacher can ask the youngster to point to parts of the picture according to the criteria being used in interpretation.
b. Having the child identify common objects and either tell about them or demonstrate their use.
c. Engaging the children in sorting, matching, or cutting activities which have been progressively sequenced according to their level of difficulty.

Assessment of Association Abilities.   To associate stimuli, to see likenesses and differences, and to be able to match a percept with an appropriate motor movement, are important skills which depend to a large degree on the accurate reception of stimuli. If an individual perceives inaccurately, it will be more difficult for him to associate stimuli correctly. Associations must take place between modalities; i.e., between auditory and visual stimuli and vocal and gestural responses. The following are activities that teachers might use and elaborate on to assess perceptual association skills:

a. Engage the youngsters in rhythm activities, such as moving in certain ways to music, which progressively increase in complexity.
b. Ask children to follow directions or to make up stories about a picture or filmstrip.
c. Provide formboard or jigsaw puzzle exercises that vary in complexity.
d. Have the youngsters group or categorize objects according to certain criteria.
e. Block designs and pegboard activities are valuable in assessing association skills. In these activities the child should be asked to copy a design by placing their blocks or pegs in an appropriate association with other blocks or pegs.
f. Sequence exercises, such as a picture sequence, will help to determine higher-level association skills in youngsters.

Assessment of Expressive Abilities.   Vocal expression will be considered only tangentially here, and only as it relates to gestural expression, since the subject is covered in depth in Chapter 6. The teacher should be alert to a number of motor skills. These include a child's skill in balance, posture, eye-hand coordination, movement in space, spatial to temporal translation, fine motor movements and left-to-right progression. The Purdue Perceptual-Motor Survey is helpful for systematic evaluation in most of these areas. Other activities for assessing expressive performance include:

a. Pegboard work, cutting and pasting, coloring, matching, sorting, copying, tracing, working with buttons and zippers, and playing with blocks, to assess eye-hand coordination and fine muscle movement.

b. Walking, running, jumping, sitting, skipping, hopping, manipulating large toys, crawling through openings, playing on jungle gyms, expressing an idea through gestures (such as catching a fish or driving a car), dancing, participating in action songs, and walking on small or narrow objects, to assess balance, posture, control of body, laterality, directionality, and body image.

c. Drawing objects such as squares or triangles, copying designs, kicking a ball, drawing a sequential story or design, hitting a baseball, doing jigsaw puzzles, constructing a block design from an actual or pictorial model, and reproducing a pegboard design, to assess ability in making spatial to temporal translations.

d. Showing the child a picture of an object and asking him to demonstrate what people do with the object, or having the student demonstrate a process such as putting on clothes, riding a bike for the first time, sewing a button on a coat, or leading a band, to assess ability in expressing meaningful ideas through gestures.

REFERENCES

Bruner, J. S., *The Process of Education.* Cambridge: Harvard University Press, 1960.

Casler, L., "Maternal Deprivation: A Critical Review of the Literature," *Monographs of the Society for Research in Child Development,* Vol. 26, No. 2, 1961.

Dewey, J., *The Child and the Curriculum.* Chicago: University of Chicago Press, 1902.

Frantz, R. L., "Pattern Discrimination and Selective Attention as Determinants of Perceptual Development from Birth," in *Perceptual Development in*

Children, A. H. Kidd and J. L. Rivoire, eds. New York: International Universities Press, Inc., 1966.

Gesell, A.,"The Otogenesis of Infant Behavior," in *Manual of Child Psychology,* L. Carmichael, ed. New York: John Wiley & Sons, Inc., 1954.

Gibson, J. J., *The Senses Considered as Perceptual Systems.* New York: Houghton Mifflin Co., 1966.

Hebb, D. O., *The Organization of Behavior.* New York: John Wiley & Sons, Inc., 1949.

Hunt, J. M., *Intelligence and Experience.* New York: The Ronald Press, 1961.

Hymes, J. L., *Before the Child Reads.* New York: Harper & Row, Publishers, 1958.

McGraw, M. B., *The Neuromuscular Maturation of the Human Infant.* New York: Columbia University Press, 1943.

Montessori, Maria, *The Montessori Method.* Translated from the Italian by Anne E. George, Cambridge, Mass.: Robert Bently, Inc., 1965.

Solomon, P., *Sensory Deprivation.* Cambridge: Harvard University Press, 1961.

Tyler, F. T., "Issues Related to Readiness to Learn," in *Theories of Learning and Instruction,* E. R. Hilgard, ed. Sixty-third N.S.S.E. Yearbook, Chicago: University of Chicago Press, 1964.

Watson, J. B., *Psychology from the Standpoint of a Behavorist.* Philadelphia: J. B. Lippincott Co., 1919.

Chapter 4

READING SKILLS

George Brabner, Jr.

Despite the constant efforts of forward-looking school systems in this country to upgrade instruction, surveys reveal that approximately ten to fifteen per cent of all the children enrolled in typical elementary schools are cases of mild or severe reading disability (Harris, 1961). Programmed instruction, special reading devices, innovations, or other methods have failed to bring about any substantial reduction in this figure.

Inadequate reading ability remains the principal reason for children being kept back in the elementary grades, and continues to plague the secondary schools, the colleges, and the military in the conduct of their programs. With our accelerating communication tempo and our increasingly complex, technological, and verbal society, the ability to decode segments of an enormous and expanding symbology quickly and accurately becomes of paramount importance, not only for the highly trained technician or scholar, but for the average man as well. Unless an individual is living in a geographically isolated area—and these are rapidly becoming non-existent—the inability to read, and to read well, will handicap him more in numerous life situations than will many physical or mental limitations.

Unquestionably, sensory handicaps, neurological impairments, low intelligence, metabolic disorders, and cultural-psychological influences will continue to be contributory factors in reading retardation for some time to come, but it is my conviction that the largest portion of children who are retarded in reading are so because of poor instruction. Where instruction is inadequate, and children still learn to read adequately, their reading ability is developed in spite of that instruction, not because of it. Too often we look for the reading problem in the child, and thereby slip into the habit of identifying the problem as the child's and not as the teacher's. It would be more accurate to say that the affliction is the child's, but the problem of cure, or amelioration, is the teacher's. Rather than talking about the instructional problems of teachers, we prefer to talk about the learning disabilities of children. Where does the focus properly belong?

We must examine both the child's behavior and our own as teachers. To accomplish the first of these objectives, we must acquire diagnostic skills so that we can identify the psychological correlates of the disability in the child's behavior; having done this, we are confronted with the instructional problem of correcting or remediating effectively, utilizing the data gleaned from the diagnosis. To use the data effectively, we must know how to manipulate the physical aspects of the learning environment, and, how to modify our behavior as teachers, which is a vital part of that environment. It may sound harsh to some, but broadly speaking, an instructional problem can be reasonably defined as any obstacle to learning created by, or persisting because of, the failure of the teacher to make the modifications of her behavior and/or materials necessary to eliminate the obstacle.

By comparison with other subject areas of the curriculum, the many rich contributions to the study of reading offer the teacher a super-abundance of methods, materials, and research findings applicable to classroom instruction. This "embarrassment of riches" poses a difficult quantitative and qualitative problem of selection, even when choices are made within a class of diagnostic techniques. To assist the teacher in the resolution of this problem, this chapter is designed to acquaint the reader with selected informal techniques of diagnosis; explain why each of these techniques deserves emphasis; and explain why these techniques are preferable in some instances to standardized instruments.

TECHNIQUES FOR ESTIMATING READING CAPACITY

Formal procedures for estimating reading capacity or expectancy level usually involve the administration of one or more standardized measures: (1) intelligence tests, which can provide a mental age index of expectancy; (2) reading capacity tests, which assess a child's comprehension of material read to him, either meaningful paragraphs or isolated words; and (3) arithmetic computation tests, to provide an indication of how well a pupil is able to perform a basic skill which does not require reading. A detailed description of the standardized tests used in formal appraisal of reading skills may be found in almost any standard text dealing with the diagnosis of reading disabilities. Two such texts which should prove to be especially helpful are *Corrective and Remedial Teaching* (Otto & McMenemy, 1966), and *How to Increase Reading Ability*, 4th edition (Harris, 1961).

Assessing Test-Taking Ability

A factor, or a complex of factors, often overlooked or taken for granted in the diagnosis of reading difficulties is what can be referred to as "test-taking" ability. For reasons too numerous and complex to expand upon here, some children may be seriously penalized, particularly by group-administered paper and pencil tests, when they are required to follow test directions and make written responses to test items.[*]

The classroom teacher can institute two important steps in her program to offset many of the test-taking handicaps that detract from a child's performance. She can (1) develop informal tests of test-taking ability to determine which pupils are deficient in specific test-taking skills; and (2) provide planned exercises for improving these skills. For example, she may furnish the class with blank IBM answer sheets and observe which children fail to fill in the banks correctly when directions are presented in either oral or written form, explaining exactly which spaces are to be blackened with the electrographic pencil. Whether the difficulty lies in the examinee's poor spatial-relational concepts, visual-perceptual deficit, or some other disability, this widely-used method for recording test responses does create unusual difficulties for certain in-

---

[*] That such may be the case with many socially disadvantaged children or with children having perceptual-motor handicaps should be apparent.

dividuals. Following this diagnostic procedure, the teacher may give specific practice exercises to the deficient pupils by having them respond to a variety of teacher-prepared tests—ranging from brief to lengthy— using the IBM answer sheets.

Informal tests of the ability to connect correctly parallel columns with a pencil line are especially important in diagnosing the test-taking ability of very young children. It is not unlikely that children with excellent word discrimination skill may have this skill obscured by their lack of a corresponding development in certain laterality concepts. Directions may cause difficulty, such as: "In the left column underline the word that is unlike the others; then draw a line from this word to the same word in the right column." The teacher should ascertain her pupils' comprehension of test terms such as: match, underline or underscore, same or different, like and unlike, upper left-hand corner, check, cross out, column, row, etc. Some children fail or do poorly on arithmetic computation tests because they either cannot read or cannot understand the single computational term (multiply, divide, subtract, etc.) which indicates the operation they are to use for solving the numerical problems.

Needless to say, the teacher should not train pupils on actual standardized test materials, or she will be guilty of coaching or rehearsing pupils for a particular test. Such precautions do not have to be as rigidly observed when informal diagnostic materials are being used, where norms are often of little consequence.

It can be argued that much of what has been described as test-taking ability depends upon general intelligence, or a capacity to comprehend what is contained in a set of verbal or written directions. In some measure this contention is probably true, for intelligence does appear to be related to the various indices we employ in estimating reading capacity. It is likely, however, that specific learning deficits not assessed by conventional tests of intelligence also affect test-taking, just as they affect other varieties of academic performance, including reading. Such test-taking deficits can and should be remedied.

The Informal Reading Inventory—(IRI)

No discussion of informal techniques for diagnosing reading difficulties would be complete without some mention of the IRI, or informal reading inventory. It receives separate treatment here because it is really a composite of many techniques which deal with reading capacity, achievement, error analysis, etc.

The IRI has been defined as "a teacher-made diagnostic reading test

based on a series of graded books, usually a series of basal readers"
(Cooper, 1956, *Criteria for Selection*). It can be used to select appropriate
reading material for use with an individual child or with several children
grouped homogeneously for reading instruction. It is also useful in detecting symptoms and correlates of reading difficulties in a given child.
The IRI is an individually administered test requiring the child to read
selections, orally and silently, from a graded series of readers. The
teacher records the errors the child makes at each level, usually on individual mimeographed copies of the test selections. Following each
reading selection, questions are asked of the child to check his comprehension of the material. This procedure is followed until the child
reaches a level of difficulty which he finds frustrating and confusing.
Cooper has provided one of the best descriptions of the IRI and its
construction, administration, and use; in addition, Smith (1959) has
authored an excellent book on the IRI, which can also serve as a guide
for the interested teacher. Her graded selections, however, are limited
to grades one through three.

Some teachers complain that the construction of IRI materials is too
time-consuming; in some teaching situations, this is undoubtedly the
case. Perhaps the construction of these materials is another one of the
tasks which can be delegated to teacher aides (where they exist), under
the supervision of the teacher.

The IRI can furnish valuable data not always available from standardized instruments. Cooper has listed four ways in which the IRI can
be used to provide realistic and meaningful information:

1. As a basis for determining the maximum level of readability of
   materials for independent reading;
2. As a basis for correcting tentative groupings established by standardized test data or other means;
3. As a basis for estimating small increments of progress not easily
   measured by standardized instruments; and
4. As a basis for determining the level at which the child becomes
   confused or blocked in the reading process.

Assessing Hearing Comprehension

To gain some idea of the level at which a child with a reading disability could be reading, that is, his potential reading level, the teacher
can make an informal appraisal of the child's hearing comprehension
of spoken language. This reading capacity, or hearing comprehension
level, is defined as the highest level at which a child can understand

what is read to him. Approximately 70 per cent of the materials read should be comprehended by the child. The teacher may test for understanding of isolated words or for comprehension of one or more paragraphs. As in the IRI technique, pre-selected word lists and paragraphs or a set of graded basal readers may be used for this assessment.

After ascertaining the point at which the child becomes confused and frustrated in his attempt to read orally—the "frustration level"—the teacher commences to read to the child, quizzing him on what she reads and continuing from one selection to the next until the child no longer grasps the meaning of the material being read to him. An estimate of reading retardation can be obtained by noting the discrepancy between reading achievement level and hearing comprehension level. Some expertise should be acquired in selecting reading materials and in constructing comprehension questions before trying the technique with a pupil, or its validity will be questionable. Cooper (1956, *Criteria for Selection*) supplies several carefully developed criteria for assisting the teacher in this respect. If the teacher can sample the listening comprehension of a child in more than one curriculum content area (science, mathematics, geography, history, etc.), it is possible to gain valuable supplemental information relating to the child's general scholastic aptitude, as opposed to his expectancy level in a particular academic skill.

Frequently, a new child may be admitted to a class during the school year and the teacher may wish to get a quick, general estimate of the child's intelligence as an index of reading capacity. Even short-form intelligence tests may not be available, and where they are, the teacher's recollection of how to administer them may be a little hazy. The teacher can make her estimate quickly by administering the vocabulary subtest of the Revised Stanford-Binet Intelligence Test. This can be done either by keeping a list of the words at hand or by committing them to memory, along with the standards for passing at each age level, so that the words can be presented to the child in proper order, inquiries made concerning their meaning, and an age-equivalent score calculated on the basis of the resulting performance. The rationale for this procedure is derived from the fact that the vocabulary sub-test on individually administered intelligence tests generally correlates higher with total test I.Q. than does any other sub-test. Socially disadvantaged children and certain other handicapped children may, of course, be penalized by this technique; however, such limitations are not so much an inherent part of informal diagnostic techniques as they are illustrations of restrictive phenomena associated with testing in general.

Assessing Vocabulary and Verbal Concept Formation

There is a consensus among reading authorities that adequate vocabulary development is crucial for good reading comprehension. For this reason, most standardized tests of hearing comprehension include a separate vocabulary sub-test; for example, the oral vocabulary sub-test of the *Gates-McKillop Reading Diagnostic Tests* (Bureau of Publications, Teacher's College, Columbia University). The teacher can keep a copy of this sub-test at her desk and read the thirty items to the pupil: "Fierce means: tame, slow, wild, easy;" "Gaudy means: certainly, wealthy, beautifully, showy," etc. A grade-level score is obtainable, but as Otto and McMenemy (1966) have pointed out, this score is not very helpful in informing the teacher as to where to begin instruction. These authors offer the following more practical alternatives:

1. *An informal inventory*—using a text judged to be at or near the pupil's instructional level of reading. By informally quizzing the pupil on the meanings he derived from context it is often fairly easy to determine not only the quantity but the quality of vocabulary work needed.

2. *An accepted frequency list*—such as that given by Durrell, which contains words for fourth through sixth grades; the Thorndike and Lorge list of 30,000 words; or any other graded list which seems acceptable. Samples from such lists enable a teacher to make a quick but accurate check on a pupil's mastery of words at various difficulty and/or frequency levels.

3. *Word lists*—obtained from a book the pupil is going to be called upon to use. This is, of course, similar to the first method mentioned; but it offers the advantage of dealing with the specific words the pupil can expect to encounter in his assigned readings. (Otto and McMenemy, 1966, p. 177)

Harris (1961, pp. 197-199), under the heading, "Informal Appraisal of Word Recognition Skills," also describes techniques similar to those above. The interested teacher may wish to take particular note of the graded word lists which he has found to be especially valuable in actual clinical practice.

A useful technique for determining whether a child in the early grades can recognize and pronounce words correctly and whether he can associate a meaningful concept with them is that which may be described as a "book analysis." The teacher analyzes a basal reader by breaking down its vocabulary into separate lists of nouns, verbs, and prepositions, and obtains pictures corresponding in meaning to the nouns, and wherever possible to the verbs and prepositions. The child is called upon to read each vocabulary word aloud and then to select the picture matching it in meaning. If the child is unable to read the word orally, the teacher tells him what it says and asks the child to select the picture that corresponds to the word. This technique is excellent for ascertaining which words can be recognized at sight and, more importantly, for determining the extent of the child's understanding of the verbal concepts that will be included in the reader used in the instructional program during the school year.

Assessing Rate of Acquisition of Sight Words

One of several criteria that can be employed to group children for reading instruction is the rate at which they can learn to recognize new words. The teacher can informally assess this rate by compiling a list of new words that can be flashed individually by cards or by some type of audio-visual device. The teacher pronounces the word for the child on the first exposure trial, and on each subsequent trial where the child is unable to recall the word. She records the number of words acquired by each child within a given time period. Instant recognition of a word on five consecutive trials can be used as a learning criterion.

Teachers interested in exploring the use of automated procedures to develop high levels of retention in word recognition and spelling may wish to read a short review of a study by Malpass (1963). In this study, he demonstrated that automated procedures were definitely more effective than conventional classroom instruction in engendering high levels of learning. These levels were maintained over a 60-day post-instruction period, although his subjects were mentally retarded children.

Assessing Arithmetic Computation Ability

As was indicated earlier in this chapter, the assessment of computational ability in arithmetic is one way of gaining an estimate of a pupil's learning ability through his performance in a basic skill not requiring reading, thus providing additional evidence that the disability is specific to reading. Standardized tests can and probably should be used, in preference to informal tests, to measure arithmetic computation. The Stanford Achievement Tests (Harcourt, Brace & World, 1953) contain computation sections for grades two through nine. This is one ability area which is probably best evaluated formally rather than informally, if the interest is estimating learning ability and not diagnosing arithmetic computation ability itself. There is little to be gained through the construction of a teacher-made achievement test. Unless a school system is experimenting with a truly radical method of arithmetic instruction—and most are not deviating to that degree from all aspects of conventional instruction, even where the "new math" has been introduced—these standardized computational tests will prove adequate for the purpose indicated.

TECHNIQUES FOR ESTIMATING READING ACHIEVEMENT

A variety of standardized tests are commercially available for the formal evaluation of both oral and silent reading achievement. Teachers become most familiar with the latter tests when they are routinely administered in a school system at the beginning and end of the school year to evaluate growth in reading for that period. Local or national norms, or both, are often employed in the evaluation.

Regrettably, many formal achievement tests suffer from at least three limitations for which compensation must be made by reliance on other techniques. These tests (1) do not correct for guessing (a child may be in the fifth grade; the test commences at the third grade level; he guesses correctly on an item and obtains a grade equivalent of 3.1, when his actual achievement level may be 1.3); (2) do not easily measure the small increments of progress for which the alert teacher is constantly looking; and (3) they can be used only for tentative grouping of children for instruction. Unfortunately, some teachers employ reading achievement scores in grouping for instruction as if they were absolute assignation criteria.

Table 3 (Cottrell, 1966) should prove valuable to any teacher interested in correcting for guessing when using standardized tests as well as her own informal tests. To use the table, the teacher need only know the number of items in the test and the number of alternatives (e.g., true or false tests have two alternatives). She can then consult the table and find the lowest meaningful score, that which is not due to chance (guessing). The .05 figure in parentheses at the top of the table merely indicates that in only five cases out of a hundred could the scores contained in the table be attributed to chance factors. On a true and false test containing ten items, the child would have to obtain at least nine correct answers before one could be reasonably sure (five times out of a hundred) that the child had not guessed. If a teacher administers a 60-item multiple choice test to her class with four alternatives for each item, a child must have

Table 3

Table of Lowest Meaningful Scores   (∞ $P \leq .05$)

Items N.	No. of Alternatives 2	3	4	5
1	–	–	–	–
2	–	–	–	2
3	–	3	3	3
4	–	4	4	3
5	5	4	4	4
6	6	5	4	4
7	7	5	5	4
8	7	6	5	5
9	8	6	5	5
10	9	7	6	5
11	9	7	6	6
12	10	8	7	6
13	10	8	7	6
14	11	9	7	6
15	12	9	8	7
16	12	9	8	7
17	13	10	8	7
18	13	10	9	8
19	14	11	9	8
20	15	11	9	8
21	15	12	10	8
22	16	12	10	9
23	16	12	10	9
24	17	13	10	9
25	18	13	11	9
26	18	14	11	10
27	19	14	11	10
28	19	14	12	10
29	20	15	12	10
30	21	15	12	11
31	21	16	13	11
32	22	16	13	11
33	22	16	13	11
34	23	17	14	12
35	23	17	14	12

Items N.	No. of Alternatives 2	3	4	5
36	24	18	14	12
37	24	18	15	12
38	25	18	15	13
39	26	19	15	13
40	26	19	16	13
41	27	20	16	13
42	27	20	16	14
43	28	20	16	14
44	28	21	17	14
45	29	21	17	14
46	30	22	17	15
47	30	22	18	15
48	31	22	18	15
49	31	23	18	15
50	32	23	19	16
51	32	24	19	16
52	33	24	19	16
53	33	24	19	16
54	34	25	20	17
55	35	25	20	17
56	35	25	20	17
57	36	26	21	17
58	36	26	21	18
59	37	27	21	18
60	37	27	22	18
61	38	27	22	18
62	38	28	22	19
63	39	28	22	19
64	40	29	23	19
65	40	29	23	19
66	41	29	23	20
67	41	30	24	20
68	42	30	24	20
69	42	30	24	20
70	43	31	24	21

Items N.	No. of Alternatives 2	3	4	5
71	43	31	25	21
72	44	32	25	21
73	45	32	25	21
74	45	32	26	21
75	46	33	26	22
76	46	33	26	22
77	47	33	27	22
78	47	34	27	22
79	48	34	27	23
80	48	35	27	23
81	49	35	28	23
82	49	35	28	23
83	50	36	28	24
84	51	36	29	24
85	51	36	29	24
86	52	37	29	24
87	52	37	29	25
88	53	38	30	25
89	53	38	30	25
90	54	38	30	25
91	54	39	31	25
92	55	39	31	26
93	55	39	31	26
94	56	40	31	26
95	57	40	32	26
96	57	41	32	27
97	58	41	32	27
98	58	41	33	27
99	59	42	33	27
100	59	42	33	28

Permission to reproduce granted by Dr. R. S. Cottrell (10-28-66).

at least 22 items correct before one could be reasonably sure that the results obtained were not attributable to chance. In this case, twenty-two would be the lowest score which could still be viewed as meaningful.

Oral Reading Achievement

A quick way to survey a class of poor readers by obtaining a sample of their reading performance has been offered by Dolch (1953, pp. 10-14), and improved upon by Harris (1961), who has suggested reading a larger sentence sample, and adding a silent-reading comprehension check. The technique, used at the beginning of the school semester, requires each child to read two or three sentences aloud, as fast as he can, from the same basal reader. If a child refuses to read, the teacher goes on to the next child, without exhibiting any signs of disapproval. If a child attempts to read but has great difficulty, the teacher immediately tells him any unknown word, says "good," and proceeds with the survey.

Following the oral procedure, the teacher can test for comprehension by having the children read silently a four- or five-page selection. As each pupil finishes the selection, he closes the book and looks up at the teacher. In this way, slow readers can be detected. When every child has finished reading, the teacher reads a prepared list of short-answer questions and the pupils write their answers. The book under consideration will prove too difficult for children scoring below 70 per cent in comprehension. This technique will reveal those children who are achieving at a level too low to use the basal reader that the majority of the class will be using, and may also indicate whether or not the book is suitable for most of the class. Harris recommends that teachers have their classes try out textbooks in various content areas, as well as basal readers.

The technique is, of course, merely a gross way of screening for reading achievement. More commonly, a teacher wishes to obtain an accurate estimate of a child's reading achievement level. For this purpose, allow the child to read aloud from a graded series of readers until the child attains that level (the instructional level) at which he can read adequately with minimal assistance from the teacher, yet still be sufficiently challenged.

Criteria for determining reading levels and suitability of reading materials are available from a number of sources. I recommend the criteria contained in the bulletin by Cooper, *Criteria for the Selection of Suitable Reading Materials*. Cooper has devised two sets of criteria for the instructional level: one for the primary grades (grades one, two, and three) and one for the intermediate and upper grades. His criteria for the primary grades read as follows:

A. Accurate pronunciation of ninety-eight per cent of the running words, or not more than one unknown word in fifty running words. (Materials in which pupils make 2-6 word perception errors per 100 running words are of questionable difficulty, and more than 6 are definitely unsuitable.)

B. A comprehension score of at least seventy per cent based on questions in the IRI.

C. Freedom from any noticeable degree of the following symptoms:
   1. Word-by-word reading
   2. Inadequate phrasing
   3. Repetitions
   4. Inattention to punctuation
   5. Strained, high-pitched voice
   6. Slow and halting reading
   7. Marked insecurity and tension movements
   8. Finger pointing
   9. Holding book too close

Again, as in assessing hearing comprehension, the teacher may want to assess oral reading achievement at varying levels within separate content areas. It is not at all unusual to find a child achieving well in one content area and poorly in another; some children may react adversely to reading problems in arithmetic and therefore read more poorly than when reading a selection in geography. In short, children read at different achievement levels in different content areas.

The teacher should not neglect to use the vocabulary list provided in the back of the reader to test the child's ability to recognize words in isolation. Intelligent children who lack sufficient word attack skills are often able to identify words within a meaningful context but fail miserably when the same words are presented out of context. When adequate clues to meaning cannot be derived from context, the bright child is unable to identify the unknown word, although it may be part of his hearing vocabulary.

Silent Reading Achievement

The procedure used in assessing silent reading achievement is similar to that for assessing oral reading achievement. Comprehension of the material read is checked by asking prepared questions; the 70 per cent comprehension score applies here also. In the upper grades (fourth, fifth, and sixth), an excellent way to improve study skills, as well as to assess silent reading achievement, is to have the pupils outline simple, well-organized reading selections. After reading each selection, the pupils are provided with blank outline forms, to be filled in with the main topics covered in the selection and certain relevant details.

Teachers are sometimes in doubt as to how to determine—even approximately—the point where a child changes from an inaudible oral reader to a true silent reader, although they understand that the child who is merely suppressing his voice while visibly moving his lips has not attained the desired skill. Actually, the transition is made when the reader reaches a level of visual and cortical integrative skill which will enable him to *think* what he is reading more quickly than he can *say* it. At this point, lip movements and barely audible whispering disappear, and visible throat-muscle movements are absent. As with oral reading, a check should be made of the student's ability to comprehend content drawn from a number of subject areas.

A highly motivating technique for assessing silent reading comprehension can be devised by preparing several pages of reading material consisting of a series of paragraphs, graded in difficulty and made up of sentence absurdities numbered consecutively. For example: (1) In the winter we slide down the hill on our pinwheels; (2) My glasses are broken so I cannot hear well; (3) I ate so much dinner, I thought my hair would burst. The pupil is shown how to do a few examples, and proceeds to do the actual test items within an allotted period of time. He is required to read the material silently and to underline the nonsense word in each numbered item that makes it an absurdity. Most children find this activity highly amusing, and consequently react to it more as a game than as a test. A test of this type, which has been found successful with socially disadvantaged children and young adults, is presently available (*Basic Test of Reading Comprehension,* S. Alan Cohen and Robert D. Cloward, Mobilization for Youth, Inc., 214 East Second Street, New York 9, New York).

TECHNIQUES FOR OBSERVING AND ANALYZING READING PERFORMANCE

Formal techniques for observing and analyzing specific reading skills and processes of the type described in this section are found in individual diagnostic reading examinations, in check lists of reading difficulties often included in such examinations, and in a variety of specialized tests which have evolved out of clinical practice. Skill in the clinical educational techniques required to analyze reading performance in a highly specific way, so that deficits can be pin-pointed, errors identified and analyzed, and idiosyncratic behaviors noted, separates the successful clinician from the test-administrator.

Analyzing Method of Word Attack

The teacher can learn a great deal about the method of word attack a child is using by informal observation of the child's oral reading performance. The skillful use of context clues is the most efficient way of unlocking unknown words; however, a child must have acquired a considerable sight vocabulary and mastery of the mechanics of the reading process before he can use context clues effectively as a method of word attack. Skill in phonic and structural analysis should, therefore, precede the use of context clues. The teacher can quickly ascertain whether or not the child is completely lacking in word attack skills by noting the characteristic silence and total absence of trial and error activity which results when the child encounters a word he does not recognize. Some children will at least spell out a word as a method of word attack, and occasionally achieve limited success in word recognition in this way.

If the teacher attends closely to the child's performance when he is trying to analyze a word, she will sometimes be able to determine whether or not he is able to sound out the word or any part of it. He may recognize initial consonant sounds only, or he may be able to break the word down correctly into its individual sound elements, but be unable to synthesize, or blend, these sounds into an auditorially recognizable whole word. Much can be learned from a child's method of guessing at an unknown word. For example, his reading the word "large" as "long" may suggest that he perceives the word as a configurational whole; similarly when "horse" is read as "house." If he substitutes a completely dissimilar word for the one encountered in print, such as "ship" for "dog," the teacher knows that the child lacks any skills for making an educated guess. The teacher should also be alert to a child's ability to utilize knowledge of prefixes, roots, and endings (structural analysis) in analyzing words when assessing the child's skill through informal observation. She may wish to use a check list of difficulties for recording her observations of the child's problems in a systematic fashion, although most lists encompass reading difficulties other than word attack behavior alone.

Assessing Deficits in Auditory Skills

Two of the many auditory skills involved in reading are mentioned here for particular emphasis. The first of these, auditory discrimination, has long received attention from reading authorities, and various tests have been developed to measure it. Monroe (1937) designed a short test for assessing this ability and included some crude norms with it, although these norms are probably now in need of revision. Monroe's test consists of pairs of words which are read to the examinee, who is asked to label them as "same" or "different;" for example, "pin—pen," and "pool—pool." The teacher can make up similar lists of paired words to read to her pupils. It is important to make sure that the child is unable to observe the teacher's lips when she is repeating the words, or he will pick up visual cues that may enable him to differentiate between words and thus score spuriously high.

The second auditory skill is by far the more neglected in the literature, but in the writer's opinion it is perhaps the most important of all the auditory abilities associated with reading. This skill is sound-blending, the ability to blend the analyzed sound components of a word, whether individual vowels and consonants or syllables, into a unified whole. It is difficult to envision how anyone not possessing eidetic imagery can learn to read at all without being able to sound-blend effectively. One cannot commit sight words to memory indefinitely; therefore, some type of analytic word attack activity must be used sooner or later if one is to become a skillful independent reader. If one analyzes a word, one must synthesize in order to hear the sound of the whole word so that it can be recognized, if it is part of the reader's hearing vocabulary.

Again, Monroe (1937) has been of assistance by publishing a short test of sound-blending ability. Here also, the teacher is free to construct her own items. Because Monroe's test is a brief one, the teacher may wish to compile a longer and more varied list of words to sample this ability in greater depth. Such a list may begin with simple two-letter words (a–t; m–e; o–n; i–t) and gradually work up to longer words (s–a–t; b–r–a–n; c–e–n–t–e–r). Again, the teacher must avoid allowing the child to observe her lips when she is pronouncing the individual letter sounds (she may have the child sit with his back to her). Children who have any sound-blending ability at all generally grasp what is being demanded of them quickly after several opportunities to respond. Precise instructions for sound-blending presentation can be found in Monroe; she recommends a rate of two sounds per second (Monroe, 1937, p. 200).

How much of sound-blending ability is learned before a child enters school, or to what extent it is dependent upon innate factors, has yet to be determined. Until research sheds more light on this phenomenon, it would probably be best for the teacher to assume that the ability is trainable. In any event, it might be well for the teacher of reading to pay a little less attention to phonic analysis and a little more to phonic synthesis.

Assessing Deficits in Visual Skills

Three visual ability areas related to reading which the teacher should be interested in assessing informally are (1) visual memory, (2) visual discrimination, and (3) visual sequencing.

Visual memory. Skill in the visual recall of letters and words is essential for the rapid development of an adequate sight vocabulary and plays an important role in spelling. Flash cards with printed nonsense words can be prepared for informal assessment of visual memory. The cards may begin with single letters and gradually advance to words of greater length. Exhibit each card for approximately five seconds, then require the child to write the flashed word. This technique only allows the detection of children with marked visual deficits, and cannot be validly used to gradate children in the skill. If the teacher suspects that the child has a motor coordination problem which interferes with rate and skill of written reproduction, she may allow the child to select, by pointing to or marking the correct stimulus word on the flash card from among several other words on a prepared response card.

Visual discrimination. Visual discrimination diagnostic tests may provide a better indication of the child's ability to read if letters and words, rather than pictures or geometric designs, are employed in their construction (Goldstein, Moss, and Jordan, 1964). One may wish to assess the ability of young children to recognize the letters of the alphabet by assigning the task of selecting out all twenty-six when they are mixed in with nonsense letters, using letter forms or letters printed on cardboard squares.

In general, visual discrimination errors can be classified as one of three types: errors based on structural details; errors based on orientational confusion; and errors that are a combination of the previous two. For example, confusing an n with an h would be an error of the first type, confusing a b with a p would be an error of the second type, and confusing a p with a q would be an error of the third category.

The present author is developing a series of sequentially organized sets of training materials designed primarily for use in the prevention and remediation of reversal errors in reading, and errors based on structural details. I hope that these materials may also be used as a clinical instrument for aid in diagnosing these problems. The recom-

mended approach is exclusively visual. At no time is the child required
to name letters or to make phonic association with individual letters or
whole words of the stimulus materials. The materials consist of sets of
stimulus cards with individual letters or combinations of letters (some
of which are actual words), and lucite (transparent) squares or rectangles with inscribed letters or combinations of letters identical in
size and shape to those on the stimulus cards. The letters or words on
the lucite squares or rectangles are printed to conform exactly, when
properly positioned, to those on the stimulus cards. The printed material on the stimulus cards appears in black, as does most ordinary
printed matter. The letters on the matching lucite squares are bright
red. These sharply contrasting colors enable the child to detect immediately any discrepancies in match when the letter or letters on a
square are superimposed on the stimulus card.

   The child's task is to match the squares with the appropriate stimuli
on the cards. (The numbers of squares equals the number of stimuli or
stimulus configurations on the cards.) Prior to each trial, the squares are
randomly scattered on the table next to the stimulus card, which is
placed before the child. The task may be performed individually or in
a group situation. In the latter case, cards are distributed to each participant and all the matching squares for each card are scattered in the
middle of the table. Each child is allotted a specific amount of time in
which to select one square which he attempts to match with the correct
stimulus on his card.* Where the goal is to prevent or correct p, d, b, q
confusion, each card may contain all of these letters, but with each
card rotated to a different position to present a variety of directional
orientations to the group:

p	d
b	q

b	q
p	d

ɑ	ᗡ
ᑫ	ᕑ

For a very slow learning child, begin with one stimulus and two different
squares from which to select the correct match. The child may then
graduate to two stimuli and two different squares, etc.

---

* A variant of this activity would require the teacher to hold up squares and ask
the group if the stimulus appears on their cards. If a child thinks the stimulus appears
on his card, he is allowed to try to make a match. It is occasionally desirable to
encourage the children to examine each other's cards to find out who has the matching
stimulus.

One cannot assume that a child who is able to match individual letters will also succeed in identifying these same letters in the context of a whole word. It is eventually necessary to provide exercises with words incorporating the practiced letters in initial, medial, and final positions. Sequentially organized exercises should be provided, which move from individually perceived letters to words consisting of two and then three or more letters.

Special exercises in matching can be given for reversal errors and for errors in discriminating letters or words whose correct recognition depends upon attention to small structural detail. For example, when the configuration q is superimposed on a manuscript *q*, the small tail at the bottom of the *q* sticks out to one side and contrasts with the red overlay. It is precisely this small detail to which the child must attend in order to succeed in distinguishing this letter from, for example, a *q* or perhaps even the numeral *9*.

The child performing the exercises in an individual situation should be able to work independently of the teacher to a considerable degree. This auto-educational aspect is made possible by a self-correcting feature of the materials. Unlike many games on the market today, the child does not have to guess that he has made a correct match—he knows. The teacher does not have to be present to verify that a correct match has been made.

Because success in reading is contingent upon attaining a certain rate, the temporal factor in the visual perceptual process cannot be ignored. The teacher may encourage the child to compete against himself through the employment of a temporal criterion, thus increasing speed of recognition. A child who is unable to tell time may still be able to respond to the signal of an automatic timer, to go off at ever-decreasing intervals. Plans are underway to modify the existing materials so that an electric circuit will be completed when a match is made, enabling the child to receive immediate reinforcement for a correct response.

Visual Sequencing. Visual sequencing is the ability to organize visual stimuli in correct spatial order. The required response may be one of recognition, recall, or reproduction, but frequently more than one of these elements is involved. For instance, in visual-motor sequencing as measured by the *Illinois Test of Psycholinguistic Abilities* (McCarthy and Kirk, 1961), both reproduction and recall play a part, as they do in written spelling.

Visual-motor sequencing is defined here as the ability to reproduce a sequence of visual stimuli from memory. A test of the ability calls for arranging in correct sequence a series of cardboard chips which have printed pictures or geometric outline forms, after a brief exposure to the sequence model.

To sound out a printed word, the pupil must be able to observe correctly the left-to-right sequence of letters before he can coordinate the temporal sequence of sound with the spatial sequence of letters. Regrettably, except for the ITPA sub-test referred to above, little has been developed in the way of formal diagnostic techniques of this ability. We can suggest only two informal techniques in this area, and can only assume that they are valid and that they assess identical or, at least, closely related abilities.

A teacher may employ a modified version of the visual-motor sequencing sub-test using letters instead of geometric forms on the chips, gradually lengthening the sequence of letters to be recalled and reproduced through the pupil's arrangement of the chips in proper sequence. The child's errors can be recorded and compared to the performance of his classmates. In constructing the letter series for such a test, it would be best to rely on a high consonant count to minimize the effect of recalling letter groups because of their similarity to known words or familiar phonograms.

The teacher can also construct an informal diagnostic test by preparing a series of stimulus cards with letter series of gradually increasing length. These cards are exposed to the child for a fixed interval, perhaps 5 seconds, and then removed. After each 5-second exposure the child is required to recognize and mark the correct letter series from among several alternative series printed on a response sheet. All of the alternative series contain the same letters, differing only in the arrangement of the letters. This technique also requires that an individual be able to discriminate visually among letter series as well as to sequence them visually in correct order. There is thus some confounding of abilities inherent in the test materials. Both informal techniques described are probably only sensitive enough to identify children having gross deficiencies in visual sequencing ability.

IMPLICATIONS OF CONTEMPORARY RESEARCH FINDINGS FOR DIAGNOSIS AND INSTRUCTION

Traditionally and correctly, educational authorities have recommended that strong emphasis be given to the development of understanding in reading. Providing children with a rich experiential background, developing meaningful verbal concepts, and improving their ability to comprehend phrases and sentences, are all activities designed to help the learner gain greater meaning from what he reads. There are, however, increasing indications that proficiency in reading may be more dependent upon perceptual and memory abilities than upon conceptual abilities.* Although there is not space here to discuss all of the related evidence which has accumulated in recent years, it is important for the teacher of reading to be acquainted with some of this evidence so that she may decide whether she wishes to re-evaluate and modify her own program in light of new findings.

Current Research in Reading Skills

1. The first of these studies (Kass, 1963, pp. 87-96) was designed to discover psychological correlates of reading disability (dyslexia). Dyslexia was defined by Kass as "retardation in reading skills which occurs after adequate instruction and which is not due to mental retardation or to sensory defects (blindness or deafness)." The Illinois Test of Psycholinguistic Abilities, which can assess ability in both the meaningful and the less meaningful aspects of language, was administered to twenty-one children between the ages of 7 years and 9 years 11 months. All the subjects were normal in intelligence, and all were retarded in reading, as measured by a battery of diagnostic reading tests. None of the children were known to have any auditory or visual defects. In addition to the ITPA, certain supplemental tests of the automatic, or perceptual factor, type were also administered.

Kass's results were intriguing. She found that the retarded readers were, in general, significantly inferior to the normal in the less meaningful, automatic-type tests, but were deficient in only one of the meaningful-type tests, or "the ability to draw relationships from what is heard." In fact, the reading-retarded subjects were better than normal in a meaningful-type test which measured the ability to understand what is seen. Kass's interpretation suggests from this finding that "children with normal intelligence who have difficulty in handling the symbols in reading compensate by garnering information from pictures (1963, p. 88)."

The principal difficulty encountered by the subjects was with closure tasks, which require that the whole be predicted from its parts. Kass points out that, because her subjects were normal in intelligence and

---

* Terms which have been used in the literature to designate these perceptual factors are: auditory and visual discrimination, auditory and visual memory, auditory and visual perception, sound blending and visualization, auditory and visual closure (Kass, 1963).

therefore had some conceptual ability, the reading disabilities probably resulted from an inability to integrate elements into a total meaningful pattern. She believes that a deficiency in the process of integration, possibly neurological in origin, may underlie the reading difficulties these children have and that training should be directed toward these processes, rather than toward the conceptual or more meaningful processes.

2. The second study was conducted by two American investigators (Birch and Belmont, 1965, pp. 135-144) who felt that one of the many causes of reading retardation might stem from an inability to integrate effectively auditory and visual stimuli; hence, an impairment in auditory-visual integration might occur more frequently in a sample of retarded readers than in their normal age-mate controls. They used 200 subjects, approximately nine to ten years of age, drawn from the total population of school children in the city of Aberdeen, Scotland. Of these students, 150 were retarded readers and 50 were normal readers.

To assess the auditory-visual integration ability of their subjects, Birch and Belmont devised an informal diagnostic technique consisting of auditory patterns which could be tapped out with a pencil on the edge of a table; and a response sheet containing visual stimuli, or patterns, on which the subject was to identify the visual equivalents of the auditory patterns presented by the examiner. The results showed that the retarded readers were significantly less able than the normal readers to judge auditory-visual equivalence. The subjects within the two groups who scored lower on the test also tended to have the lower reading scores. Birch and Belmont found that the significant difference in auditory-visual test performance remained even when subjects with low normal IQ were eliminated from consideration. They concluded that auditory-visual integration ability is specifically related to reading performance, although it is not the only factor contributing to reading retardation.

3. Graubard (1966) attempted to identify some psycholinguistic correlates of reading disability in emotionally disturbed children. The subjects were twenty-three children who had been institutionalized for behavior disorders. They ranged in age from 8 years 6 months to 10 years 11 months, were of normal intelligence, and their reading achievement was at least one year below expectancy. Performance on various psycholinguistic measures and tests, including the ITPA, Monroe's Sound Blending, Wechsler's Mazes, and Harris' Test of Lateral Dominance, was used as a basis of comparison with the normative popula-

tions. Graubard's results showed that his delinquency prone subjects deviated from normal communication processes; most of their deficits appeared at the integrational level and in the visual-motor channel.

Among other disabilities, he discovered a deficit in visual-motor sequencing (the ability to reproduce a sequence of visual stimuli from memory). This is one of the psycholinguistic abilities considered basic to the reading process. He found that fine discriminations, such as between a circle and an octagon, were imperceived by many Ss in the sample. As the test items were offered, the successful Ss tended to use mnemonic devices to solve the test tasks; for example, some Ss labelled disks with the names of card suits to aid them in identification and memory. He suggested several techniques, most of them perceptual-motor in nature, which could be used to remediate the deficits encountered in his sample. He called attention, however, to the need for developing new training methods which can be used to remedy integrational deficits, particularly of the visual-motor type. Graubard concluded from his findings that the special population from which he sampled did have special strengths and weaknesses related to reading achievement, and that special teaching is required to remedy the weaknesses.

4. A less recent study by Simpson (1960) includes a perceptual training program designed to improve reading readiness. While studying the reading readiness problems of first grade pupils, Simpson observed that the copying sub-test on the Metropolitan Readiness Test seemed to predict reading performance better than did those designated as reading readiness sub-tests. She attempted to determine the relative contribution of perceptual ability to first grade reading achievement, as measured by the Metropolitan Readiness Test and the Primary Mental Abilities Test. Simpson correlated the sub-test scores of 312 first grade pupils on the Metropolitan Readiness Test and the Primary Mental Abilities Test with total scores earned on the Metropolitan Reading Test and found that the perceptual sub-tests (numbers, matching, copying, quantitative, and space) correlated more highly with reading achievement than did traditionally designed reading readiness sub-tests such as "sentence meaning" and "information."

Using an experimental group of twenty-four first graders of normal intelligence and a comparable group of twenty-four control children, Simpson directed the teacher of the experimental group in implementing a perceptual training program which was added to the regular first grade curriculum activities for one school year. At the conclusion of the study, a comparison of the reading achievement of the perceptual training group with that of the control group showed the average reading achievement of the training group to be significantly greater (3.33 months). Simpson concluded from her findings that the perceptual development of first grade children can be increased through appropriate perceptual training activities, with a resulting increase in reading achievement.

Her sentiments echo my own when she remarks at the end of her study, "at least at the first grade level, [and probably earlier] there is statistical justification for increased emphasis on the teaching of reading as if it were a PERCEPTUAL ART as well as a LANGUAGE ART." Serious consideration must be given to the balance between perceptual and conceptual aspects of the reading readiness program and, during the first grade instruction and later, to the specific nature of the training provided.

5. In a study by Goldstein, Moss and Jordan (1964), using six-year old mentally retarded subjects, the experimental group was exposed to a reading readiness program for the entire first year in a special class setting, while the control children received instruction in the regular grades in the first grade reading program. (It should be noted that the initial stages of this instruction included some reading readiness activities.) At the end of the first year, the control group surpassed the experimental group in reading achievement. Although the experimental readiness program used in this investigation did progress through a pre-established sequence of perceptual training activities, which culminated in "differentiating letters and letter groups," most of the activities did not involve the use of printed letters or words. Hence, after observing the superior results of the control group, which received directed reading instruction, the investigators concluded that "the conceptual and perceptual exercises in learning a new word may have as much or more value to the child as differentiating an equilateral triangle from a right triangle or an oval from a circle" (Goldstein, Moss and Jordan, 1964, p. 107). Their findings cast doubt on the validity of the assumption that much time in readiness programs must be spent on perceptual training with ambiguous stimuli prior to practice with actual letters, groups of letters, or words.

Summary

Admittedly, the evidence produced by these five investigations is far from conclusive, but it must be remembered that these are only a sample of some of the recent findings which have appeared in the research literature. Further research into the nature of perceptual and memory-type abilities may eventually disclose the answers to some of the baffling reading difficulties confronting the teacher, particularly in the behavior of children of normal intelligence. New kinds of diagnostic and remedial techniques will have to be developed to identify these factors and their role in the reading process. For example, what might be the relationship between the abilities measured by the auditory-visual integration test of Birch and Belmont and the abilities required in the crucial skill of sound blending as a word attack technique? Why do some children with normal hearing master this technique with little or no difficulty, while others never respond to instruction at all?

Naturally, some children are distinctly more advanced than others in perceptual and memory abilities long before they enter school. Cognitive training practices, intentional and unintentional, vary widely from one home to another. If the public schools eventually extend their program downward to include preschool instruction for all children, and not just for the disadvantaged, as in Operation Head Start, systematic exercises emphasizing perceptual–memory–integrational training may come to occupy a prominent position in the educational program. This kind of instruction could continue through kindergarten and the primary grades, gradually decreasing in amount while accompanied by a corresponding increase in more conceptual, meaningful instruction (Figure 4). At present, we are contending with many perceptual prob-

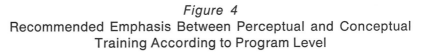

Figure 4
Recommended Emphasis Between Perceptual and Conceptual Training According to Program Level

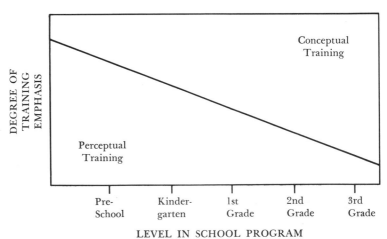

lems in the classroom which could be eliminated, or greatly minimized, through an early intensive program. Two or three years of intensive diagnosis; the establishment of a solid foundation of perceptual memory skills; and gradually increasing attention to conceptual development, could result in an excellent reading readiness program. Story-telling time and trips to the farm and museum are not enough.

REFERENCES

Birch, H. G., and L. Belmont, Auditory-Visual Integration in Brain-Damaged and Normal Children, *Developmental Medicine & Child Neurology,* 7 (1965).

Cooper, J. L., *Criteria for the Selection of Suitable Reading Materials.* Unpublished mimeo bulletin. University of Connecticut, 1956.

Cooper, J. L., *The Informal Reading Inventory: Its Construction, Administration, and Use.* Unpublished mimeo bulletin. University of Connecticut, 1956.

Cottrell, R. S., Table of Lowest Meaningful Scores (personal communication) October, 1966.

Dolch, E. W., "How to Diagnose Children's Reading Difficulties by Informal Classroom Techniques," in *The Reading Teacher,* 6 (1953).

Goldstein, H., J. W. Moss, and L. J. Jordan, *The Efficacy of Special Class Training on the Development of Mentally Retarded Children.* Cooperative Research Project No. 619, Office of Education, U. S. Department of Health, Education and Welfare, 1965.

Graubard, P., "Psycholinguistic Correlates of Reading Disability in Disturbed Children." Paper presented at the American Psychological Association, New York, New York, September 2, 1966.

Harris, A. J., *How to Increase Reading Ability* (4th edition). New York: David McKay Company, Inc., 1961.

Kass, Corrine E., "Some Psychological Correlates of Severe Reading Disability (dyslexia)," in *Selected Studies on the Illinois Test of Psycholinguistic Abilities,* D. J. Sievers, *et al.* Madison, Wisconsin: Photo Press, Inc. 1963.

Malpass, L. R., A. S. Gilmore, M. W. Hardy, and C. F. Williams, *Automated Teaching for Retarded Children: A Summary Comparison of Two Procedures.* Cooperative Research Project No. 1267, Office of Education, U. S. Department of Health, Education and Welfare, 1962.

McCarthy, J. J. and S. A. Kirk, *Illinois Test of Psycholinguistic Abilities.* Urbana, Illinois: University of Illinois Press, 1961.

Monroe, Marion, *Children Who Cannot Read.* Chicago: University of Chicago Press, 1937.

Otto, W., and R. A. McMenemy, *Corrective and Remedial Teaching.* Boston: Houghton Mifflin Company, 1966.

Simpson, Dorothy M., *Perceptual Readiness and Beginning Reading.* Unpublished Doctoral dissertation, Purdue University, 1960.

Smith, Nila B., *Graded Selections for Informal Reading Diagnosis: Grades One through Three.* New York: New York University Press, 1959.

Chapter 5

WRITTEN EXPRESSION AND SPELLING

G. Phillip Cartwright

PART I: WRITTEN EXPRESSION

The appraisal of written expression has long been a serious problem for teachers of all grade levels. It is well known that teachers will often disagree when asked to evaluate the quality of a written composition. One teacher may unconsciously place a premium on the grammatical correctness of a composition, while another may stress the originality of the ideas expressed. Typically, it is quite difficult to define exactly the criteria or standards which a teacher may use to score a composition. It is the purpose of this chapter to bring together some ideas and techniques which may reduce the inconsistency often found in the appraisal of written expression.

Written expression is defined here as the use of the English language for the purpose of communication. It does not include handwriting or motor ability, although these factors may be important prerequisites for a child to be able to place his thoughts on paper. Written expression would include daily written assignments of many kinds: letter writing; creative or original writing of stories or experiences; factual or abstract essays; book reports; and even essay tests. The emphasis is upon the child's ability to use the English language to convey thoughts and experiences, and to use the language to demonstrate his ability to deal with abstract and concrete relationships.

REQUISITES FOR ADEQUATE APPRAISAL

Two major areas seem to be important in the accurate appraisal of written expression: reliability and validity. Any method of grading students' written work should have built into it a high degree of consistency or reliability. A highly reliable method would be one in which all teachers using the method on a given group of compositions would score or grade all the compositions in the same manner and arrive at precisely the same grades. Almost by definition, such a method would be quite objective and could not rely on subjective or ill-defined factors. When a teacher grades a series of written assignments, it is extremely important that she have clearly fixed in her mind a systematic and objective procedure for the appraisal of the assignments. This procedure should be such that all the assignments will be graded or scored according to the same frame of reference, and will not change from student to student.

The second area of importance is validity. A valid measure of writing ability is one which actually assesses the child's ability to use the language. Valid measures can operate at many different levels, and will vary according to the purpose of the written assignment and the interests of the person who scores the assignment. It is not possible, therefore, to say that a certain method of appraisal is the "most" valid; a given method may be quite satisfactory for one aspect of written expression but not at all suitable for another aspect. At the present time, there is lack of agreement among language authorities concerning which procedures are most suitable for different purposes.

Some of the problems involved in choosing appropriate appraisal procedures can be eliminated by carefully defining the purpose of the written assignment. A careful formulation of an answer to the question, "What are the objectives of the assignment?" will set the stage for evaluation of the assignment in terms of the satisfaction of the objectives. It is not enough to say, "The papers will be graded for creativity and originality." Some teachers might grade such papers on how well-formulated and well-stated the original ideas might be, while other teachers might put a premium on words or phrases that convey vivid meanings or sensual impressions. An example of one properly stated objective for a written assignment following a lesson on subject-verb agreement is: "The student will demonstrate his ability to write complete sentences in which subject and verb are in agreement." Another appropriate objective might be: "The student will use words which convey vivid visual or auditory impressions."

TECHNIQUES OF APPRAISAL

The techniques of appraisal of written expression can be logically clustered into four areas of composition abilities. The organization of the following sections is based on the premise that these four areas must be assessed in order to obtain an adequate evaluation of a child's overall ability in written expression. The four areas have been arbitrarily labeled Fluency, Vocabulary, Structure, and Content (Cartwright, 1967). Adequate and objective measures have been developed for the first three areas; completely objective measures of content have not yet been developed for classroom use. The techniques suggested are not necessarily mutually exclusive; they may be combined or substituted, augmented or reduced. The procedures are designed to be flexible and to allow for the ideas of the creative teacher.

Fluency

Fluency, as used here, means quantity or verbal output. Numerous research studies have shown fluency as measured by sentence length, sentence complexity, etc., to be related to age (McCarthy, 1954; Meckel, 1963). As a child grows older he tends to write longer compositions, to use longer sentences, and to use more complex sentences. In addition to greater proficiency with the language, the older child has accumulated more experiences which can be drawn on for a particular written assignment, and thus he has more to say. Besides sheer quantity of words, variety in sentence length and in types of sentences seem to be important factors in fluency.

Average Sentence Length. The average sentence length is obtained by: (1) counting the number of words in the composition; (2) counting the number of sentences in the composition; and (3) dividing the number of words by the number of sentences. In general, longer sentence lengths indicate more mature writing. As a very rough guide, the author, in a study of the language of 160 normal children, found that children between the ages of eight and thirteen gained on the average about one word per year in sentence length (Cartwright, 1968, *Written Language*). Eight-year-old children wrote sentences averaging about eight words in length; nine-year-olds averaged slightly less than nine words per sentence and so on, up through age thirteen (slightly less than thirteen words per sentence). A deviation of about two words was fairly standard; the average departure from the normal for a given age group was about two words above or below the normal. Thus, if an eleven-year-old child attains an average sentence length of eight words (three words less than we would expect), he would appear to be below par in fluency. This finding might suggest that the child did not fully understand the assignment; that he did not have the relevant experience to do justice to the assignment; that he was using only short, choppy sentences; or that he was actually writing at the level of a nine- or ten-year-old child.

A beneficial by-product is obtained when number and average length of sentences is calculated, for, in order to determine where a given sentence should begin or end, the teacher is often forced to evaluate each sentence in terms of its content and grammar.

Sentence Variety. Sentence variety is closely related to sentence length, inasmuch as the child who writes very short sentences will not be able to use compound or complex sentences. A short sentence almost automatically precludes the use of dependent clauses. A rough check on a child's progress can be determined by the percentage of usage of each of four sentence types: incomplete, simple, compound, and complex. For example, if a child has written a twenty-sentence composition composed of three incomplete sentences, eleven simple sentences, four compound sentences, and two complex sentences, the percentage of usage of the four sentence types would be: incomplete, 15 per cent; simple, 55 per cent; compound, 20 per cent; and complex, 10 per cent. The use of percentages permits comparisons based on different numbers of sentences. We would expect the percentage of simple sentences to decrease, and the percentage of compound and complex sentences to increase, as the child grows older.

A related analysis of sentence structure can be made by examining clauses within sentences and using the clause as the unit of analysis. LaBrant (1933) found that both the ratio of the number of dependent clauses to the total number of clauses, and the average number of clauses per sentence, increased with chronological age. Sentence variety might also be interpreted as variation in the length of sentences: mixing long sentences with medium length and short sentences. Page (1966, pp. 238-243) provided research support for this idea when he found that variety in sentence length was related to teachers' evaluations of compositions.

Vocabulary

Adequate written expression in any form, whether it is letter-writing, a composition assignment, or an answer to an essay question, depends a great deal upon the variety of words known to the writer. A small vocabulary forces redundancy; the writer must use some words repeatedly. The writer with a large vocabulary may choose from a larger collection of words and is less likely to be redundant. Also, the size of a child's vocabulary, and thus his word variety, increases as he grows older.

Type-Token Ratio. Variety of word usage can be measured by use of the type-token relationship. The type-token ratio is the ratio of different words used (types) to the total number of words (tokens) (Johnson, 1944). The sentence, "The boy ran to the corner to get the ball," contains ten words (tokens). The word "the" is used three times, "to" is used twice, and the remaining words once each. The ten-word sentence is composed of only seven different words (types). The types divided by the tokens gives a type-token ratio of .7. A low type-token ratio would indicate that a child is using some words repeatedly, and might indicate that the child's vocabulary is inadequate for the assignment. In such a case, it would be worthwhile to provide exercises in vocabulary building for the child.

If the type-token ratio is used to compare the written expression of different children or of the same child at different times, it is essential that the same number of words from each child be used to calculate each type-token ratio. The first fifty or one hundred words of the composition might be used for this purpose. Carroll (1938, pp. 379-386) has pointed out that as the number of words in a composition increases, the percentage of different words decreases. Thus, the type-token ratio based on the first one hundred words will almost always be less than the type-token ratio based on the first fifty words of the same composition. Carroll (1964, p. 54) also states that "A measure of vocabulary diversity (the type-token relationship) that is approximately independent of sample size is the number of different words divided by the square root of twice the number of words in the sample."

Index of Diversification.   The index of diversification (Carroll, 1938, pp. 379-386; Miller, 1951), also a measure of vocabulary variety, is easier to calculate, but is also influenced by composition length. It is obtained by finding the average number of words which appear between each occurrence of the most frequently used word in the composition. In the author's experience, and as indicated by Miller (1951), the word "the" can be safely used as the most frequently occurring word in most compositions. As an example, consider the following fictitious passage:

> The boy ran to the corner to get the ball. The ball was not there.
> The boy ran back down the street. The ball was there on the grass.

The number of words between each occurrence of the word "the" is 3,3,1,4,4,1,4. (Do not count words occurring before the first "the," nor after the last.) The number of words between successive "the's" totals twenty, and the number of intervals between successive "the's" is seven. Twenty divided by seven gives an index of diversification value of 2.85. (The type-token ratio is .52.)

An alternative method of obtaining the index of diversification can also be used. To the number of "the's" in a composition, add the number of words which appear before the first "the," and after the last. Subtract this sum from the total number of words in the composition. Divide this difference by one *less* than the number of "the's" in the composition. The two different methods yield the same results. A third method will give slightly higher values for short compositions, but is easier to calculate than the other two methods. Simply divide the number of words in the composition by the number of "the's," or by the number of occurrences of the most frequently used word.

The index of diversification is similar to the type-token ratio since the higher the index value, the more diverse or varied the vocabulary. Both measures can be used to compare the written expression of different children or of the same child at different times. It should be emphasized that the index of diversification, like the type-token ratio, will give different results depending on the number of words on which it is based. Compositions or composition segments of approximately equal length should be used when comparing the writing abilities of two or more children.

Unusual Words.   The breadth of a student's vocabulary or the extent to which the student uses uncommon or unusual words may be of considerable importance. One way to measure breadth of vocabulary is to determine the extent to which a student uses words not found on published lists of the words most frequently used by children. For a young child, the Dolch list (1955) of two hundred and twenty common words might be used. The teacher should make a note of how many of the first fifty or one hundred words of a composition do not appear on the Dolch list. For older children, the Dolch 1,000-word list (1960, *Primary Reading*) or the Dolch 2,000-word list (1960, *Better Spelling*) are more appropriate. Once again, the teacher is reminded to use approximately the same number of words from each composition when making comparisons.

Structure

The English language has a number of rules which govern its structural and mechanical aspects. Adherence to the rules puts both the reader and the writer in the same frame of reference and facilitates the primary purpose of language, communication. It is not enough for a student to be able to recognize the correct statement of grammatical rules or to be able to pass a test on the rules of grammar, punctuation, or capitalization. Indeed, many research studies have demonstrated that children who score high on grammar tests do not necessarily write the best compositions (Cartwright, 1966). Rules of grammar, including syntax, morphology, diction, capitalization, and punctuation, must be internalized by the student to insure adequate written expression. Internationalization implies correct application of the rules in a writing assignment rather than recognition or replication of the rules in a test of grammatical knowledge.

At first glance, punctuation and capitalization may appear irrelevant in a discussion of the structure of language. In practice, however, faulty punctuation or capitalization may be indicative of a lack of understanding of sentence structure and basic grammatical rules.

So many different procedures for grammatical and structural analysis have appeared in the literature that it is impossible to enumerate them here. Instead, two general approaches will be suggested. One approach is global, the other analytical. These approaches are characterized by their flexibility; an individual teacher can modify or adapt the procedures to suit a particular situation.

Global Approach.   The Grammatical-Correctness Ratio (GCR) was suggested by Stuckless and Marks (1966) as a quick and effective method of estimating a student's facility with grammar. It is presented here as representative of the global approach to the problem. The method is implemented by identifying the number of grammatical errors in the first fifty words in a given composition. The number of errors is subtracted from 50, and this difference is divided by 50. The resulting decimal is multiplied by 100 to obtain a percentage. The percentage is useful if the GCR is based upon a different number of words in the compositions of different children. In the author's experience, GCR's based on either fifty or one hundred words give comparable results (Cartwright, 1968, *Discriminating Power*).

The flexibility of this technique is evident when one realizes that grammatical errors can be defined very broadly or very narrowly, depending upon the objectives of a particular written assignment. It is possible that a teacher might want to look at only one or two types of errors and calculate several GCR's, each based on a different set of grammatical errors. Punctuation and capitalization can also be treated in the same manner. When the procedure is used to compare the written work of two or more students, or different samples of one student's work, the errors examined should be carefully defined in advance so that the ratios will be based on the same type of errors for each composition.

Analytic Approach with Student Profiles. The analytic approach consists of tabulation of various types of errors in a systematic manner. Again, the types of errors tabulated will depend upon the interests of the teacher and the objectives of the written assignment. Errors can be treated individually or combined into categories. In addition to grammatical errors, such as disagreement between subject and verb, various types of errors in sentence structure and punctuation can be tabulated. The teacher can obtain individual and class profiles of specific strengths and weaknesses by using a standard format to record the frequency of different types of errors. A sheet of paper is ruled with a series of columns, each column representing a particular type of error, and each student's name is placed down the side of the paper. As each student's paper is scored, each error is tallied in the appropriate error column.

The analytic approach is illustrated by the error analysis chart in Table 4. The chart is a record of each student's errors in each of the areas listed at the top of the chart. Each row is a profile of one student's relative strengths and weaknesses. John N., for example, appears to be having a great deal of difficulty with verbs but little trouble with capital letters. Sam W. is having more difficulty with sentences than with any of the other areas. The totals at the bottom of each column indicate that, as a whole, this group of students needs work with verbs, modifiers, and punctuation. Table 5 provides a brief list of the types of errors that

Table 4

Grammatical Error Analysis Chart: Individual and Class Profiles

	Verbs			Pronouns		Words[1]						Sentence		Punctuation				Capitals			Totals
	Form	Agreement	Tense	Antecedent	Usage	Additions	Omissions	Substitutions	Substandard	Modifiers	Plurals	Incomplete	Run-on[2]	Period[2]	Comma	Apostrophe	Other	Sentence	Proper Nouns	Overuse	
John N.[3]	5	2	4		2			1	1	1		1	1	3				1			22
Joe S.	2		1			1					1			1	1	1	1				9
Millie M.		1	1		1		1			1	1					1					7
Don W.			1		1						1				1						4
Bob M.		1							1	1						1			1		5
Sam W.	1	1	1		1					2		3	3	2	1						15
Mary D.			1	1						2					1	1					6
Sally B.			1							2					1		1				5
Tom T.	2	2	1	2	1					1	1	1		1							12
Ann H.			1												1	1					3
Totals	10	7	12	3	6	1	1	1	2	10	4	5	4	7	6	5	2	1	1		88

1 Categories of additions, omissions, and substitutions: Myklebust (1965).
2 Certain errors may be recorded twice; e.g., run-on sentences will result in lack of periods.
3 All errors based on first 50 words.

might be included. Since a long composition contains more opportunities for error than a short one, tabulations of errors should be based upon compositions of approximately the same length, or upon composition parts containing about the same number of words.

Content

There should be little question that content is an area of great interest to most teachers. It is well known, however, that teachers often do

Table 5

Examples for Error Analysis Chart

A. VERBS
   1. Form: lay for lie, drank for drunk
   2. Agreement: They was going home.
   3. Tense: Inappropriate tense shift between sentences.

B. PRONOUNS
   1. Ambiguous Antecedent: John and Jack were there and he saw him do it.
   2. Usage: It was him. Him did it hisself.

C. WORDS
   1. Additions: My dog he barked.
   2. Omissions: He went the store.
   3. Substitutions: Tom sat on the there.
   4. Substandard: ain't, gonna

D. MODIFIERS: The boy talked loud.

E. PLURALS: The two dog played.

F. SENTENCE ERRORS
   1. Incomplete: Going to the store on Saturday.
   2. Run-on: We went to the store we went home and ran upstairs and ran downstairs and played house and we had fun oh boy did we have fun.

G. PUNCTUATION
   1. Period: Omission after sentence or abbreviation; inappropriate placement.
   2. Commas: I left, it in the car.
              He likes to run swim jump and play.

H. CAPITALIZATION
   1. Beginning of sentences
   2. Proper nouns: English, Fifth Avenue, Monday
   3. Overuse: My Mother was there and We went to a Movie.

---

not agree on the quality of content in a given composition. Similarly, researchers studying writing skills have not always agreed as to which procedures should be used to evaluate content. Although there has been some progress in this area, most of the recent work is still experimental, and many procedures have not yet been refined to the point where they are practical for the classroom situation.

Although some teachers and researchers prefer to evaluate content by a single global impression, using such a procedure makes it difficult to define the attributes of the composition. A better method is to formulate specific criteria for appraising the composition and follow the analytic approach. Specification of criteria will yield greater reliability and validity to the appraisal of written expression (see Braddock, Lloyd-Jones, and Schoer, 1963). The major purpose of the analytic approach is to help the teacher separate the various components involved in written expression, facilitating identification of specific weaknesses and strengths related to each of the components. As is the case with the analytic approach to structure, both individual and class profiles of strengths and weaknesses can be obtained.

Unfortunately, completely objective techniques for the appraisal of content are not yet available. The technique most often used is the rating method. The successful use of this method depends a great deal upon the careful formulation of the criteria used to evaluate the written material. Precise expression of the objectives of the writing assignment, and equal precision in the specification of evaluation procedures, will augment the reliability and validity of the appraisal process.

The accompanying rating scheme (Table 6) illustrates the analytic approach to composition appraisal, and suggests three criteria: Accuracy, Ideas, and Organization. The names of the areas are arbitrary; different circumstances may call for the substitution or addition of different names and criteria. Depending upon the specific assignment, relatively more weight could be given to one or two of the areas. The essential feature of the checklist is the identification of anchor points along the rating scale. The anchor points should be defined as precisely as possible; this specificity in definition will facilitate the consistent appraisal of a series of compositions. Each composition should be scored on accuracy, ideas, and organization, with points from 0 to 10 assigned in each of these areas according to their criteria. Relative weaknesses and strengths in any of the three areas can thus be readily identified.

A number of different patterns of strengths and weaknesses may emerge when using the rating scheme. For example, a particular student might be rated fairly high in accuracy and ideas, and low in organization. This pattern might indicate that the student should practice outlining and writing from an outline. A pattern of low accuracy and moderate to high ideas and organization, could indicate good organization of some original ideas but a minimal command of relevant factual information. (Evidence for the validity of this particular pattern can be obtained from

Table 6

Rating Scheme for Evaluation of Content

ACCURACY (Appropriate for all forms of discourse.)

The composition completely satisfies all the objectives of the assignment. All the necessary facts and concepts included and correctly interpreted.	10
	9
	8
Most of the relevant concepts are included. The composition satisfies most of the objectives of the assignment.	7
	6
	5
Several relevant facts or concepts omitted. Some assignment objectives not satisfied.	4
	3
Superficial coverage of topic; factual content very limited.	2
	1
Exhibits little or no understanding of the topic. Composition does not meet any of the objectives of the assignment.	0

IDEAS (Increases in importance as form of discourse proceeds from narration to exposition or argumentation.)

Ideas suggested are pertinent to the topic, and/or represent a high degree of originality. No cliches or hackneyed phrases are present.	10
	9
	8
	7
Presents a variety of good but standard ideas.	6
	5

Ideas not clear or are inadequate. Often resorts to cliches.	4
	3
	2
Exhibits neither originality nor understanding of the task. Does not meet any objectives of the written assignment. Presents only cliches or re-statement of the ideas of others.	1
	0

ORGANIZATION (Necessary for all types of discourse.)

Ideas developed in logical sequence. Appropriate emphasis given to different ideas when necessary. Paragraphing is appropriate to content. Successful use of topic sentences, suspense, and climax if relevant to type of discourse.	10
	9
	8
	7
Some improvement could be shown in sequence of idea development. Paragraphing not always consistent with content.	6
	5
Does not carry out a logical progression of ideas. Paragraphing and overall organization indicates haziness in thinking although parts of the composition show some internal relationship.	4
	3
	2
Very poor arrangement of ideas; no logical relationship between sections or ideas. Paragraphing non-existent or inappropriate to content. Sentences bear little relationship with each other or with paragraphs. Unimportant or irrelevant ideas emphasized.	1
	0

---

anyone who has read essay examinations of students who have not committed themselves to much study prior to the examination.)

The rating scheme can be modified by omitting a particular section, by adding another section, or by substituting criteria or anchor points within a given part of the checklist. In an assignment encouraging originality and creativity, such as a science fiction story, the accuracy section might be omitted and the ideas section weighted double. If the assignment is a factual essay on some historical event, accuracy might be given more weight than ideas. An additional section on critical thinking or

Table 7

Individual and Class Profiles

Name	Fluency: Sentence Length	Vocab- ulary: TTR[1]	Structure: GCR[2]	Accuracy	Content			Total Content
					Ideas	Organ- ization		
John N.	7.7	.48	.68	3	5	2		10
Joe S.	10.2	.72	.82	6	6	5		17
Millie M.	11.1	.70	.86	8	4	6		18
Don W.	12.8	.80	.92	9	9	8		27
Bob M.	9.8	.66	.90	7	6	6		19
Sam G.	10.6	.64	.70	4	5	4		13
Mary D.	11.4	.58	.88	8	8	7		23
Sally B.	10.9	.74	.90	6	5	5		16
Tom T.	9.1	.60	.78	4	8	4		16
Ann M.	12.2	.76	.94	9	6	7		22
Averages	10.6	.67	.84	6.4	6.2	5.4		18.1

[1] Type-Token Ratio
[2] Grammatical-Correctness Ratio

analysis might be included when the writing topic is the critique of a play or a controversial essay.

Individual Profiles

Student profiles or records can indicate relative strengths and weaknesses in the four main areas of Fluency, Vocabulary, Structure, and Content. Table 7 illustrates an abbreviated version of a class profile, comprised of a number of individual student profiles. These ability profiles are useful to the teacher in at least three ways:

1. The profiles will reveal how well a student performs in comparison to the other students in his class.

2. One student's profile may indicate that his writing abilities are unevenly developed, or that he is having difficulty in one area but not in the others.

3. Evaluating the class several times during the year can provide a check on student progress in each of the areas. Such a progress check can be applied to the class as a whole, and may reveal that a certain area is a continuing source of difficulty for a number of students.

SUMMARY

We can see, then, that the accurate appraisal of written expression demands the selection of reliable and valid evaluative procedures, and the teacher's careful delineation of the objectives of a particular writing assignment. The student's ability is most effectively appraised by giving separate attention to four elements in his written work, which we have labeled Fluency, Vocabulary, Structure, and Content. The use of individual and class profiles can help pinpoint a student's strengths and weaknesses, in relation to his own previous performance in written work, and to the performance of his classmates. The teacher may also find helpful some published aids for the appraisal of written expression, four of which are listed here:

1. *Sequential Tests of Educational Progress: Writing*. Princeton, N. J.: Cooperative Test Division, Educational Testing Service, 1957.
   The STEP Writing test is available in two forms and in four levels, from grade four through junior college. The test consists of objective items which measure conventions, organization, critical thinking, effectiveness, and appropriateness.

2. *Writing Skills Test*. Chicago: Science Research Associates, 1961.

Single form objective test for grades 9–12. The objective items measure vocabulary, spelling, punctuation, mechanics, sentence recognition, and sentence building.

3. *Writing Skills Laboratory*. Chicago: Science Research Associates, 1964–1965.

Two levels of the *Writing Skills Laboratory* cover grades 4–9. The Laboratory contains systematic sequences of instruction designed to improve the writing ability of students. Specific objectives are formulated for the various lessons and procedures are suggested for the evaluation of student performance.

4. Myklebust, H., *Development and disorders of written language. Volume One: Picture Story Language Test*. New York: Grune & Stratton, Inc., 1965.

Three writing ability scales are introduced: Productivity, Syntax, and Abstract-Concrete. Students are asked to write a story based upon a picture. Scoring procedures and examples are provided, as are norms for ages 7, 9, 11, 13, 15, and 17.

PART 2: SPELLING

The appraisal of spelling ability presents a different set of problems from those involved in the appraisal of written expression. In any composition or on a spelling test, correctly spelled words can be discriminated from incorrectly spelled words with high validity and reliability. The primary purpose of appraisal of spelling ability is to discover consistent patterns of strengths and weaknesses. Knowing that a student consistently makes certain types of errors, the teacher can initiate a remedial program enabling him to generalize to new spelling situations with minimum difficulty.

In the next two sections, two approaches to the appraisal of spelling ability are suggested. Explicit in each are methods for remedial instruction; the appraisal procedures can be converted directly into remedial techniques. The third section illustrates specific testing techniques, applicable to all the appraisal procedures. The objectives mentioned at the beginning of the chapter are also pertinent here. The objectives of a spelling program should center around utility and facilitation of communication. The view of spelling as an exercise in mental discipline is no longer recognized as a legitimate objective.

Blair (1956), Brueckner and Bond (1955), Dolch (1960, *Better Spelling*), Fitzgerald (1955), and Otto and McMenemy (1966), have suggested a number of factors which may be related to spelling difficulties, including low intelligence, emotional problems, poor speech, or severe perceptual, auditory, or motor difficulties. Informal techniques for assessing difficulties in these areas can be found in other chapters of this book and will not be repeated here.

SPECIFIC APPROACH TO SPELLING APPRAISAL

The specific or inductive approach to the appraisal of spelling difficulties does not necessarily depend upon the identification of correlates of spelling disability. As the name implies, the inductive approach proceeds from the analysis of specific errors to the identification of patterns of strengths and weaknesses in spelling. The approach is implemented by testing children on specially-constructed spelling lists which reflect common spelling errors. In their research with computer-assisted instruction in spelling, Mitzel and Brandon (1966) suggested areas of difficulty from which spelling lists can be constructed. One such area is word endings, including forming plurals, adding suffixes, and adding endings to words which end in "e" or "y." Words which contain the "ei" or "ie" combination are also a source of difficulty to some students as are homonyms, compound words, and contractions.

Profiles of Spelling Abilities

Word lists can be constructed based on the general rules of spelling found in most spelling books. Choosing the spelling rules and words to include in a given list will depend upon the age of the students. As suggested in the sections concerning written expression, student profiles of strengths and weaknesses is usually a very helpful analytic procedure.

The spelling error analysis chart is constructed in the same manner as the grammatical error analysis chart, and provides a set of profiles of spelling strengths and weaknesses for the students in a class and for the class as a whole. Table 8 is an example of this procedure; the table is not intended to be an exhaustive source of potential areas of spelling difficulties. Teachers may wish to make changes or additions to accommodate students' needs in particular situations. Regardless of the sources of potential difficulty chosen for inclusion in the profile, each source should be based upon approximately the same number of words to permit direct comparisons among the various types of errors.

Examination of Table 8 reveals that, as a whole, this fictitious class is having difficulty forming plurals and is confusing "ei" and "ie" words. The relatively high rate of double letter errors was due to just two

Table 8

Abbreviated Spelling Error Analysis Chart: Individual and Class Profiles

Name	Plurals[1] (girles, man's for men)	"ie" or "ei" words (seive, friend)	Silent letters (no for know)	Homonyms (to for two)	Contractions (cann't)	Double letters (reel for real, speling)	Totals
John N.	5	2			1	1	9
Jay R.	2		1				3
Bob S.	3	1		1	1		6
Ed B.	4	1	1	2			8
Bill T.		2	1	1		5	9
Jack B.	3	2		2	1		8
Carol C.		1	1		6		8
Jerry R.	3	2	1				6
Mary M.	4	3	1	1		4	13
Totals	24	14	6	7	9	10	70

[1] Each column based on a 20-word list.

people, Bill T. and Mary M. Carol's spelling problem centers on her inability to form contractions.

GENERIC APPROACH TO SPELLING APPRAISAL

The generic or deductive approach to spelling appraisal is based on the premise that a student who understands certain rules of spelling (linguistic principles) will be able to apply them in a spelling situation and generalize to new words. For example, understanding of the often stated rule: "*i* before *e*, except after *c*, or when sounded like *a* as in neighbor and weigh" should help the student spell a variety of words which he may not have been specifically taught. To use the generic approach, the teacher tests the students on spelling rules. Theoretically, one question about a specific rule eliminates the necessity for testing students on all the possible spelling words governed by the rule. Testing can be carried out by asking the students to supply the rule or to recognize a properly stated rule.

This approach does have certain weaknesses. First, as teachers, we are really concerned with whether or not a student can spell certain words, and not with his ability to recite spelling rules. Some students may be able to spell quite well but unable to tell which rules they are using. On the other hand, some students may be able to recite the rules perfectly but still not be able to spell very well. Second, there are almost always exceptions to the rules of spelling. With these reservations in mind, most authorities do not recommend spending a great deal of time teaching spelling generalizations (Dolch, 1960, *Better Spelling*; Fitzgerald, 1955).

The generic approach is effective only when used in conjunction with the specific approach. That is, a student's poor performance on a certain group of spelling words can be checked against his knowledge of the spelling principles involved. The teacher may find that the student has little knowledge of the linguistic principle, or that he does not know how to apply the principle. Some children may improve their spelling abilities by concentrating on spelling rules while others, especially those weak in the ability to generalize, may make little headway.

TECHNIQUES FOR TESTING SPELLING

Dictated Spelling Test

The dictated test is by far the most common testing procedure and does not need to be described here. Its primary advantage is that, except for word selection, it takes very little advance preparation on the part of the teacher, and all the students in the class can be tested at the same time. The dictated spelling test also provides some indication as to whether a student is having spelling difficulties because of auditory problems. Initial appraisal should include dictated tests requiring the child to discriminate correctly and spell such words as pin and bin, mat and mad, mail and nail, gem and Jim, join and joint. The critical task is the selection of words which represent various types of errors.

The Cloze Procedure

The Cloze procedure is quite versatile, and has been used both in research and in the teaching of reading for a number of years (Kirk, 1940; Taylor, 1954; Weaver, 1964). The procedure can be used successfully as a visual means of testing spelling. Students are required to supply a missing word from a sentence by filling in a blank with the correct word. Consider the sentence, "The boy hit the baseball and ran to first _____." The correct response is "base." Alternatively, the child could complete a word, as in b_____ (base); or fill in missing letters, as in b_s_b_ll (baseball). Items of this nature can be presented orally by the teacher, with a written response by the student, or with all the items written down for the student.

A more efficient use of the Cloze procedure is in the appraisal of specific spelling difficulties and in the evaluation of a student's knowledge of spelling generalizations. Specific areas of strengths and weaknesses can be pinpointed, and remedial procedures can be based directly upon the findings. The student is asked to fill in blanks, which in this case deal only with trouble spots and general rules. The following items illustrate the procedure:

> The boy was L_t_ to school.
> Go fly a k_____.
> I borrowed a cup of sugar from my n____ghbor.
> There were five wo_____ and three girls in the group.
> Don't get t____ close to the hot stove.

For students who have difficulty constructing the answer, the teacher may provide a multiple choice format.

He is my best fr____nd.	He is my best _____.
1. ie	1. friend
2. ei	2. freind
3. e	3. frend
4. i	4. frind

He is my next-door _____.

    naybor   nieghbor   neighbor   neybor

The teacher would be wise to use the Cloze procedure in conjunction with the dictated spelling test, especially when she wishes to obtain detailed diagnosis of a student's spelling ability. The visual Cloze procedure is highly complementary to the auditory dictated spelling test.

Proofreading

Students can be asked to proofread specially prepared stories for spelling errors. Although the teacher can control the number and types of errors in the stories, she cannot observe the possible errors of the students unless they are required to correct the misspelled words.

Free Writing

To determine the types of errors most often made by students in free writing or composition assignments, keep a systematic spelling record for each student. The systematic record is most useful when it is in the form of individual and class profiles illustrated in Tables 4, 7, and 8. A permanent record of this kind will permit periodic evaluation of student progress.

SUMMARY

From our discussion of spelling appraisal, the teacher may conclude that a specific approach, focusing on actual spelling errors, will give her a more accurate picture of the student's spelling ability than will the generic approach. The latter, however, since it will reflect the student's understanding of generalized spelling rules, is a useful supplement to the specific assessment. Individual and class profiles can be as helpful to the teacher here as they were in identifying strengths and weaknesses in written expression. We may also expect the use of the dictated spelling test, in conjunction with the flexible Cloze procedure, to prove most effective in assessing spelling ability by auditory and visual means.

REFERENCES

Blair, G. M., *Diagnostic and Remedial Teaching*. New York: The Macmillan Co., 1956.

Braddock, R., R. Lloyd-Jones, and L. Schoer, *Research in Written Composition*. Champaign, Illinois: National Council of Teachers of English, 1963.

Brueckner, L. J., and G. L. Bond, *Diagnosis and Treatment of Learning Difficulties*. New York: Appleton-Century-Crofts, 1955.

Carroll, J. B., "Diversity of Vocabulary and the Harmonic Series Law of Word-Frequency Distribution," *Psychological Record, 2,* (1938).

Carroll, John B., *Language and Thought*. Englewood Cliffs, N. J.: Prentice-Hall, Inc., 1964.

Cartwright, G. P., *Techniques of Analysis of Written Language*. Paper presented at the Annual Meeting of the American Educational Research Association, February, 1966.

Cartwright, G. P., *Multivariate Analyses of the Written Language Abilities of Normal and Educable Mentally Retarded Children*. Paper presented at the Annual Meeting of the American Educational Research Association, February, 1967.

Cartwright, G. P., "Written Language Abilities of Normal and Educable Mentally Retarded Children," *American Journal of Mental Deficiency, 72,* 499-508, (1968).

Cartwright, G. P., *Discriminating Power of Several Objective Measures of Writing Ability*. Paper presented at the Annual Meeting of the National Council of Measurement in Education, February, 1968.

Dolch, E. W., *Methods in Reading*. Champaign, Illinois: Garrard Publishing Co., 1955.

Dolch, E. W., *Teaching Primary Reading*. Champaign, Illinois: Garrard Publishing Co., 1960.

Dolch, E. W., *Better Spelling*. Champaign, Illinois: Garrard Publishing Co., 1960.

Fitzgerald, J. A., "Children's Experiences in Spelling," in *Children and the Language Arts,* V. E. Herrick and L. B. Jacobs, eds. Englewood Cliffs, N. J.: Prentice-Hall, Inc., 1955.

Johnson, W., "Studies in Language Behavior. I. A Program of Research," *Psychological Monographs,* 56, No. 2, (1944).

Kirk, S. A., *Teaching Reading to Slow-Learning Children.* Cambridge, Mass.: Houghton Mifflin Co., 1940.

LaBrant, L., "Studies of Certain Language Developments of Children in Grades Four to Twelve Inclusive," *Genetic Psychology Monographs,* 14, No. 5 (1933).

McCarthy, D., "Language Development in Children," in *Manual of Child Psychology,* L. Carmichael, ed. New York: John Wiley & Sons, Inc., 1954.

Meckel, H. C., "Research on Teaching Composition and Literature," in *Handbook of Research on Teaching,* N. Gage, ed. Chicago: Rand McNally & Co., 1963.

Miller, G. A., *Language and Communication.* New York: McGraw-Hill Book Co., 1951.

Mitzel, H. E., and G. L. Brandon, *Experimentation with Computer-Assisted Instruction in Technical Education.* Semi-annual progress report, Project No. 5-85-074. University Park, Pa.: The Pennsylvania State University, 1966.

Myklebust, H., *Development and Disorders of Written Language: Picture Story Language Test,* I. New York: Grune & Stratton, Inc., 1965.

Otto, W., and R. A. McMenemy, *Corrective and Remedial Teaching.* Boston: Houghton Mifflin Co., 1966.

Page, E. B., "The Imminence of Grading Essays by Computer," *Phi Delta Kappan,* 47, (1966).

Stuckless, E. R., and C. H. Marks, *Assessment of the Written Language of Deaf Students,* U.S.O.E. Cooperative Research Project 2544, University of Pittsburgh, 1966.

Taylor, W. L., *Application of Cloze and Entropy Measures to the Study of Contextual Constraint in Samples of Continuous Prose.* Doctoral Dissertation, University of Illinois, 1954.

Weaver, W. W., *Theoretical Aspects of the Cloze Procedure.* Paper presented at the 14th annual meeting of the National Reading Conference, Southern Methodist University, Dallas, Texas, 1964.

Chapter 6

SPEECH AND LANGUAGE DISORDERS

Betty Jane McWilliams

Discussion of diagnosis and treatment of speech and language disorders should, ideally, emerge out of an orderly consideration of human development in all its complexity. The ability to acquire language, a system of symbols fundamental to thinking, reading, writing, speaking, and listening, is intricately associated with every other aspect of development. It is impossible to understand the unique nature of either language or speech apart from a more basic comprehension of children, their genetic constitutions, their innate developmental potentials, the possible influence of infinite numbers of events which may operate to disrupt the developmental process, and the baffling, often insidious ways in which various factors may combine to the developmental disadvantage of a particular child.

SPEECH AND LANGUAGE AS LEARNED BEHAVIORS

The acquisition of a linguistic system, or language, proceeds within a learning structure. As in all other types of learning, language growth depends upon the presence of an appropriate developmental foundation. The components of this foundation include (1) intact sensory mechanisms capable of receiving stimuli, (2) mental abilities of sufficient magnitude to make possible the interpretation and integration of experience, (3) the capacity to translate experience into symbolic structures, (4) the faculty for retention, and (5) the ability to recall and use previous experiences in the form of concepts. Weakness or breakdown in any one or combination of these abilities may result in difficulties in language acquisition. Even when these foundations are adequate, poor emotional integrity or serious social and economic deprivation may render the child incapable of mobilizing his capacities so that he may reach the expected level of language learning

Speech is also learned behavior. It is the verbal expression of the symbol and, as such, lags behind the symbolic structure. This situation remains throughout life. Passive vocabulary, or words which can be understood or recognized, is always larger than active vocabulary, which is made up of the words that are readily available for use in typical verbal output. The expressive act, of course, is symbolic; but the act itself is accomplished through a motor modality requiring an exceedingly complicated organization of behaviors. Although speech is uniquely characteristic of human beings, they possess no specific system of organs with primary responsibility for speech. Instead, speech is an overlaid function which utilizes and adapts structures serving other more basic biological needs. Stated simply, speech results when the exhaled air stream passes across the vocal folds, setting them into vibration and creating undifferentiated voice. When the air stream involved in vibration is further modified by the articulators—the tongue, lips, teeth, hard palate, soft palate, and mandible—and is channelled through a major resonating cavity, recognizable speech sounds emerge. These sounds can be reproduced or imitated by recreating the same anatomical and physiological conditions and, in predictable combinations, constitute the spoken words of our language. The accuracy with which an individual reproduces the sounds of his language and combines them in the appropriate order will depend upon a number of variables. Speech and language disorders must be discussed within the framework of capacities essential to their unimpaired development. Understanding those deficits that contribute to the speech and language difficulties leads to meaningful approaches to management.

A Word of Caution

Before continuing, it must be emphasized that the classroom teacher should not approach this experience with the idea that he will learn to diagnose and treat disorders of communication. No written material can provide the training necessary for listening to speech effectively and differentially, nor can a brief survey of simple diagnostic procedures help the teacher to become an expert diagnostician. The whole process of communication is an exceedingly complicated part of human behavior. It involves complex anatomy and physiology, intricate learning mechanisms, confusing interrelationships among the various perceptual systems, obscure facets of personality, and cultural-social phenomena. Indeed, it is often impossible for a specialist in the field of communications disorders to arrive at a precise and unequivocal diagnosis. He can often do little more than describe the problem, speculate on its causes, and plan and execute a therapy program that can be modified according to the demands of the patient. The specialist must have extensive training which meets the certification requirements of the American Speech and Hearing Association (Membership Directory, 1967, pp. 23–24), good clinical practice under competent supervision, and years of professional experience. The classroom teacher cannot be expected to serve in lieu of an individual with all the credentials necessary to work in a clinical field. On the other hand, an informed teacher can do a great deal for the child who does not have access to professional help, and can work more effectively with clinicians who serve in the school system.

SPEECH DISORDERS: THEIR NATURE, IDENTIFICATION, AND MANAGEMENT

The 1950 White House Conference estimated that 6% of the total population has some type of communication deficit. Other data emerging from studies of specific populations place the incidence among school children at from one to twenty-two per cent (Hull and Timmons, 1966, p. 359). These large variations in the reported statistics can be explained in terms of (1) the variety of sampling techniques used, (2) the different criteria chosen for determining the presence of a problem, and (3) the differences in the ages of the children studied. In any event, it is reasonable to conclude that there are more children with disorders of communication than there are children with any other single type of handicapping condition (Johnson, et.al., 1967, p. 2). We may assume, therefore, that no teacher is likely to escape the necessity for understanding something of these problems.

Definition of Speech Problems

In order to deal effectively with children who have problems in communication, the classroom teacher must differentiate between defective speech and speech which is sub-standard by the teacher's cultural yardstick, but which is a simple reflection of the child's environment. While both types of speech may require alteration, they are not precisely the same. If a child says, "If I'da knowed I coulda rode, I woulda went," he certainly needs help with grammar, word selection, pronunciation, and enunciation, but he has demonstrated his ability to acquire the verbal patterns of his culture. To the extent that he accurately reproduces those patterns, he reveals his ability to respond to the normal stimuli of his environment. We may wish to alter the stimuli so that the youngster can learn new responses acceptable in other cultural communities and capable of freeing him from the limitations to which he was born, but we cannot interpret his inadequate verbal behavior as symbolic of inadequacies with the child. On the other hand, if this same child were to say, "If I'da n-n-n-knowed I coulda wode, I w-w-woulda went," we would have evidence of his cultural deprivation, as in the first instance, as well as evidence of his repetitious and faulty consonant production, both symptoms of speech disorders. It is imperative for the teacher to determine whether or not a problem actually exists. A practical definition of a speech disorder is helpful (Van Riper, 1963, p. 16) : "Speech is defective when it deviates so far from the speech of other people that it calls attention to itself, interferes with communication, or causes its possessor to be maladjusted."

Speech calls attention to itself when it contains elements that differ sufficiently from the accepted standards to be noted by the casual listener. For example, a ten-year-old boy was referred for clinical help because he talked about the "sun up in the <u>ch</u>ky," his new "micro<u>ch</u>cope," and the "<u>ch</u>kies" he got for Christmas. Since the <u>sk</u> consonant blend with which he had trouble occurs infrequently, he encountered only occasional difficulty, but his speech was bizarre to his listeners nonetheless. What he had to say was lost because of the way he said it; his speech pattern called undue attention to itself.

An eight-year-old girl, omitting almost all medial and final consonants, had trouble making anyone understand that she was trying to say, "My big sister goes to college," when it came out, "My bi titte doe to da-e." Under most circumstances, communication was an impossibility for this child. Her seriously disrupted speech pattern met two of Van Riper's criteria. It both called attention to itself and interfered with communication. There was also the distinct possibility that the third criterion was met as well.

A college freshman looked out at the world across the toes of his own shoes, answered questions with a shrug of the shoulders or, at best, with a single word, and demonstrated extreme embarrassment when he could not avoid an encounter with communication. He is an example of an individual whose speech, while not calling attention to itself or interfering directly with communication, did cause its possessor serious adjustment problems. This boy, a halting oral reader, had been mislabeled a stutterer by an unthinking and misguided teacher. He accepted her evaluation of his speech, became upset when he had to reveal his problem to others, exaggerated the normal non-fluencies which occurred in his speech, and gradually became increasingly poorly adjusted.

Articulation Disorders

Clinical experience and research evidence show that articulation problems are the most frequent disorder of communication. Over half of most case loads are made up of articulation disorders, with at least one estimate as high as 90.5 per cent (Johnson, Darley, and Spriestersbach, 1963, p. 81). Articulation is concerned with the sounds of speech—the consonants, vowels, and diphthongs which go together to make up the words we say. If a child says "thun" instead of "sun" or "wed wabbit" instead of "red rabbit" or "birfday" instead of "birthday," we know that he has sound substitutions. A substitution occurs when a standard speech sound is used instead of another standard speech sound, as in the examples given above. A distortion refers to a sound that can be recognized as belonging to the appropriate family of sounds but which is produced in a manner that makes it sound odd. For instance, if the consonant [s] is channelled through a narrow groove in the middle of the tongue, the sibilant quality which we recognize and accept as [s] is heard. If the groove is lateralized, the [s] can still be recognized, but it will sound "slushy" and different from what the ear is accustomed to hearing. An *omission* is the absence of any sound when one should be present. The child who says "nake" for "snake" is omitting the initial [s] in the

[sn] blend. (A blend is two consonants occurring together.) "Da-ie" for "doggie" or "ca" for "cat" are other examples of the same type of error.

It must be remembered that when children first begin to talk their speech is liberally sprinkled with inaccuracies which characterize particular ages and about which it would be foolish to be alarmed. As age increases, however, articulation patterns improve. Many different studies over a period of years, involving a number of different groups of children, have shown this to be true. By the time a child enters kindergarten, his speech should be understood by most listeners, and by the age of eight years, children should have well developed consonant patterns. Table 9 summarizes Templin's work on the age levels at which 75 per cent of the children she tested were able to produce correctly the various consonants.

Table 9

Earliest Age Levels at which 75 Per Cent of Children Tested Correctly Articulated Consonant Sounds*

Age Levels Yrs.		Consonants					
3.0	m		n	ng	p	f	h	w
3.5	j (as in yellow)						
4.0	b		d	k	g	r	
4.5	s		sh	ch			
6.0	t		l	v	th (voiceless)		
7.0	th (voiced)		z	zh (as in azure)	dzh (as in jug)		

* Templin, M. C., *Certain Language Skills in Children,* Monograph Series, Institute of Child Welfare, Minneapolis: University of Minnesota Press, No. 26, 1957. (Used with permission.)

Judging the Nature of Articulation Defects. In order that the teacher's ear will not play tricks, it is important that there be some basic understanding of the consonant sounds, since they are the sounds most likely to be defective. Table 10 provides a summary of the major characteristics of the consonants. While this brief presentation will not substitute for a course in phonetics, it will provide a foundation for the teacher faced with the problem of determining exactly what is wrong with speech that sounds wrong. Perhaps it would be helpful, as was done in the original paper, to explain this chart by example. It will be noted by reference to Table 10 that the consonant sound [p] can be classified according to the anatomic parts which are used to produce it. The sound is called bi-labial because two lips are involved in its production. The sound can also be classified according to the place of resonance. Thus, the consonant sound [p] is an oral sound. It is emitted through the oral cavity as opposed to the nasal cavity. The [p] is also a voiceless sound, meaning that the air stream proceeds from the thoracic cavity to the point of articulation before it is interrupted. In other words, the vocal folds are not active in the production of this sound as they are in the production of the voiced counterpart, the consonant sound [b]. In addition, [p] is a stop-plosive; the articulators come together, air is impounded behind them, and there is a sudden expulsion for the formation of the sound. It is obviously a different mechanism from that used in the production of [s], where there is an opening through which air is forced in a continuing manner. This sound, therefore, is classified as a continuant or fricative. Careful study of Table 10 will reveal that the classification of consonant sounds is reasonable, understandable, and necessary in the evaluation of speech disorders occurring from faulty consonant articulation.

The only way to decide what a child is doing that makes his speech different from accepted standards is to listen to him talk and judge the manner in which he produces each of the consonants in each of the positions in which they occur in our language. The examiner who does this over a long period of time will usually find that children tend to do several things with the same sound so that they are not consistent. The sound may be in error in several different ways and may even be correct some of the time. Because there are twenty-five consonant sounds with which to be concerned, and because of the variability with which errors occur, the wise teacher will listen to these sounds one at a time in various combinations, and will write down all that is heard. This process is known as articulation testing. A skilled examiner will make these observations from conversational speech and will supplement this testing with a picture articulation test, such as the Templin-Darley Test of Articulation, or with sentences loaded with the sounds to be tested. There is nothing magic about one group of sentences as opposed to another or one picture in contrast to another so long as they elicit the desired response. A simpler method, and one that saves time for the busy teacher, is the word-repetition test. To administer this test, the teacher asks the child to repeat words after him. He must provide a model that is not stressful in any sense so that the child is not encouraged to imitate the teacher's production, thus providing a faulty picture of his own articulation abilities. This method has been shown to yield generally reliable results, and it has the advantage of time conservation (McWilliams and Matthews, 1965, pp. 69-71; Templin, 1947, pp. 293-300) .

Table 10

Classification of Consonant Sounds Found in American Speech*

Consonant Sound	Voicing: Voiced	Voiceless	Resonance: Oral	Nasal	Place of Articulation: Bi-labial	Lingua-alveolar	Lingua-velar	Labio-dental	Lingua-dental	Lingua-palatal	Glottal	Sound Classification: Stop-plosive	Affricate	Fricative	Glide	Nasal	Lateral	Initial Position	Medial Position	Final Position
p		x	x		x							x						pie	supper	cup
b	x		x		x							x						boy	maybe	tub
t		x	x			x						x						tiny	into	cat
d	x		x			x						x						do	under	bed
k		x	x				x					x						kind	making	bake
g	x		x				x					x						go	wagon	egg
tʃ		x	x			x							x					chair	pitcher	peach
dʒ	x		x			x							x					jam	edging	bridge
f		x	x					x						x				for	coffee	laugh
v	x		x					x						x				very	television	save
θ		x	x						x					x				thank	birthday	tooth
ð	x		x						x					x				them	brother	smooth
s		x	x			x								x				see	missing	mass
z	x		x			x								x				zoo	amazing	maze
ʃ		x	x							x				x				shoe	pushing	mash
ʒ	x		x							x				x					azure	garage
h		x	x								x				x			hat	ahead	
r	x		x							x					x			ring	around	car
j	x		x							x					x			you	onion	
w	x		x		x										x			window	twin	
hw		x	x		x										x			white	anywhere	
m	x			x	x											x		man	summer	come
n	x			x		x										x		nice	funny	sun
ŋ	x			x			x									x			mink	sing
l	x		x			x											x	like	balloon	ball

* McWilliams, B. J., E. J. Forrest, and J. Matthews, "Speech and Its Pathologies," *Journal of Dental Education*, 29, No. 1 (1965), pp. 16-22. (Used with permission.)

Figure 5 is a sample recording form. The material and the notations made by the teacher are valid only if the teacher's ear is accurate and if the recording is accurate. A particularly interested teacher may wish to make tape recordings of several children's speech and listen to them repeatedly to gain practice in making judgments about the accuracy of sound production. This system is far from foolproof. It has some of the same inherent flaws which are apparent in newspaper medical columns, and sometimes lead readers to diagnose themselves and others with disastrous results. However, it is assumed that the reader will bring mature judgment to this task, and will recognize that the testing provides a guide rather than a hard-and-fast, irreversible diagnosis with which the child must live whether it applies or not. If possible, it is helpful for the teacher to discuss the speech profiles with a trained speech clinician. If a clinician is not available, it might be wise to encourage the school system to consider speech evaluation as a topic for an in-service training program.

The articulation profile shows which sounds are in error, but it does not provide information about the ease with which the errors might be corrected under the appropriate circumstances. A second type of testing, known as stimulatability testing (Milisen, 1954, pp. 6-17), can help to assess this factor. In this test, the examiner attempts to see if a child can produce the defective consonants in isolation; in nonsense syllables, in words, in sentences, after listening and watching carefully exactly what the examiner says. For example, if a child has a defective [s], and the chances are good that this will be one of his defective sounds, he is given instructions to listen and watch exactly what the teacher does. The [s] is produced, (not es, but as the voiceless channelled air stream by itself, the sound the snake makes—sssss) three times while the child watches the minute visible facial and oral movements and listens carefully to the sound itself. He is then asked to do it. If he fails, he is given two or three additional trials before it is decided that he cannot do it. The next step is to try the [s] in combination with vowels, as in sah, ahsah, or ahs, proceeding as was done with the sound in isolation. After the nonsense syllables have been tested, the examiner attempts to elicit the sound in words and then within the context of a simple sentence. It seems logical that a defective sound that can be imitated correctly within the framework of a simple sentence is closer to emerging into the habitual speech pattern than is a sound that cannot be imitated in isolation. Stimulatability testing thus provides some basis for determining the depth of the problem and for predicting within limits the ease with which it should yield in therapy.

Figure 5

Articulation Test

Name_____ Birthdate_____ Date_____

Sound	Position in word			Stimulatability				Blends			
	I	M	F	Isolation	Nonsense Syllables	Words	Sentences				
p								br-		-sm	
b								tr-		-ks	
t								dr-		-pt	
d								kr-		-mps	
k								gr-		pr-	
g								pl-		fr-	
tʃ								kl-		ɵr-	
dʒ								gl-		sr-	
f								sm-		fl-	
v								sn-		sl-	
ɵ								sp-		sw-	
ð								st-		kw-	
s								sk-		spl-	
z								tw-		spr-	
ʃ								bl-		skr-	
ʒ								-lf		str-	
h											
r								Correct = ✔			
j								Distortion = dis			
w								Substitution = Indicate Sound			
hw											
m								Omission = o			
n											
ŋ											
l								Comments: _____			

By:_____

Varied Etiologies.   We have considered an informal means for arriving at a descriptive analysis of defective sounds when the problem seems to be one of consonant articulation, but we have not suggested why this defect may have occurred. There is no clear-cut information about the precise causes of such problems, although many investigators have sought explanations. It is known that articulation disorders may occur as a result of neuromuscular problems commonly seen in cerebral palsy and in other less profound neurological disturbances. In certain cases, neurological deficits are manifested in the form of apraxia, which, as far as speech is concerned, is the inability to understand what movements are necessary for the production of a particular sound even though the muscles are capable of the appropriate behavior. Disorders such as cleft palate, submucous cleft of the palate, and other deficiencies in the velarpharyngeal valving mechanism may make it impossible for the child to impound enough air in the oral cavity to produce the sounds requiring high intra-oral pressure. Certain dental anomalies, while they do not bear a one-to-one relationship to speech adequacy, may make it difficult to perfect related sounds. For example, severe dental deviations in the central and lateral incisors may lead to difficulty in producing sibilant sounds. This is an uncommon occurrence, but it can happen.

There is some evidence suggesting that a reduced ability to retain auditory impressions, often referred to in the literature as poor auditory memory span, may create barriers to perfecting articulation skills in certain children. Others may experience difficulty in auditory discrimination. In short, they may be unable to hear fine differences in speech sounds even though auditory acuity is normal. Poor ability to discriminate the sounds of speech may, of course, accompany reduction in hearing sensitivity, which is also a major contributor to articulation difficulties. Still another possible explanation for disorders of articulation is immaturity. The speech may reflect the child's level of social–emotional–mental development more accurately than it does his chronological age.

It is usually impossible for an experienced diagnostician to state unequivocally the cause of a problem in a particular child. The classroom teacher should not attempt to do so, but should be cognizant of the developmental problems that might contribute to articulation disorders and should be on the alert to identify them.

The Role of the Teacher in Correction.   Most speech clinicians who work with articulatory problems recognize the value of auditory stimulation in therapy. Regardless of the cause of an articulation problem, children appear able to change their own speech by listening carefully to the speech of others and then attempting (1) to imitate it; (2) to evaluate the results of their own efforts; (3) to make necessary modifications; and (4) to work diligently at perfecting a newly-acquired sound for use in conversation. Teachers can help with this process by (1) stressing phonics; (2) emphasizing consonant sounds during presentation of spelling words; (3) asking children with known problems to underscore in red those reading words containing the deviant sound; and (4) having them read aloud, quietly interjecting a correct model following an incorrect production. In casual conversation, the teacher may personally utilize the child's problem word two or three times without necessarily pointing out to the child that he was wrong. Stressing one sound will simplify the process for the child, who may become confused if asked to change his entire speech pattern at once. Speech improvement activities for the entire classroom are helpful. Particularly useful is creative dramatics, which can be beneficial to all the children as well as to those with speech troubles. Such planned programs as *Listening with Mr. Bunny Big Ears* (Wilcox and McIntyre, 1965) can give the teacher direct guidance in planning speech stimulation activities in the classroom.

A child's ability to imitate the teacher's model does not mean that the child can recall the appropriate pattern and use it independently. Mothers and teachers often complain that a youngster is lazy because, after he is reminded, he can say certain words much better than he does in conversation. This so-called laziness indicates that he can be stimulated to produce the correct sound in a word, but that it has not been incorporated into free and automatic conversational speech. The teacher can help the child transfer sounds into conversational speech by establishing simple reminders. Asking him to read a certain paragraph aloud and to produce correctly all of the [s] sounds that appear in the passage is one example. These sounds may be underscored in red as an extra clue.

The teacher may wish to move from this situation into certain pre-arranged settings, such as asking the child to make an announcement to the rest of the class, during which he is to concentrate on producing correctly a particular word that he is trying to make habitual. He and the teacher may share some "magic word" which the child uses as he enters or leaves the classroom. The teacher may occasionally err in pronunciation to see if the child can catch and correct the error. It is important to refrain from criticizing general conversation, lest the child begin to feel that how he talks is more important than what he has to say. These sample techniques are based upon the idea that children must become aware of their defective speech patterns, learn to change them when they are thinking about it, recognize the correct production, and carry it into free conversation. The teacher can help most by being relaxed, patient, somewhat structured, and willing to give the child many opportunities to try.

Hearing Loss

While hearing loss is not a speech disorder in the sense that an articulation problem is, it has much to do with the way consonants develop and with the way speech is generally perfected. Hearing loss constitutes a major problem in communication and must be considered here, although it will be necessary to discuss various other aspects of hearing in later sections of this chapter as well.

Children who lack usable hearing do not learn to talk. Speech fails to emerge when it is not heard. Language concepts, which constitute the foundation of verbal communication, also do not develop. Deaf children, therefore, are severely handicapped in their language development. Less severe hearing deficits may also be devastating if the child can hear only fragments of words or only stressed words. The longer clinicians deal with problems of this sort, the more convincing the evidence becomes that even what seems on the surface to be a clinically insignificant hearing loss may be an important contributor to retarded language development and to the level of skill obtained in speech. As is true of most other problems, severe hearing loss, which, for all practical purposes, is total, will probably not be overlooked. A child with a problem of this magnitude does not usually find his way to the regular classroom. However, many mild hearing difficulties go undetected. These children do constitute educational problems.

The Need for Teacher Sensitivity to Hearing Impairment. The most likely candidate for trouble is the child with a mild to moderate hearing loss, perhaps of a fluctuating nature. This child seems to hear sometimes, not to hear at other times, to hear when he wants to, and to be a difficult behavior problem. The observant teacher can often determine when the child is having auditory difficulty by his behavior. There are no specific diagnostic tests to recommend, except careful audiometric and otological study by trained specialists. These services certainly are not to be found in the classroom, nor will the teacher have the skill to use the techniques. The teacher must depend upon observation, common sense, and knowledge of how people with poor hearing tend to behave. Certain clues imply a loss of hearing. Any one or all of them may be present, although the same symptoms may indicate other kinds of disorders as well. The teacher must not assume that certain behavior always indicates the presence of a hearing loss. Nevertheless, the following symptoms often occur in children with hearing problems; and the teacher should be alert to them:

1. Responding consistently to sound when it is quite loud, but failing to respond to normal environmental noises, including speech.
2. Responding when looking at the speaker, but failing to respond in the absence of visual cues.
3. Responding better to sound presented on one side than to sound presented on the other.
4. Turning one ear toward the source of sound.
5. Responding with an expression of surprise after the teacher has spent some time attempting to attract attention and has finally repeated the message in a louder voice.
6. Confusing classroom instructions, assignments, or words in spelling. (This is particularly important when words that sound alike are confused or misunderstood.)
7. Increased restlessness during activities that involve listening.
8. Any evidence of draining ears.
9. Alteration in auditory behavior following an illness.
10. Repeated earaches.
11. Frequent requests for repetition.
12. Puzzled expression when placed in a listening situation.

These signs are indicative of possible reduction in auditory acuity. Again, this problem cannot be handled by the classroom teacher directly. If a school nurse or a speech clinician has access to an audiometer which is kept in calibration and used in an acoustically reasonable environment, the child should have an audiogram to determine if the symptoms are actually related to loss of hearing. When the audiogram shows hearing loss, or when such a testing program is unavailable, the parents should be consulted and the youngster referred to an otolaryngologist. Some states provide help in this area under the aegis of the State Department of Health. If an otolaryngologist is not available, a pediatrician or family doctor should be consulted. The teacher can assist further by providing the physician with a brief summary of observations.

The teacher's primary responsibility in this case is to refer the child to a hearing specialist. Many hearing losses in the mild to moderate range can be helped by treatment. Losses which are irreversible may require the use of amplification and special guidance for both the child and his parents. In the meantime, the teacher can assist the child by altering the classroom environment to compensate as much as possible for the deficit. The following suggestions may be helpful:

1. The child should be seated in the classroom so that he is as close as possible to the source of major sound. If this sound is the teacher's voice, and if the teacher spends considerable time at his desk, the child should have a position close to the teacher's desk and located so that he will be encouraged to watch the teacher's face. Many children with hearing losses develop expertise in speech reading, and anything the teacher can do to help this process is to be encouraged.

2. The child should be given freedom to move about the room in order to place himself in the most desirable position. This should be done quietly and with some understanding on the part of his classmates.

3. The teacher might take extra precautions to see that the youngster with a hearing problem has a special opportunity to check assignments. This attention might take the form of a brief conversation during or after class, a note to take home, or an assignment notebook which the teacher can check quickly when it seems necessary.

4. Children who do not hear well sometimes misbehave in the classroom because they are bored, because they are out of sorts with themselves and the world, or because things have not gone well. They also sometimes misbehave because they do not understand what constitutes acceptable behavior. It is important for the teacher to decide whether the behavior is part of the symptom complex or whether it has more to do with "a mad little boy with a short fuse." These children are entitled to discipline in the same way that other children are. The hearing-impaired child constitutes a unique problem, because it is easy to believe that he has been uncooperative and inconsiderate when, in reality, he has not understood that the situation demanded something else from him.

5. The teacher who works with a hearing-handicapped child should watch for words which are mispronounced or misunderstood in reading, spelling, and other subjects. It may be necessary to list these words separately and keep them as a special assignment for vocabulary building. Eliciting the aid of the mother is desirable here. The child should be encouraged to check the words in the dictionary, find them in reading assignments, write them in sentences, and use them in informal conversation.

Again, it should be recognized that the classroom teacher will have neither the time nor the training to provide a fully developed classroom program for a hard-of-hearing youngster; but a teacher who understands some of the symptoms, observes wisely and well, seeks appropriate help, and creates a favorable classroom environment, is taking a giant step toward providing genuine support and help.

Stuttering Problems

Stuttering is another of the communication deficits which the teacher is likely to encounter. Estimates of incidence differ from one study to another, but it is probably not greater than one per cent of the school population. Since this problem has a relatively low incidence, it will not require the major emphasis in the classroom demanded by articulation problems. This disorder of the rhythm of speech, however, has the potential for emotional trauma for both child and teacher.

Normal speech is never completely fluent. Even those speakers whom we most admire encounter mild repetitions of words or of sounds, sometimes have difficulty initiating a word, vary the pace of their utterances so that there are occasional time disruptions, and demonstrate other slight fluency breaks. Although these characteristics are typical of the normal speech pattern, most adults consider themselves to be fluent speakers. They are not aware of the moderate imperfections which occur regularly in their own speech and in the speech of others. However, just a little more than normal hesitation or stoppage makes them conscious of the lack of fluency, and they become uncomfortable in its presence. In fact, many people, teachers and parents among them, do not hesitate to call a child stutterer if he demonstrates these fluency disruptions. The only trouble with applying labels to human behavior is that the labels may not really be appropriate, but may make their own unique contribution to a child's emerging concept of himself—sometimes to his destruction. If a little girl grows up hearing that she has beautiful hair, eyes like blue pools, skin like fine china, and that she embodies all of the most attractive feminine characteristics, she is likely to have a better self-image than the child who hears that her hair is straight as a poker, her eyes too small for her face, her skin a little sallow, and her behavior like that of a bull in a china shop. Children somehow tend to become that which we tell them they are—good or bad, tense or relaxed, gay or sober, good speakers or poor. This statement is, of course, over-simplified; but the point is made to stress the hazards involved in telling a child what he *is*.

Classroom Management in Terms of Level of Stuttering.   Van Riper (1963, pp. 328-333) has identified four levels of stuttering. The first stage is known as "primary stuttering." Children in this stage of development may go for weeks or months without difficulty and then encounter times of real disturbance. The teacher's responsibility in this case is simply to recognize that this child cannot accurately be called a stutterer because he does not behave like a stutterer most of the time. If labels must be applied, they should be realistic enough to describe the behavior observed most consistently. In this case, it is fluent speech, not stuttering. The best means that the average teacher can adopt for handling problems such as this one is to become a slave to his own powers of observation. Children with this type of non-fluency will obviously speak better under some conditions than under others and are likely to display non-fluency when their speech efforts are directly criticized by the teacher. The teacher who observes, understands, and is concerned about a child's feelings can hardly help making program modifications which will minimize his problems. For example, if a particular youngster has trouble answering "present," the teacher will not demand this specific response from any of the children. If certain non-fluencies are more pronounced after the child has spent considerable time in concentrated work at his desk and just prior to a play period, the teacher may decide to wait until after the break in the routine to call upon him. The teacher who shows insight will suffer no discomfort if non-fluent speech is encountered, and the child will be extended the same respect and courtesy that would be extended to anyone else wanting to communicate. On the other hand, if the teacher is uncomfortable in the presence of stuttering, he may allow a non-fluent child to sit in the classroom learning that silence is more acceptable than speech. Some teachers find it impossible to take stuttering in stride and thus create impossible attitudes toward the non-fluent child on the part of other children. "Shut up until you can talk right," is an example of one such teacher's response. It is understandable that the other children laughed and made fun of the little boy to whom the comment was directed. Their behavior was merely a reflection of the teacher's attitudes. They may even have laughed in response to the obviously high tensions that existed.

As the child experiences again and again the periods of non-fluency, he begins to evaluate his own speech output and to register concern over his inability to manage himself verbally. Van Riper calls this the second stage of stuttering. It is slightly different from the first stage in that the repetitions are likely to speed up and to become less and less an integral part of the total speech pattern. The classroom teacher can help this child in many of the same ways that are useful with the child in the very early stage of non-fluency. However, the added dimension of the child's occasional awareness of his difficulty must not be ignored by the teacher who would render the most effective help. Under ideal circumstances, a speech clinician would be involved along with the teacher and the parents, and would help to broaden everybody's understanding of this child, his family, and his relationships to himself and others. If help is not available, the teacher must work alone, remembering that conservative approaches may not bring about dramatic changes in speech, but that they also lack the potential for tragedy inherent in more flamboyant techniques. A teacher handling a non-fluent child must do everything possible to keep him talking happily, to reward him for volunteering, to encourage him in group activities where he is likely to have marked success, and to give him quiet support and understanding when he falters. If the teacher can accept the failures easily and without dismay, and has the patience and time to let the speech unwind as it will, he will make a major contribution toward helping the child feel that he is capable of successful communication.

The transitional stage of stuttering is more severe than the first two stages. It is marked by the onset of speech-centered anxiety and struggle behavior. The child, now aware that his speech is unacceptable to other people, begins to struggle to keep from stuttering. In this stage, children attempt to ease themselves over a difficult speech situation by slapping their legs, blinking their eyes, or adopting some little trick word or phrase to get themselves started. The first two stages of non-fluency are fairly common among pre-school and early elementary children. The transitional stage is probably more typical of youngsters in the primary grades, but may persist among older children. As one bad speech experience follows another and social penalties accumulate, it becomes increasingly difficult for the child to contemplate speaking without experiencing panic and fright. When he anticipates speech failure and is afraid to talk even before he undertakes the task, he has entered the final stage in the severity of stuttering. This is secondary stuttering.

There are certainly other ways of looking at the problem of stuttering. The interested teacher will wish to pursue the subject in much greater depth. Most theories recognize a gradual increase in both the severity of symptoms and the speaker's awareness of these symptoms. Indirect approaches to management and manipulation within the framework of the classroom are far more successful in the early stages of stuttering than in the more advanced stages. It is not recommended here that the teacher undertake any formal therapeutic techniques with advanced stutterers. Instead, the teacher should encourage parents to seek professional help with difficult problems, but to remember that all stutterers will be helped to function more successfully by:

1. Encouraging a great deal of talking in situations likely to bring success—even if this has to begin with choral reading or role playing.
2. Accepting a child's best speech effort without criticism, anxiety, guilt, or anger.
3. Helping the non-fluent child to achieve as much success as possible in non-verbal areas where he is likely to do well.
4. Assisting the non-fluent child in adjusting to his peer group.
5. Avoiding the use of precise labels.
6. Proceeding with caution.

Etiology.   Let us review briefly the causes of stuttering. The most accurate statement that can be made is that no one really knows what causes excessively non-fluent speech. The wise teacher will not try to solve that problem for a particular child. There is some evidence to suggest that some children may have a constitutional predisposition to awkward speech. Other theories attribute the cause to emotional instability, possible neurological differences, or to speech-centered anxiety resulting from inappropriate and improperly timed attention to normal hesitations found in the speech patterns of most pre-school children. Other suggested causes include improper learning and a variety of opinions and theories which might fit under any one of these major headings. Clinical experience suggests that the most reasonable position is that of Van Riper (1963, p. 327), who believes that stuttering has many possible causes. In fact, it is usually impossible for an experienced clinician to view a particular stutterer and determine with any degree of security the cause of his problem. The important factor is the feeling of the individual with the stuttering problem toward his speech, how it alters the course of his academic and social life, and the manner in which other people respond to it. Regardless of the cause of the problem, in all likelihood the aberrant speech has become a source of anxiety and fear. These feelings are of paramount importance in management. We cannot reiterate too frequently the dangers involved in the misapplication of diagnostic and causal labels to children. It is preferable to treat symptoms knowingly than to force any problem into a preconceived mold which may ignore the flesh-and-blood child.

Voice Disorders

Voice disorders occur when some difficulty is present as the exhaled air stream passes over the approximated vocal folds and enters the oral and nasal cavities. If there is an inadequate air stream; if the folds are too taut; if there are various pathologies of the vocal cords; if there is faulty function; if the air stream is inaccurately channelled because of velarpharyngeal insufficiency, permitting air to enter the nostrils inappropriately during speech; or if there is an excessive adenoidal mass which prevents air from entering the nasal passages, voice disorders will occur. Problems with the breath stream may result in a voice that sounds as if too much breath is being used, as if too little breath is available, as if the breath stream is under improper control, or as if the individual is speaking from air trapped too high in the chest cavity. Difficulties with the folds themselves may make the speech sound hoarse, harsh, or inappropriate in tone for the age and sex of the individual. These problems may be functional in nature, meaning that they result from the inadequate use of an adequate mechanism; or they may be pathological in origin, resulting from conditions such as nodules on the vocal cords, contact ulcers of the folds, benign or malignant tumors, or thickening of the folds from infection at that level or higher in the respiratory tract. The inappropriate channelling of air may lead to inappropriate expulsion of air through the nostrils when the individual does not have a satisfactory method of separating the nasal passages from the oral cavity. This problem occurs when there is a cleft palate, a paralysis of the soft palate, a submucous cleft of the palate, a short palate, or a deep pharyngeal wall. Too little air is sent through the nasal cavity when the individual has a severe head cold, and when there is an excessive adenoidal mass or other growths closing or partially closing the passage.

Once again, the best aid the teacher has for dealing with these problems is his ear and his ability to observe. We shall not include any simple diagnostic test to determine the nature of voice disorders, and we shall cover no simple therapy procedures which may be used in the classroom. Disorders of the voice are often confusing and complicated. They may run the gamut from a voice that is too loud to one that is too soft, from a voice that is too high pitched to a voice that is too deep, from a voice that is hypernasal to one that has too little nasal resonance. Regardless of the problem, the teacher should encourage the family to seek professional advice. While it is true that some voices are more pleasant, more efficient, and more nearly appropriate to the age, sex, and social status of the individual than are other voices, it is also true that a real voice disorder always demands professional attention. The classroom teacher cannot discover or treat nodules on the vocal cords, nor can a teacher find and repair an unobservable cleft in the palate.

The words of warning that run throughout this discussion are not intended to imply that the teacher should not be alert to the needs of children, nor that the teacher should adopt the philosophy that since there is nothing he can do to cure a child of his hoarse voice or of his stuttering problem, the only alternative is to do nothing. The teacher with insight will do a great deal to explore problems with parents, to encourage them to seek the help the child needs, and will work diligently to provide a classroom environment that will be conducive to the child's best social and emotional development and to his continuing interest in and concern about communicating with other people.

Language Disorders

At the beginning of this chapter we defined language as a system of symbols. This symbol system is used in verbal expression or speech, but language has a much broader application. It is essential for the reader to understand that a consideration of language is necessary in a discussion of communications problems and that it will differ in many ways from discussions of speech per se.

Factors of Importance in the Acquisition of Language. The infant begins the process of language acquisition at the moment of his birth, when he starts to experience events, contacts with other people, and feelings which he will gradually internalize, organize, interpret, store in his memory, symbolize, recall, and express. While the average baby says his first meaningful word at about one year of age, the evidences of language, the precursors of true speech, are apparent almost from the beginning of his life. His early responsiveness to bright moving objects, a social smile, the panic that possesses him when his mother leaves him with a stranger, the cessation of crying when the bottle appears, the somewhat disorganized motor responses to the word "bye-bye," the hand movements that can be observed when he hears "pat-a-cake"—all of these are clues to the developing symbol system. He gradually attaches meaning to events in his life, recalls them in comfort or discomfort, responds accordingly, and understands simple words several months prior to saying his first true word. The baby who does not demonstrate this understanding cannot be expected to use words as early or as skillfully as the child who does show these early signs of learning.

If teachers, whose business it is to understand the learning process, will consider for a moment, they will realize that language acquisition is not a simple process. Language is learned when the baby is exposed to it in his regular environment. If his exposure is in any way interrupted or modified, the process of language learning will be affected.

Mental Ability. The word "learning" carries the implication that mental abilities play an important part in the onset of language. Language represents the highest level of cortical behavior known, and remains a reliable indicator of mental ability throughout life. Retarded children always show some reduction in language skills while average children usually demonstrate average vocabularies. Superior people who have had an opportunity to broaden their educational experiences show a higher level of language development than less gifted people exposed to the same environment. We can expect, therefore, that the language abilities of children in a classroom will differ in accordance with their ability to deal intellectually with the experiences to which they are exposed. A child of borderline intelligence will never be able to develop language skills comparable to those of a gifted child, even in the presence of expert teaching. Thus, one aspect of language evaluation is the appraisal of intelligence. This is not to say that the two are precisely the same or that, in a given child, an evaluation of intelligence will yield an adequate measure of language. An evaluation of intelligence does, however, provide a reasonable base upon which to build levels of expectation and understanding of language strengths or weaknesses. It would be safe to say that almost all well-ordered centers where language is studied on a clinical basis use tests such as the Cattell Infant Scale, the Merrill-Palmer, the Leiter International, the Stanford-Binet, the Wechsler Intelligence Scale for Children, the Columbia Scale of Mental Maturity, the Goodenough Draw-a-Man Test. Hopefully, children with language disorders will have the benefit of such testing over a period of time, in the hands of competent examiners. Chapter 2 deals with this particular topic. The teacher should be able to utilize the psychologist's reports as aids in determining whether or not language behavior is within reasonable limits for a particular child.

Children whose language is disordered because of slow mental development will generally demonstrate language behavior more typical of their mental than of their chronological ages. Clinical experience suggests, however, that scores on intelligence tests represent a wide variety of activities; and since some tasks on the tests are less demanding than others, language behavior may reasonably be somewhat below over-all mental age. In other words, language usually appears to be more seriously retarded than do certain other capacities. For example, there will be a greater relative delay in the onset of true words in a retarded child than in onset of walking, provided there are no accompanying neuromotor problems.

Visual Ability. Given the necessary intelligence for the learning of language, a child must be able to receive the stimuli from his environment. Visual perception is involved at a very early age. Evidence strongly supports the conclusion that blind children will have a slower onset of verbal language than will sighted children. This developmental difference is probably related to the fact that visual disturbances reduce a child's experiential world and distort his understanding of the environment which he is not capable of taking in with his eyes, evaluating, and visually interpreting. The discussion of receptive abilities in Chapter 3 is relative here.

Some disturbance in early language development may be noted in children who are sighted but who have visual acuity problems severe enough to upset visual input. Children with severe myopia or extreme hyperopia live under visually limiting conditions. The myopic child deals most satisfactorily with stimuli that fall within his field of vision, and he must exclude those experiences that fall outside the periphery of his visual ability. The hyperopic child, on the other hand, must chase the rainbows that fall within his visual realm and discount the visual stimuli at close range. The myopic child may enjoy the stimulation of looking at books, coloring, and playing with a variety of small toys. The hyperopic child will find these events distressing and may reject this kind of activity in favor of more gross behavior that is less challenging to his impaired vision.

The teacher concerned with communications and language deficits must be alert to signs of visual distress in children. Although these problems cannot be treated by the teacher, he can encourage the parents to take the child to an ophthalmologist. Many of the disturbances which we are considering here may not reveal themselves in the usual school screening procedures. Let me illustrate. A six-year-old boy with faulty language patterns involving confusion of pronouns, immature sentence structure, omission of helping words, and poor consonant articulation was brought to the clinic. His history revealed poor progress in reading. He was noted to have a facial tic isolated to the region around the eyes and resembling a wink. He had passed a school screening test and had been given a clean bill of visual health by a competent ophthalmologist. However, using observation as the chief clinical tool, it was noted that he read with only one eye at a time. He never focused on a printed page with both eyes. As he read, the examiner got down on the floor and followed his tracking. From this vantage point, it was possible to observe that his eyes were crossing markedly and that he solved his subsequent problems by using only one eye at a time. When these observations were reported to the ophthalmologist, he carried out a more complete visual examination and subsequently recommended that the child have glasses. There was almost immediate improvement in academic performance, in over-all maturity, and in language and speech usage.

Visual perception must also be taken into account. Again, Chapter 3 deals with this question in more detail; but it should be stressed that visual perceptual skill is part of the equipment necessary for acquiring mature language patterns. When visual perception is faulty, the best language treatment involves perceptual education. The techniques suggested in other chapters of this volume are not a formula for every child who has slow speech development and poor language structure; but visual perception does play an increasingly apparent role in this process.

Auditory Perceptual Capabilities. In addition to hearing losses, other less understood aspects of audition also influence the development of language. Auditory perception is considered in this connection.

Some children seem deaf at times, and at other times seem not to be deaf. They constitute an enormous diagnostic problem in the audiologic and speech clinic. The final solution to their problem will not be found in the classroom. Children with these difficulties should be referred to special diagnostic centers where experienced personnel, sophisticated equipment, and a great deal of time can be devoted to differential diagnosis. However, the teacher has the responsibility for careful observation in the classroom, so that specific information may be made available to the diagnostic clinic. The sensitive teacher will be able to make an important contribution to eventual diagnosis. Here, specific observations should be carefully recorded, with examples rather than interpretations of behavior reported. A recent letter from a classroom teacher provides an example of what *not* to do. A letter had been written asking for some indication of the school progress, particular learning difficulties, and the behavior of a little boy who was encountering difficulties in many areas of development. The teacher was prompt and courteous in answering, and included information about the child's inability to withstand frustrating experiences and his frequent crying under stress. This part of the report was helpful. She continued, however, by indicating that, after many conferences with the child's mother, she had concluded that the boy was rejected by his parents. This may have been a valid conclusion, but the teacher gave no evidence to support it. It would have been much more helpful had she reported the content of the school interviews and the reasons for feeling that this was a rejected child.

In the area of hearing, specific examples of auditory behavior in the classroom will provide the best help to the diagnostic clinic. The confusing child who suffers from auditory perceptual deviations may show some of the following symptoms which the teacher is in a unique position to observe:

1. He may respond better to the speech of others in a one-to-one situation than he does in the confusion of the classroom.
2. He may appear to understand some words that are spoken to him but seem not to hear or to be concerned with others. His vocabulary may show the same inconsistencies.
3. He may be unable to deal with any kind of question asked of him or may answer only the simplest ones.
4. He may use echolalia.
5. His hearing may appear to come and go.
6. He may respond occasionally to soft tones while ignoring loud ones.

Auditory hyperactivity may be a part of this syndrome. Unable to focus his attention on the most important stimuli in the environment, the child may flit from one auditory impression to another, attending to each one briefly and as if it were of primary importance to him. He may show marked reduction in hyperactivity when placed in a less complex auditory environment. The teacher can experiment to extend observations. A child with these auditory problems may have serious reductions in both receptive and expressive language. In its more serious forms, this problem is likely to be discovered before the child enters school. In its milder forms, however, the classroom teacher may be the one to recognize the subtle clues of its existence and to assist the child both in the classroom and in his search for more significant aid. While the teacher is helping the parents to find the kind of assistance required, certain changes may be initiated to ease the classroom situation. They include:

1. Seating the child so that he is removed from as much of the classroom stimuli as possible. The front of the room is probably a better place than the back for this purpose.
2. Doing as much teaching as possible through visual channels if these remain intact.
3. Attempting to give a concrete example when a difficulty with understanding is encountered, such as pointing to boots and saying the word several times, when instructing the child to put his boots on.
4. Recognizing that the child with this kind of auditory disturbance will show marked erraticism in intellectual functioning and that this erraticism is related to his unpredictable perceptual equipment, rather than to stubbornness or poor motivation.

5. Working closely with the child's mother, if she is cooperative and interested, to develop a basic vocabulary that will be important in the subject matter of the classroom. Experimental repetition, finding pictures of particular objects and pasting them into a scrapbook with the mother's help, is one simple procedure that will tend to draw attention to and stimulate words that need to be learned.

6. Having the child underline trouble words with a red pencil when they occur in his textbooks and attempting, by demonstration, writing, and frequent use, to help him become more familiar with that particular symbol.

7. Allowing him some freedom to move about the classroom, both to reduce the internal tension likely to accompany this problem, and to move himself to better physical positions relative to the source of sound.

8. Learning to extend special activities to suit the particular child.

9. Becoming familiar with literature that deals with this and related problems. The reader is referred to Johnson, et al., 1966.

Aphasia.   It would be a naive teacher indeed who did not associate a discussion of language disorders with such terms as childhood aphasia, aphasoid children, children with the Strauss syndrome, brain injury, interjacent children, children with learning disorders. We have avoided the use of these terms because of the confusion that surrounds them, and because they are not terms that should be applied without the use of thorough and sophisticated diagnostic procedures. Even then, there is striking evidence to support the contention that these diagnostic categories are considerably less precise than one might wish. There are many children whose problems are not clear-cut. They do not have the neuromotor problems found in cerebral palsy, yet they do present complaints of perceptual deviations, bizarre learning patterns, behavioral aberrations, hyperactivity, or some combination of these symptoms. Their language deficits do not have a clear neurological base, although many professional people would apply that term to them. They are not clearly mentally retarded, but neither are they clearly normal in intelligence. They may constitute management problems at home and at school, but one would be reluctant to attribute the over-all problem to emotional disturbance. These children exist in the midst of professional confusion over the nature of their problem. However, one thing seems certain. Systems of education which are applicable to average children are not applicable to these children. A specific case will illustrate this point.

When Susan was four years old, she had essentially no expressive language, and often acted as if she were totally deaf. It was difficult to assess her receptive ability. Psychological testing was almost impossible because of her severe hyperactivity and erratic behavior. She was tested on the floor, with the examiner moving materials into her line of vision as she traveled about. Even with these extreme testing measures, she showed at least borderline intelligence although there was wide variability in her functioning. By the time she was six, her I.Q. scores fell within average range, but her patterning of successes and failures was completely atypical. She had wide areas of difficulty well below her chronological age and evidence in other areas of strengths at and above her chronological age. She functioned better in visual perception than she did in areas of auditory perception. She learned to read extremely well and developed a vocabulary notable for its concreteness, lack of color, and, often, slight inaccuracy. Numerical concepts were a total impossibility for her. As a result, the arithmetic presented to the rest of the class was always well beyond this child's level of maturity, so she fell farther and farther behind. Had her teachers in the early grades been able to recognize that she was not ready for the kind of mathematical work that was offered, at least a portion of her problem might have been alleviated. However, it would have required tutoring, individual instruction on the part of the teacher, and careful cooperation with the home. The program could well have ended in the school's deciding to have an ungraded educational plan for this child. For example, she could have gone to the kindergarten for work on numerical readiness and to a third grade class for reading.

The arguments usually advanced by a school against handling a problem this way are that it destroys the child's peer relationships, gives him a sense of failure, makes it impossible for anybody to determine where he really belongs, and upsets his educational program as far as high school graduation is concerned. These arguments are easily refuted when we see that, although this child has proceeded apace with her age group in a public school, she has encountered every one of these problems and has been almost totally sacrificed educationally. She is paralyzed by anything that has to do with arithmetic, is not truly a member of any peer group, and will never be able to complete a regular high school program because of the number of courses that are now beyond her. It should have been possible, short of sending her to an expensive private school, to make adjustments in her educational program. Perhaps a classroom teacher could not have handled all the difficulties this little girl has in social perception—and they are marked. I think it would not even have been reasonable, in the absence of a language and speech-centered curriculum, to expect the teacher to have handled her language problems. It might have been possible, however, to make a marked contribution in both of these areas by the school's creative willingness to undertake its major mission with this child, as it must with all children. The school's major mission is education. The teacher is the expert in this field and can make the greatest contribution to troubled children through the mechanisms which he knows best. This contribution can be made while the "experts" outside the school program fight the battle of etiology, terminology, and prognosis for these children about whom almost nobody agrees. Learning more about teaching such children may lead eventually to the establishment of badly needed programs geared to their needs.

Emotional Problems.   Emotional development has a special relationship to language learning. All communication involves an exchange between two human beings. If a child's early experiences with people have been unpleasant and threatening to him, he may withdraw from social intercourse, cutting himself off from auditory stimuli and behaving as a deaf or perceptually handicapped child. He may permit himself to receive certain verbal stimuli and to make them his own in the form of language concepts, but refuse to use them in a verbal manner himself.

Specialists disagree about the types of emotional problems found in children, and the reasons for them. One little girl was successively diagnosed as mentally retarded, aphasic, brain damaged, symbiotic, and character defective. So many different opinions could hardly contribute to Lois's educational management. Her harassed older brothers, her troubled parents, and her weary teachers still had the problem of trying to live with her, and of deciding how to help her learn something other than egocentric speech, which was an outgrowth of her self-centered view of the universe.

The observant teacher will be able to ascertain certain behaviors suggesting that at least part of a child's problem lies in the area of emotional well-being. Once these observations are made, the teacher must remember that they are not unique to emotional disturbance but may occur with other disorders and at times in normal children as well. The teacher should be aware of the following indications of a child's possible emotional disturbance:

1. A capacity for speaking which is demonstrated only in selected situations or with specific people.
2. The use of some words, often echolalic in nature, or expressed in a flat, empty, inflectionless pattern.

3. The inability to use speech when it is directly requested, but fairly good ability to use it when it may be inappropriate to the activities of the rest of the class.
4. The use of self-talk suggesting that the child is engaging in fantasy. Fantasizing occurs when the child seems to be conversing with himself (although he may use no voice), unaware of what else may be going on in the room. (This is different from the self-talk which normal children use during intense imaginative play.)
5. Stereotyped motor behavior, such as rocking or head banging.
6. Preoccupation with some part of a toy, such as the wheels on a wagon, to the exclusion of the toy itself.
7. Demand for sameness in clothing, routine, or physical environment.
8. Destructive behavior beyond the normal destructiveness of small children.
9. Fire setting.
10. Wetting or soiling.
11. Inability to fit into a peer group.
12. Excessive fear or anxiety.
13. Temper tantrums.
14. Excessively quiet, uninvolved, passive behavior in the classroom.
15. Poor affect.
16. Learning problems apparently unrelated to intellectual limitations
17. Poor attention
18. Poor motivation.

Children react in many different ways when they are troubled. Some of their behavior is directed against society; some is directed against self. When their problems are sufficiently severe, there is almost always a communication deficit of one kind or another. Mutism and serious language retardation may occur as manifestations of the extreme forms of emotional disorder. Once again, these are not problems that can be effectively treated in the classroom, although the teacher can do much to help a troubled child by creating an atmosphere of acceptance and understanding. The teacher should do everything possible to minimize the weaknesses of the emotionally disturbed child and to bolster his confidence by providing opportunities for success; by accepting and reinforcing any efforts which the child makes; and by attempting to develop situations which will encourage him to try. This, believe it or not, is language therapy.

Interrelated Etiologies.   It should be clear to even the casual reader that the causes of language disturbance in children are overlapping and are certainly not discrete. A child with neurological impairment may have mental retardation or perceptual deficits which are not commensurate with his level of mental functioning. A child whose basic problem is emotional may also have perceptual difficulties, resulting from his tendency to withdraw from environmental stimuli and his refusal to deal with them on a meaningful level. The reverse is the child who has perceptual deficits that are not a part of a picture of mental retardation, but which are severe enough to impair his ability to handle the problems of living. This child is likely to be emotionally upset as well as perceptually involved. We cannot discuss causes of language disorders in children with the idea that it is possible to sift the evidence and relate a particular deficit to a specific cause. We must instead be cognizant of the many factors that operate together to permit language learning or to interfere with it.

Evaluating Language Skills.   We have suggested that severe problems in language acquisition require careful differential diagnosis in an effort to understand the disorder as well as present technical limitations will permit. Mental development, various aspects of perception, neurological condition, and emotional state must all be investigated through case history, clinical testing, observation, and exchange of ideas. When the results of these investigations are examined in a clinic or are considered by the classroom teacher, the problem of dealing with the language disturbance still remains. Regardless of the origin of poor language development, remedial steps are necessary; and before remedial steps can be taken, some information about the level of language functioning is needed. There are many ways to appraise language, but the most frequently discussed formal test is probably the Illinois Test of Psycholinguistic Abilities (McCarthy and Kirk, 1961). This test attempts to evaluate receptive, associative, and expressive abilities. It is a rather complicated test to give, so it should be administered by a skilled psychological examiner rather than by a classroom teacher. Data from instruments such as the ITPA are likely to be much more meaningful when they are administered as part of a battery of psychological tests.

Language development and verbal skills are after all related to the intellectual process. This is not to say that language problems do not exist apart from intellectual problems, but that a differentiation must be made. The Peabody Picture Vocabulary Test (Dunn, 1959) may be administered as a part of a total psychological battery; but is also a useful instrument for a teacher's use, if he follows directions consistently and carefully. This test is not a measure of total language functioning, but will give some idea of the level at which words are understood by the child. It provides a partial guide to receptive language ability and permits the examiner to consider the probability that expressive language will not operate on a higher level. If expressive language were better than receptive skills, the teacher would suspect a hearing loss, an emotional problem, or some other condition which prevented the child's cooperating on the test. The test is not time-consuming, but it must be administered individually.

Other methods of appraising language involve greater skills of observation than of testing technique. The teacher should listen for evidences of immaturity in school children by their selection of pronouns. "I" and "me" should be clarified by the time a child enters school. "He" and "him," "she" and "her," "we" and "us," and "they" and "them" should also be used appropriately. Sentences become more complicated in both structure and length as children grow older. This part of language skill is a reflection of environment, among other things, and is likely to differ from one socio-economic level to another. Templin (1957) has shown in her study of 480 children, ranging in age from three to eight years, that the average sentence length increases from 4.1 words at three years to 7.6 words at eight years The increase is gradual, with the largest jump occurring between five and six years, when the average child moved from 5.7 to 6.6 words. Templin has also shown that increase in average sentence length carries with it an increase in sentence complexity and a gradual reduction in the use of single word responses. The classroom teacher can use this information by keeping a running record of the actual words which children say over a period of time. Templin used fifty utterances, a formula adopted for many subsequent research projects. This might be difficult to do in a classroom, but it is possible if the teacher does not attempt to keep a running record of the comments of too many children simultaneously. The teacher can count the words in each utterance and arrive at an average for the fifty utterances. This count will provide a crude indication of the length of sentences as well as of the frequency with which the child enters into verbal communication. For information about the process of counting utterances, the reader is referred to McCarthy (1930).

Language-disturbed children frequently have difficulty with consonant articulation. They seem to learn words imperfectly and to extend immature articulatory and structural patterns into their later years, some arriving in secondary classrooms with deviations of this type. A language disorder is not always accompanied by articulation disturbance, nor is articulation disturbance always a sign of language disorder. The two frequently do exist together, however, and probably have the same causal foundation. Where they do co-exist, both problems must be treated in order to help the child communicate more effectively. It is advisable, however, to stress language first and to perfect articulation after the symbolic understanding is well established. The articulation test thus becomes an important part of the language evaluation.

Classroom Management.   The magic formula for handling and treating language problems in the classroom is missing from this discussion, because there is no such formula. McWilliams (1965) has suggested that each child with a language deviation will provide his own model and his own educational requirements, based upon the extent to which he is atypical in his language development and the manner in which his problem is typical of the classification into which he fits. Effective teaching of children with language problems requires a teacher who recognizes that academic achievement must always come after the child is helped to a position where he is able to learn. The language-handicapped child often needs individual teaching, and must be allowed to move at his own pace. He requires consistent and understandable limits, both in the classroom and the home. He demands consistency in management and instruction. Repetition of stimuli appropriately presented sometimes constitutes the secret password to the mind of a language-disturbed child. This child must be consciously *taught* to live and to do those things which other children acquire incidently.

CONCLUSION

The process of communication is the foundation upon which all educational experience rests and out of which emerges the only known evidence of academic success or failure. Educational input will depend upon the child's ability to receive, interpret, store, recall, and express the stimuli provided by his environment. To understand this concept is to recognize that communication skills are basic to all learning and to all living. Educational systems have too often failed to stress these fundamental abilities as they have attempted to build superstructures out of the learning of more traditional academic subjects, all of which depend upon successful communication. Awareness of the requirements of learning and insight into child growth and development point to a need for reappraising educational philosophies and for placing communication at the core of all learning programs, for both normal and handicapped children.

In the classroom, the teacher sets the communication pace for all the children. The teacher who is a successful communicator by nature or by art will do most to stimulate children, and will understand their failures as well as their successes. This teacher will know that positive personal attitudes toward children and love for them provide solid support for successful use of techniques, whatever they may be. This teacher will recognize before administering a single test that all public-school children must learn to listen to others, must develop confidence in themselves, must be given opportunities to encounter new experiences in order to broaden the scope of language development, and must be helped to acquire the language structures necessary for dealing successfully with those experiences. This teacher will provide a classroom environment conducive to a genuinely meaningful exchange with and among children who differ in many dimensions, and who emerge unique as individuals. This teacher fits well the image of the "good" teacher who has achieved a "clinical point of view in education" (Johnson, 1967, pp. 28-110).

REFERENCES

Dunn, L. M., *Peabody Picture Vocabulary Test*. Minneapolis: American Guidance Service, Inc., 1959.

Hull, F.M., and R. J. Timmons, "A National Speech and Hearing Survey," *Journal of Speech and Hearing Disorders*, 31, No. 4 (1966), 359.

Johnson, D. J., and H. Myklebust, *Learing Disabilities, Educational Principles and Practices*. New York: Grune & Stratton, Inc., 1967

Johnson, W., S. F. Brown, J. F. Curtis, C. W. Edney, and J. Keaster, *Speech Handicapped School Children*, (3rd Edition). New York: Harper & Row, Publishers, 1967.

Johnson, W., F. L. Darley, and D. C. Spriestersbach, *Diagnostic Methods in Speech Pathology*. New York: Harper & Row, Publishers, 1963.

Membership Directory, American Speech and Hearing Association, 1967.

McCarthy, D., *The Language Development of the Pre-School Child*. Institute of Child Welfare Monograph Series, No. 4. Minneapolis: University of Minnesota Press, 1930.

McCarthy, J. J., and S. A. Kirk, *Illinois Test of Psycholinguistic Abilities*. Urbana, Illinois: University of Illinois Press, 1961.

McWilliams, B. J., "The Language Handicapped Child and Education," *Exceptional Children*, 32, No. 4 (1965), 221-228.

McWilliams, B. J., E. J. Forrest, and J. Matthews, "Speech and Its Pathologies," *Journal of Dental Education*, 29, No. 1, (1965), 16-22.

McWilliams, B. J., and H. P. Matthews, "Visual Versus Aural Stimulation in Articulation Testing," *Speech Pathology and Therapy*, 8, No. 2 (1965), 69-71.

Milisen, R., "A Rationale for Articulation Disorders," *Journal of Speech and Hearing Disorders*. Monograph Supplement 4, (1954), 6-17.

Snow, K., and R. Milisen, "The Influence of Oral Versus Pictorial Presentation Upon Articulation Testing Results," *Journal of Speech and Hearing Disorders*, Monograph Supplement 4, 1954.

Templin, M. C., *Certain Language Skills in Children, Their Development and Interrelationship*. Institute of Child Welfare Monograph Series, No. 26, Minneapolis: University of Minnesota Press, 1957.

Templin, M. C., "Spontaneous Versus Imitated Verbalization in Testing Articulation in Pre-School Children," *Journal of Speech Disorders*, 12, (1947), 293-300.

Templin, M., and F. Darley, *The Templin-Darley Tests of Articulation*. Iowa City, Iowa: The State University of Iowa, 1960.

Van Riper, C., *Speech Correction Principles and Methods*, (4th Edition). Englewood Cliffs, N. J.: Prentice-Hall, Inc., 1963.

Wilcox, E., and B. McIntyre, "Listening with Mr. Bunny Big Ears," *Educational Activities*, Freeport, N. Y., 1965.

Chapter 7

ARITHMETIC SKILLS

Elizabeth F. Spencer
Robert M. Smith

Arithmetic is a form of language involving the communication of concepts through symbols. Among the concepts embodied in this unique language are quantity, size, order, relationships, space, form, distance, and time. The prerequisites for satisfactory achievement in each of these facets of arithmetic are identical to the basic skills required for proficiency in many of the other areas considered in this volume. Particular stress has been placed on the importance of establishing an appropriate level of development in various perceptual-motor factors. Children who experience problems in any of these skills will probably encounter difficulty in mastering certain arithmetic concepts.

For students to do their best in arithmetic, they must understand and apply properly the fundamental skills and processes. Because of the complexity involved in manipulating the unique symbols of this subject area, the unfamiliarity of the language to many youngsters, and the enormous variability in student's competencies and weaknesses, many children have serious problems in arithmetic. The level of students' achievement is influenced by how well their teachers understand the fundamental concepts embodied in arithmetic, and the degree to which they can effectively communicate them to the students.

Arithmetic skills are so complex in their interrelationship that youngsters may have difficulty in achievement for a variety of reasons. Skillful teaching of arithmetic is based on the teacher's ability to "fraction-down" the larger areas of performance into their basic components, and design evaluative techniques to identify which skills or competencies are causing difficulty. Because of the variety of characteristics represented in each classroom, various children will have different problems and will thus need unique remedial programs. The students' heterogeneity and the wide variation of competence among teachers, underscore the educators' need to develop diagnostic skills for identifying the nature of each child's arithmetic difficulty, and to design appropriate remedial strategies before the disabilities become too serious.

This chapter considers two major areas of potential weakness in arithmetic: (1) those skills that are necessary for an adequate understanding of quantity, including the development of a minimum level of skill in computation; and (2) the application of quantitative concepts and computational skills in the solution of arithmetic reasoning problems.

In earlier chapters, it has been stated that teachers should use many of the available formal appraisal techniques. A number of these formal tests do not require special training or supervised clinical experience. The content of these instruments can be employed in part or whole, according to the type and amount of information needed by teachers. Formal tests can also serve as models for further development of informal evaluative techniques. There is little merit in a teacher's spending time and effort designing informal tests when sections of existing standardized instruments will serve the same purpose. The teacher will find it useful, however, to develop alternate forms, using a standardized test as a model, when she wishes to make frequent informal checks of pupil progress.

ADVANTAGES IN DIAGNOSING ARITHMETIC PROBLEMS

The desire for teacher competence in educational diagnosis should be obvious. Satisfactory achievement in any subject assumes that a pupil can perform satisfactorily in the many sub-skills embodied in the subject matter. The identification of weaknesses in any of these specific skills will help the teacher to provide each pupil with the most desirable curriculum, with appropriate instructional devices. Identifying arithmetic difficulties will provide information concerning where particular emphasis should be given in the instruction.

If a number of pupils in a class do poorly on certain skills in computation but better in understanding meanings and relationships, one might assume that previous instruction had not allowed the students to develop mastery in this vital area of arithmetic. Such weaknesses may result from: (1) earlier instruction not sequentially developed; (2) pupils not given enough time to practice the skills; (3) lack of reinforcement for correct responses, resulting in many youngsters practicing their errors; or (4) lack of emphasis on careful work habits. Another class may have just the opposite problem. The pupils may do well in computational skills but have no understanding of why they perform certain computations; nor may they realize how computational skills can be applied in various situations. Principles, relationships, and meanings may not have been a clear part of their instruction. The teacher of a class with weaknesses of this type must help the pupils develop basic concepts in arithmetic reasoning.

A third problem is exemplified by students who have difficulty with both arithmetic computation and reasoning. These youngsters, when forced to attempt work beyond their level of functioning, will often become discouraged, frustrated, and anxious over anything related to arithmetic. This syndrome must be diagnosed promptly, or the teacher will have to focus on both arithmetic difficulties and changing student attitudes as well. Children with problems of this type should be introduced to an arithmetic sequence which will allow them immediate success.

Periodic informal assessment of students' arithmetic problems will help teachers identify difficulties which might influence the youngsters' performance in other subject areas. This clinical awareness will help identify basic causes of children's school problems. Among difficulties experienced by pupils in a typical classroom, the teacher might expect to encounter:

1. Students with a hearing loss;
2. Pupils who have moved so frequently that they have not been exposed to an appropriate and systematic arithmetic sequence;
3. Children who have experienved severe environmental deprivation or family upheaval;
4. Youngsters who have problems concentrating because of mild emotional difficulties;

5. Children who avoid the subject because of previous failures in related areas;
6. Pupils with perceptual-motor disturbances; and
7. Students with reading weaknesses.

Each of these problems rarely occurs in isolation—they characteristically appear in various, subtle combinations. This range of difficulties can seriously influence the youngsters' performance in arithmetic. A clinically sensitive teacher should employ a continual and systematic schedule of informal diagnostic activities designed to identify weaknesses and establish appropriate remedial programs for various disabilities.

TECHNIQUES FOR DIAGNOSING ARITHMETIC WEAKNESSES

Many of the general techniques available to teachers for observing student behavior have been reviewed in Chapter 1 and elaborated upon in chapters that have considered specific subject areas. Most of these suggestions are appropriate in the study of children's performance in arithmetic. The systematic collection of relevant data will help to validate any hunches a teacher might have concerning possible problem areas. These data should be gathered from as many sources as possible, using a variety of observational strategies in a realistic setting.

Teacher Observation

Consider a typical third grade class which has just been given an assignment in subtraction involving borrowing. As the teacher moves about the room she observes the following:

1. Jimmy is counting on his fingers but ceases to use this procedure when he sees the teacher standing beside his desk. The teacher notices that Jimmy can do the assignment without counting on his fingers but that he works problems at a much slower pace.
2. Mary is observed to be reversing numbers to avoid having to borrow. After questioning, the teacher realizes that the youngster does not fully understand the process of borrowing.
3. Sam crowds numbers on his paper, erases a great deal, and makes frequent errors in computation.
4. Charlie is adding the algorithms instead of subtracting.

With a large class the teacher has been busy, and unable to observe the work of all of the youngsters. She has, however, seen four students in action; and on the basis of their behavior, she should have generated some hypotheses concerning areas of difficulty for each student. The tabulation of these problems is not as difficult or time consuming as one might expect. Most of the students in a class will not have such large problems and will not require a great amount of the teacher's time for observation. Students with weaknesses must have the immediate diagnostic and remedial attention of the teacher before their erroneous methods become firmly established. They must not be allowed to practice their errors. To collect data systematically on the students, the teacher might:

1. List five or more operations in the arithmetic process in which each of the pupils is unsure, weak in comparison with other children, or in error. In the example given above, the teacher's list might have included the following notations:
   a. Pupil seems to have difficulty in understanding the concept of numbers.
   b. Youngster has not moved to an abstract level of conceptualizations, and requires concrete objects in calculating algorithms.
   c. Student can subtract when all of the numbers in the minuend exceed the value of numbers in the subtrahend but cannot borrow from one column to the other.
   d. Child omits a column because numbers are crowded and often misplaced.
   e. Youngster confuses addition and subtraction.
2. List all of the operations involved in a specific arithmetic process, and record next to each of the operations the names of those youngsters who are significantly weak. The list might include:
   a. Makes an error in combinations.
   b. Subtracted minuend from subtrahend.
   c. Failed to borrow and gave zero as the answer.
   d. Omitted a column.
   e. Did not borrow when necessary.
   f. Used trial-and-error addition.
   g. Reversed digits.
   h. Borrowed when unnecessary.

In observing a youngster's arithmetic performance, the teacher should be specific in describing the nature of a pupil's weaknesses. This care necessitates frequent checks of each student's work, and the information can help the teacher regroup students according to their difficulties and not according to levels of achievement alone.

Examination of Written Assignments

Checking papers for correct answers is a clerical chore that can be done rapidly with the aid of an answer sheet. These checks are very important; the teacher should not view them solely as busy work. A student's written work can provide valuable information in assessing specific arithmetic weaknesses. Any youngster who makes more than ten per cent errors on a paper should receive a more comprehensive assessment. Subsequent evaluations should include (1) inspecting all the missed problems to ascertain their degree of similarity; (2) determining which operations the youngster executed in error; and (3) asking each student to solve several problems in which some previous weakness had been observed. Again, a written record of the difficulties various pupils are encountering will help the teacher plan for subsequent grouping and determine the need for more comprehensive evaluative measures.

Teachers usually ask that children correct their mistakes on arithmetic papers. This procedure can be valuable for the pupil if he can depend on a stable source for explanation and help. To be told flatly that he is wrong in his answer, without any hint of why or how he can correct his response is a frustrating experience. For perceptive students, an example in a text will be sufficient. Other pupils may need more specific guidance to learn the proper steps in an arithmetic sequence. If several pupils have made similar mistakes, a group session on the chalkboard is recommended.

Answers to Oral Questions

A private interview with a child who seems to be confused by some phase of arithmetic will be most revealing. Returning to a level at which the child has been successful and proceeding to the level where correct functioning breaks down is a revealing diagnostic technique. Having the child explain aloud his reasoning methods will also provide promising clues. Oral questioning with a child who realizes he is doing failing work in a subject area can occasionally trigger an emotional outburst. It is essential, therefore, that rapport between teacher and child be firmly established; that a scolding manner be neither employed nor implied; and that the cooperation of the child be secured before initiating serious questioning. The interviewer should remember that the purpose of oral questioning is to determine whether the pupil understands the basic principles involved. Does arithmetic have meaning for him?

Asking the pupil his feelings toward arithmetic can be revealing. Motivation is an ingredient that cannot be overlooked in examining a pupil's learning difficulties. Studies have demonstrated that some youngsters have an intense dislike for arithmetic. The teacher should identify and try to change these feelings before continuing instruction to higher conceptual levels. The frequent dislike of arithmetic centers typically in the students' lack of conceptual understanding of a process, difficulty in translating word problems into appropriate form for computing, and weakness in prerequisite skills necessary to arithmetic achievement.

Board Work

Asking children to work problems at the chalkboard, singly or in groups, is a good way to identify areas of difficulty in their early stages. The technique has the advantage of allowing a teacher to survey the work of several youngsters simultaneously. The efficiency of this method should be capitalized upon by the teacher's systematically recording any of the children's weaknesses in attacking problems. It is important that consistent errors be identified.

Other Strategies for Diagnosis

Modern textbook writers usually provide several evaluative procedures to aid teachers in determining the amount of review needed before students proceed to new work, and in identifying various arithmetic weaknesses. These sources should be used throughout the diagnostic process. Other procedures include teacher-made tests, standardized evaluative instruments, formal diagnostic measures, and check lists.

BASIC SKILLS FUNDAMENTAL TO ARITHMETIC ACHIEVEMENT

The dramatic changes which have occurred in arithmetic instruction since the middle 1950s are not news to most teachers. A complete reorientation has taken place at all levels of instruction. Children are no longer required to spend hour after hour committing multiplication tables to memory, in the way so familiar to many parents. Instruction in arithmetic has changed in content, by taking higher-level concepts into the early elementary grades, and there has been a complete shift away from old, routinized instructional procedures. Much more emphasis is now given to the firm establishment of basic concepts at an abstract level.

Mathematicians consider success in arithmetic to be based on a complete understanding of numerical concepts. This skill includes more than simple memorization and rational counting. According to the mathematicians, children will not fully understand quantity unless they first appreciate the full meaning of numbers. The repetitive practice and chanting of numerical combinations, which characterized past arithmetic instruction, frequently resulted in a child's developing the ability to call numbers but not necessarily gaining full meaning of quantity. This situation is analogous to that of youngsters who have learned to word call in reading without developing a consistent method of word attack.

A number of promising approaches have been suggested to help youngsters develop an understanding of numbers. Piaget (1952) and others (Lovell, 1961; Churchill, 1961) have indicated the need for students to understand first the concepts of classification, seriation, combination, and conservation before proceeding to high-level operations. They believe that the more mechanistic techniques of the past are inadequate if arithmetic is to be understood at a conceptual level. Instruction in modern mathematics assumes that pupils have been exposed to activities which encourage understanding in these vital areas.

Teachers must be aware of the many fundamental skills that are precursive to subsequent instruction in arithmetic. In fact, many youngsters will fail to achieve adequately in arithmetic because of basic weaknesses in one or more of these skills. By identifying the root of the problem, the teacher will be able to plan effective instruction. The table below lists the more important fundamental skill areas, with an illustration of an activity for each, that might be used to assess informally the extent to which each skill has developed.

Table 11

Basic Skills Requisite for Satisfactory Achievement In Arithmetic

SKILL	INFORMAL DIAGNOSTIC ACTIVITY
LANGUAGE OF ARITHMETIC (All, More, Take-away, Less than, Add, Subtract, Borrow, Carry)	Using blocks, sticks, or counting frame, ask children questions which require them to respond with an expression characterizing a quantity or relation. Switch the task around by asking the students to show piles of sticks which are more than or less than the teacher's pile.

Table 11 (continued)

SKILL	INFORMAL DIAGNOSTIC ACTIVITY
CLASSIFICATION	See how well children can group objects according to criteria such as color, size, shape, use, or other characteristics. Ask them to classify according to more than one criterion. Develop a sequence of activities that require progressively more difficult and abstract classification.
CORRESPONDENCE (Relating elements in one group to elements in another group)	Have the youngsters match an object in one set to an object in a second set. Use objects that are similar, then objects which are dissimilar. As they are able to execute the task, place different numbers in each set and ask which set contains more or less than the other set.
CONSERVATION (The number of units within a set, or the amount of some material, remains the same regardless of changes made in arrangements)	Using stick or blocks organized according to some configuration, move the arrangement around to form a different configuration. Ask the pupils to indicate if the original number of objects has been changed. Variations of this activity can be developed using materials such as the Cuisenaire Rods. Conservation of quantity can be assessed using bottles of water, the water subsequently distributed into other containers, or using clay to form various shapes.
REVERSIBILITY (Units can be restored to their original position without changing their nature or relationship to other groups of objects)	Using objects such as blocks, alter the position of the units, asking the pupils to place them in their original order. Question the pupils to determine if they realize that it is possible to place the units in their former configuration without changing their characteristics or relationship to other units or groups of objects.
ORDERING	Using materials of different sizes such as the Cuisenaire Rods, ask the youngsters to order the rods according to their length, from smallest to largest. The difficulty of this task can be increased by using more than three or four objects, or by using materials which are inconsistent in their progression from smaller to larger.
ASSOCIATING NUMBERS WITH APPROPRIATE NUMERALS	Place a number of objects on a table. On another table place cardboard cutouts of numerals. Ask the children to inspect the objects and to choose the numeral which correctly

SKILL	INFORMAL DIAGNOSTIC ACTIVITY
	tells how many objects are visible. Increase the complexity of the task by asking the pupils to write down the appropriate numerals without access to the cutout numerals.
AUDITORY MEMORY	Ask the children to follow directions which are presented to them vocally.
VISUAL MEMORY	Present a series of objects ordered in a logical sequence. Ask the youngsters to shut their eyes. Mix up the sequence, and ask the students to order the objects as they were earlier observed.
PERCEPTUAL-MOTOR SKILLS	(See Chapter 3)

Each of these foundation areas assumes that the youngsters are able to function effectively in even more fundamental areas, such as visual discrimination, auditory discrimination, auditory-visual integration, spatial orientation, etc. For youngsters with severe difficulties, it may be necessary to evaluate their ability to function in these areas.

STANDARDIZED TESTS OF ARITHMETIC ACHIEVEMENT

There are a variety of achievement tests that include sections on arithmetic. These instruments can be administered either individually or in groups; obviously, individual administration will yield a more accurate measure of arithmetic achievement, since the examiner is able to exert greater control over the testing situation. In every case, however, the standardized administration procedures should be followed. Most of these tests are available to teachers:

1. California Arithmetic Tests (Ernest W. Tiegs and Willis W. Clark, California Test Bureau, 1963.) Subtest of California Achievement Tests. Grades 1–2, 2.5–4.5, 4–6, 7–9; three scores: reasoning, fundamentals, total. Diagnostic leads are afforded by the item classification and difficulty data.

2. Iowa Tests of Basic Skills: Arithmetic Skills (E. F. Lindquist and A. N. Hieronymous, Houghton Mifflin Co., 1956). Grades 3–9; three scores: arithmetic concepts, problem solving, total. A convenient, easy-to-use format. Tests functional skills. Evaluates generalized arithmetical skills. Emphasizes understanding. Does have considerable verbal content.

3. Metropolitan Achievement Tests: Arithmetic (Walter N. Durost, *et al*, Harcourt, Brace, & World, Inc., 1962.) Subtest of Metropolitan Achievement Tests. Grades 3–4, 5–6, 7–9; two scores: computation, problem solving and concepts. A traditional test of arithmetic.

4. Seeing Through Arithmetic Tests (Designed for use with Scott, Foresman Series, *Seeing Through Arithmetic*, 1962.) Grades 3, 4, 5, 6; seven scores: problem solving, computation, selecting equations, information, concepts, total. Valuable for assessing pupil achievement in modern arithmetic programs.

5. Stanford Achievement Test: Arithmetic Tests (Truman L. Kelley, *et al*, World Book Encyclopedia, Inc., 1964.) Grades 4–5.5, 5.5–6.6, 7–9; three scores: computation, concepts, application. A traditional test of arithmetic.

6. SRA Achievement Series: Arithmetic (Subtest of SRA Achievement Series; for grades 2–6, title is *Let's Figure This Out*, 1960.) Grades 1–2, 2–4, 4–6, 6–9; three or four scores: concepts, reasoning, computation, total. Has a helpful teacher's handbook for diagnostic work after testing. A formal test as low as grade one is unique. Tests arithmetic as taught in a traditional program.

Standardized arithmetic achievement tests are designed to help teachers determine how well a child scores in various arithmetic areas by comparing each youngster's performance with a large normative group. These data, then, determine if each child is performing at his expected grade level.

Teachers can obtain more information from standardized arithmetic achievement tests than just an inter-individual comparison. Most tests include subsections which allow the data to be profiled. This procedure provides an indication of the major areas in which each pupil is relatively stronger or weaker. In profiling, an individual's performance on each of the subtests is compared with achievement in the other areas. A relatively even profile is, of course, desirable, approximating a child's expected grade level.

The profile sheet on many tests is often routinely removed from the student's booklet, placed in his cumulative folder, and the remainder of the booklet discarded. This procedure results in the loss of potentially valuable diagnostic information. Teachers should recover the sheets on which the students have worked their problems and analyze their performances to determine which areas and skills presented some difficulty for most of the class and consistent trouble for certain children. If 40 per cent or more of a group makes a certain type of error, the teacher can legitimately assume that the concepts embodied in the activity are not generally understood. In such cases, the teacher should consider re-teaching the concept using a different methodology than she employed previously. She should also determine whether the scores for individual pupils are at approximately the same level on the various subtests, and whether individual and group patterns emerge which might be valuable in planning subsequent instruction.

FORMAL DIAGNOSTIC MEASURES

While achievement tests will provide a general picture of areas in which youngsters may be having difficulty in arithmetic, the teacher should recognize that their diagnostic value is limited. These survey tests are not designed to evaluate specific difficulties in depth—they do not include a formal means for assessing the strategy a child might use in solving a problem. This assessment is highly important in identifying the reasons for arithmetic weaknesses.

When a teacher suspects that certain pupils are weak in certain areas of arithmetic because their achievement test profiles are uneven, she must make a further effort to determine the reasons for the weaknesses. The best means for identifying the causes is the administration of a formal instrument allowing an intensive study of students' arithmetic performance in various areas. The tests should be administered individually, and require clinical sensitivity on the part of the examiner to identify the subtleties of a child's approach to a problem. Some teachers will have the necessary background and experience but not the time to administer a diagnostic instrument in arithmetic. Other teachers should seek the advice and assistance of more skilled diagnosticians or subject specialists. The diagnostic arithmetic tests are not as involved in their administration as are diagnostic reading tests. Some of these diagnostic tests which require specialized ability for administration are:

1. Diagnostic Tests and Self-Helps in Arithmetic (Brueckner). Grades 3–8; examines addition, subtraction, multiplication, division, operations with whole numbers, operations with fractions, operations with decimals, percentage, and measurement.

2. Los Angeles Diagnostic Tests: Fundamentals and Reasoning. Grades 2–9; examines addition, subtraction, multiplication, division, and reasoning.

3. Diagnostic Chart for Fundamental Processes in Arithmetic. All

elementary grades; examines arithmetic habits, procedures, and types of errors made in computation.

4. Easy Steps in Arithmetic. Grades 2–6; examines addition, subtraction, multiplication, division, and money computation.

5. Essential Arithmetic Tests. Grades 2–7; examines computation and problem solving.

The teacher should avoid overgeneralizing about any pupil's arithmetic weaknesses solely on the basis of his performance on one of the above instruments. We emphasized in the first chapter that a child's performance must be adequately sampled. Although diagnostic tests are valuable, other types of observations are still necessary before characterizing a child's typical performance in any area. If a youngster has trouble with borrowing when subtracting, make sure that you observe him in various situations requiring use of this skill.

TEACHER-CONSTRUCTED EVALUATIVE TECHNIQUES

There are many times during the school year when the teacher may wish to evaluate informally a student's progress in some aspect of arithmetic. It may be that a certain computational concept has been giving a student trouble; or perhaps that a youngster has difficulty with word problems because he cannot translate them into appropriate computational form. Other instances where quick, informal evaluation is helpful are the appraisal of different methods of instruction, the establishment of groups, the placement of new pupils entering the class from different school systems, or student readiness for proceeding to a new level of instruction.

Prior to constructing an informal test, the teacher should give some thought to the reason for developing such a measure. To develop a test blindly, just because it seems like a good idea, is really meaningless. If the teacher is interested in surveying her pupils' understanding of certain computational concepts, the test should reflect this objective, and control as far as possible other compounding variables, such as reading or reasoning. Specifically, if the objective is to see how well the youngsters can carry in addition, any teacher-developed instrument must include a disproportionate number of problems requiring this skill. An attempt should be made to sequence the items from problems in carrying requiring the most fundamental understanding to more difficult problems demanding higher levels of skill. For example, addition which involves two-digit numbers, requiring the pupil to carry only once, is easier than multiple carrying, as in numbers of three or more digits.

Teacher-made tests can be administered in either group or individual sessions. Group administration does not provide the means for intensive analysis of the processes or habits a youngster uses in working a problem. Individual administration gives an idea of how the child arrives at an answer and provides indications of other weaknesses, such as in counting, measurement, discrimination, reversals, or combinations. Unfortunately, even the time it takes to administer a short test individually is prohibitive in many classrooms.

An example of a teacher-constructed test is given below. This test is for subtraction, and would be used after the youngsters have been introduced to borrowing that involves two numbers in the subtrahend and minuend. Notice that the tasks proceed from the relatively simple to the more complex. This sequence is important in any diagnostic effort, for it provides a clue to the exact location in the breakdown of a pupil's understanding.

Table 12

A Teacher-Made Test in Subtraction

SKILL TO BE ASSESSED	EXAMPLES OF PROBLEMS				
Number facts up to 10	8 − 5	9 − 2	7 − 4	8 − 6	6 − 4
Number facts above 10	11 − 8	17 − 9	17 − 8	13 − 7	12 − 4
No borrowing	38 − 5	79 − 8	57 − 3	68 − 8	95 − 3
With borrowing	40 − 7	63 − 9	56 − 7	70 − 4	21 − 6
Two numbers no borrowing	57 − 37	68 − 45	87 − 24	88 − 30	59 − 36
Two numbers with borrowing	51 − 18	72 − 38	81 − 29	73 − 24	46 − 28

Let us assume that a youngster is able to solve correctly all the above problems with the exception of those with a zero in the minuend. This fact would immediately stand out in a careful inspection of his work, and would indicate a need to alleviate this weakness before the youngster moves to another level of instruction. If a child misses several problems throughout the test, he probably understands the processes involved but makes errors through carelessness or sloppy work habits. These habits should be corrected to increase his efficiency and accuracy. Children who miss many problems will require more thorough analysis of their difficulties and evaluation in areas that are sequential prerequisites to the skills in which they have failed.

In constructing informal tests, teachers will find an adequate sample of tasks in arithmetic workbooks or texts. Various forms of tests can be developed, typed on large cards, and used over and over again. The pupils' responses should be kept for comparison with their performance on formal arithmetic achievement tests. This comparison will provide a consistent picture of each child's unique arithmetic strengths and weaknesses.

When a teacher analyzes a youngster's performance on an informal test, she must consider certain key questions:

1. What is the rate at which he works?
2. Is he rigid in the procedures he uses to attack a problem, or does he have no consistent method for solution?
3. What is his attitude toward arithmetic, and toward his being evaluated in arithmetic? Does he panic, get tense, feel hopeless, or is he unconcerned?
4. Is he too dependent on the teacher, answers in the back of a book, or on other students?

Discovering and eliminating errors in the mechanics of computation will not solve all the problems in arithmetic learning. This is much too simple and too narrow an approach. Adequate understanding of principles on the part of the pupil is necessary if he is to achieve self-confidence. Appropriate application of arithmetic operations is the primary goal of arithmetic instruction. If a pupil only multiplies, when he sees the appropriate sign on his work sheet, the mechanical operation of multiplying becomes an end in itself and has little utilitarian meaning for him. We must thus give some attention to the students' arithmetic reasoning abilities.

When assessing arithmetic reasoning skills, the teacher can control the possible influence of reading difficulties by reading problems to the children. At the most elementary level the problems should require only a single computational process to determine if the pupils grasp the process of translating the components of a situation to an algorithm. The teacher might gradually introduce problems that require the use of multiple processes. Initially the problems should contain no irrelevant information and should be sequenced roughly according to each child's level of computational skill. The reasoning problem can be made more difficult by the introduction of irrelevant information. In these situations the pupil must weed out the important data and translate the information into correct computational form. The teacher must be careful to separate computational difficulties from reasoning errors. From her analysis the teacher can decide the most effective method for subsequent instruction.

The importance of checking a child's day-to-day arithmetic work cannot be emphasized too strongly. This daily evaluation will help to reduce errors of production, and to indicate areas in which instruction is failing. A constant check will help to prevent the reinforcement of incorrect procedures. Early detection of student difficulties means easier remediation. Diagnosis, then, should be a constant activity.

IDENTIFYING ERRONEOUS ARITHMETIC HABITS

As the teacher inspects students' arithmetic work, she may find it helpful to use a check sheet for recording the results of her observations. A check sheet allows the teacher to compile a systematic collection of data, and thus helps her to focus on specific weaknesses. The table on pp. 168-169 lists habits in addition, subtraction, multiplication, and division that might be observed in pupils' work. The alert teacher should be able to devise similar check lists in other areas of arithmetic. Many of the arithmetic habits listed in the table can be observed by inspecting students' work without their being present. A comprehensive appraisal of habits, however, should be done on an individual basis.

SUMMARY

To be realistic, it is impossible for teachers to devote to every child the time necessary for a complete individual arithmetic diagnosis. Fortunately, every child does not need such a diagnosis. Many youngsters will be able to handle adequately the instructional objectives in the arithmetic program without special diagnostic or remedial attention. Others, however, will falter in very basic areas, and will require continual evaluation and assistance. It is the latter group for whom the diagnostic activities suggested in this chapter are applicable.

Table 13

Types of Arithmetic Habits Observed in Elementary School Pupils*

ADDITION

Errors in combinations
Counting
Added carried number last
Forgot to add carried number
Repeated work after partly done
Added carried number irregularly
Wrote number to be carried
Irregular procedure in column
Carried wrong number
Grouped two or more numbers
Splits numbers into parts
Used wrong fundamental operation
Lost place in column
Depended on visualization
Disregarding column position
Omitted one or more digits

Errors in reading numbers
Dropped back one or more tens
Derived unknown combination from familiar one
Disregarded one column
Error in writing answer
Skipped one or more decades
Carrying when there was nothing to carry
Used scratch paper
Added in pairs, giving last sum as answer
Added same digit in two columns
Wrote carried number in answer
Added same number twice

SUBTRACTION

Errors in combinations
Did not allow for having borrowed
Counting
Errors due to zero in minuend
Said example backwards
Subtracted minuend from subtrahend
Failed to borrow; gave zero as answer
Added instead of subtracted
Error in reading
Used same digit in two columns
Derived unknown from known combination
Omitted a column
Used trial-and-error addition
Split numbers
Deducted from minuend when bor-

rowing was not necessary
Ignored a digit
Deducted 2 from minuend after borrowing
Error due to minuend and subtrahend digits being same
Used minuend or subtrahend as remainder
Reversed digits in remainder
Confused process with division or multiplication
Skipped one or more decades
Increased minuend digit after borrowing
Based subtraction on multiplication combination

* G. T. Buswell and Leonore John, *Diagnostic Chart for Fundamental Processes in Arithmetic.* Indianapolis Indiana: The Bobbs-Merrill Co., Inc., 1925. (Used with permission of publisher and author.)

MULTIPLICATION

Errors in combinations
Error in adding the carried number
Wrote rows of zeros
Carried a wrong number
Errors in addition
Forgot to carry
Used multiplicand as multiplier
Error in single zero combinations, zero as multiplier
Errors due to zero in multiplier
Used wrong process—added
Error in single zero combinations, zero as multiplicand
Confused products when multiplier had two or more digits
Repeated part of table
Multiplied by adding
Did not multiply a digit in multiplicand

Based unknown combination on another
Errors in reading
Omitted digit in product
Errors in writing product
Errors in carrying into zero
Counted to carry
Omitted digit in multiplier
Errors due to zero in multiplicand
Error in position of partial products
Counted to get multiplication combinations
Illegible figures
Forgot to add partial products
Split multiplier
Wrote wrong digit of product
Multiplied by same digit twice
Reversed digits in product
Wrote tables

DIVISION

Errors in division combinations
Errors in subtraction
Errors in multiplication
Used remainder larger than divisor
Found quotient by trial multiplication
Neglected to use remainder within problem
Omitted zero resulting from another digit
Counted to get quotient
Repeated part of multiplication table
Used short division form for long division
Wrote remainders within problem
Omitted zero resulting from zero in dividend
Omitted final remainder
Used long division form for short division
Said example backwards
Used remainder without new divi-

dend figure
Derived unknown combination from known one
Had right answer, used wrong one
Grouped too many digits in dividend
Error in reading
Used dividend or divisor as quotient
Found quotient by adding
Reversed dividend and divisor
Used digits of divisor separately
Wrote all remainders at end of problem
Misinterpreted table
Used digit in dividend twice
Used second digit of divisor to find quotient
Began dividing at units digit of dividend
Split dividend
Counted in subtracting
Used too large a product
Used endings to find quotient

Diagnosis is but the first step involved in effective instruction. Appropriate remediation is the desired goal. The instructional strategies selected for remedial procedures should emerge from the information collected through teachers' diagnostic efforts. Arithmetic is a common area of weakness for pupils, and teachers should be familiar with a broad range of assessment procedures in order to modify their instructional programs effectively.

REFERENCES

Churchill, E. M., *Counting and Measuring*. Toronto: University of Toronto Press, 1961.

Lovell, K., *The Growth of Basic Mathematical and Scientific Concepts in Children*. London: University of London Press, 1961.

Piaget, J., *The Child's Conception of Number*. London: Routledge and Kegan Paul, 1952.

Chapter 8

PERSONAL-EMOTIONAL-
SOCIAL SKILLS

James L. Lister

The personal, social, and emotional aspects of a child's
makeup profoundly influence his ability to enjoy and
profit from the school experience. Without early detection and remediation, problems in these areas can lead
to serious difficulties which will reduce the child's over-
all ability to learn and to relate effectively with others.
The teacher who is sensitive to the child's feelings about
himself and others is better equipped to create an effective learning environment, to aid him in relating effectively with other children, and to play a vital role in
obtaining additional professional help.

171

HUMAN BEHAVIOR: ITS NATURE AND DEVELOPMENT

Requirements for Healthy Development and Functioning

Personal, social, and emotional skills are a reflection of a child's level of mental health. Although there have been numerous definitions of mental health (Jahoda, 1956), there is general agreement concerning the nature of the psychologically healthy individual. Combs (1926) has described the adequate person in terms of his perceptions: the way he views himself, others, and his world. As a framework for viewing personal-social-emotional functioning, Combs' four characteristics of the psychologically adequate personality are helpful. Working from the basic assumption that all behavior is a function of the way things appear to the person, Combs describes the healthy person as: (1) having a positive view of self; (2) being identified with others; (3) being open to experience; and (4) having a rich and available perceptual field.

Positive View of Self.   The psychologically healthy child feels good about himself. He believes that he is generally liked by those who know him; that he is a worthwhile person in his own right; and that he is generally capable of adequately meeting the challenges which confront him from day to day. The child does not have an exclusively positive view of himself; there are certainly times when he does not feel at all good about himself, and he may at times even feel that he is not very well-liked by some adults and peers (Combs, 1962, p. 51). But it is the positive view of self which predominates in the psychologically healthy child.

Identification with Others.   The complete egocentrism of the infant gradually gives way to recognition of the existence and importance of other human beings. Psychologists are generally agreed that the capacity to recognize and feel related to other human beings is a valid index of psychological health. As the child matures physically, he also increases his capacity to identify with others in a non-demanding, non-dependent fashion. The child comes to find that he shares a great deal in common with others around him; many of his strongest feelings, fears, and dreams are shared by other people. The child who has a sense of identification with others does not necessarily fit the stereotype of the highly social or gregarious personality. On the contrary, he may occasionally prefer to spend time with one or two best friends, or to be alone. The healthy child, however, has the capacity to be alone without experiencing alienation or separation. The child who is developing the capacity to extend himself to include others can often behave apart from his immediate peer group because he identifies with a greater range of persons.

Openness to Experience and Acceptance. Those who work with very young children are familiar with the young child's capacity to deny the reality of unpleasant facts and events. Of the many mechanisms for psychological self-defense which children and adults employ, denial is often considered the most primitive, representing a lower level of psychological maturity than, say, rationalization. A clear index of psychological health, therefore, is the child's ability to face facts, even when the facts do not fit his wishes and beliefs. The child's ability to absorb and accept most of his experience; that is, organismically admit the truth of his experience; is one of the basic aspects of the adequate personality. Openness to experience refers to the child's search for information, his readiness to listen to divergent opinions, and his ability to resist acting or choosing with insufficient information. Acceptance of one's experience does not suggest acquiescence or resignation. Rather, it describes the sense of confidence that comes from a wish to know the facts and the ability to meet the challenges of new events.

A Rich and Available Perceptual Field. It is easy to see how a rich and available perceptual field contributes to the child's psychological economy. To have available a clear perception of himself and the world in which he lives gives the child a great reservoir of information, skills, and understandings upon which to draw. The psychologically healthy child has a rich background of perceptions from many experiences, including formal school learnings, to which he has free access. The capacity to relate one's knowledge and experience to an immediate problem situation is as vital to effective functioning as the knowledge itself. The psychologically healthy child has a large store of life data, and he knows how to use it.

Levels of Human Effectiveness

In assessing the psychological health of children, one may consider their behavior according to levels of human effectiveness. Blocher (1966) has described this approach to diagnosis in terms of the degree to control the individual can maintain over his environment and his reactions to it. The five levels are only a convenient way of describing a unitary dimension, and refer to typical or average levels of functioning, not to momentary or short-term behavior which varies from time to time and place to place.

Panic. The child who functions at this level requires protection, institutionalization, or very close personal supervision, for he has lost control to such a degree that he may endanger himself and others. Behaviorally, the child may either strike out physically or verbally against others, or attempt to avoid everyone around him. He may engage in physical self-abuse, such as head banging, hair pulling or cutting, and scratching his skin. In terms of Combs' model of the psychologically healthy personality, it is easy to see that the child who functions at this level has anything but a positive view of himself and his ability to cope with his world or to relate warmly to those around him. From his behavior, we can infer that he feels incapable of coping with a very threatening world; that he is alienated from others; and that he must either shut out much of his experience or be overwhelmed by it.

Inertia.   At this level of functioning, the child exerts little control over his environment, remaining passive to immediate problems and situations. This level is characterized by a lack of goal-oriented, organized behavior. Behaviorally, we might expect the child to depend upon others to organize his behavior; to give him suggestions and directions and check to be sure that he has followed them. He might, for example, make an initial effort to follow his teacher's instructions on a small project but fail to try his own ideas or ask for further assistance. This child cannot postpone satisfactions for more than a short time, and directs his efforts toward immediate satisfaction without concern for others around him. Such a child is below his age norms on initiative, creativity, and acceptance of responsibility for his behavior. He is very much an "outer-directed" person.

Striving.   At this middle level of human effectiveness, the child has a fair degree of control over his emotional reactions. He can work on a difficult problem for some time rather than react to frustration with rage, crying, or withdrawal. There is a degree of planning and goal-direction, but the child is usually concerned with meeting a crisis or emergency which would not have arisen had he planned and organized more effectively. From the child's behavior, we can infer that his view of himself holds many negative evaluations. While this child has some capacity for identification with others, he views himself as sufficiently different and alienated that his relationships with adults and other children are continuously precarious ones. He must be carefully attuned to others' feelings toward him, so that he can act in a manner acceptable to them. He finds it difficult to admit many perceptions into his awareness, and these incomplete and distorted perceptions render him less effective than he might otherwise be. As a result of his distortion and denial of certain experiences, the child may find that essential perceptions are missing, or that he cannot draw readily upon the experience which he has had. The child of any age who functions at the striving level has serious doubts about himself. He finds it difficult to trust and identify with others; he cannot face facts and act accordingly; he lacks many of the perceptions essential to optimal functioning; and he cannot easily relate his knowledge and experiences to the daily business of living.

Coping. At this level of human effectiveness, the child works actively to change his environment. He is capable of long-range planning and organization, and views life more as challenge than as crisis. The child may appear highly effective on the surface, but may experience frequent feelings of uncertainty and anxiety. At the coping level, the child is never quite convinced that he is successful, or accepted and valued by others.

Mastery. Comparatively few individuals attain the highest level of human effectiveness. It is, however, the level of functioning toward which people strive. This person plans and executes long-range goals successfully and responds to immediate challenges. He does so with feelings of adequacy, security, and mastery much of the time. Living is fun. Persons approaching this level of functioning have a distinctive view of themselves, other people, and the world in which they live. Their reservoirs of positive perceptions of self are adequate to sustain occasional failure. They are closely identified with a great range of humanity, and can identify with their peers, but they do not depend upon them for validation of their own ideas and behaviors. Such persons do not merely tolerate, but actively seek, a wide range of new experience inconsistent with prior experience. They can readily come to terms with new facts, even when the new information requires a substantial shift in beliefs or behavior. Persons functioning at the level of mastery are so intimately in touch with great amounts of information and experiences that they can readily draw upon them in their immediate lives.

SOURCES OF DATA: OBSERVATIONAL
TECHNIQUES CLASSIFIED

The teacher has immediate access to a vast amount of data useful in determining the level of effectiveness at which a child functions. Other useful data can be easily obtained through simple procedures. To avoid a bewildering welter of facts gathered through a potpourri of techniques, we shall offer a brief classification of assessment procedures.

Each procedure yields a particular kind of information about the child, and each kind of information has its unique values and limitations.

A note of caution should be sounded here regarding the level of training and experience essential for the independent administration and interpretation of the standardized and informal procedures presented in the following sections. The American Psychological Association (1954) has stated the training and supervised experience required to administer psychological tests and diagnostic techniques. The statement classified tests according to three levels: (1) those which can be administered and interpreted on the basis of a careful study of the manual by those without formal training in measurement, testing, or psychological theory; (2) those which can be administered and interpreted by persons with basic courses in measurement, testing, and psychological theory; and (3) those which require, in addition to formal study of measurement, testing, and psychological theory, a substantial amount of supervised experience in administration and interpretation. Tests of personal–social–emotional development are classified at the second and third levels. Most teachers will not have had the training and experience necessary to use such techniques independently. It is therefore essential that consultation and supervision be obtained from qualified persons in the school. The school counselor can be expected to have training in the use of all tests except those at the highest level, the individually administered tests of personality such as the Rorschach Ink Blot Test and the Thematic Apperception Test. The school psychologist can be expected to be qualified to use tests at the highest level. Consultation with specialists will insure that appropriate techniques are being employed and that sound conclusions are being drawn.

The following classification (drawn heavily from Adams, 1964) should aid in avoiding the interpretive pitfalls which characterize much of the data teachers gather about their students.

Self-Report Techniques

Self-report data are obtained from children in ways which allow them to describe themselves and their relationships with others.

Standardized Instruments. Several standardized self-report techniques are currently available. The following are presented as examples of the published materials available to supplement assessment by informal procedures.

1. The Mooney Problem Check List (Mooney and Gordon, 1950) is designed for children in grades seven and above and requires about

30 minutes to administer. Problems typical of the age group are included in such areas as social relations, home adjustment, health, sexual adjustment, and others. The check list provides a simple inventory of the problems as students view them.

2. The SRA Junior Inventory (Remmers and Shimberg, 1957), like the Mooney Problem Check List, lists problems children commonly experience in five areas: (1) about myself; (2) about me and my school; (3) about me and my home; (4) getting along with other people; and (5) things in general. It is designed for use with children in grades four through eight and can be administered in about 45 minutes.

3. The California Test of Personality (Thorpe, et al, 1953) is one of the few available inventories designed to measure the personality characteristics of young children. Separate scores are provided in twelve areas, such as school relations, sense of personal worth, and withdrawing tendencies. The test can be used from kindergarten through high school and adult levels. It requires 45 to 60 minutes to administer.

Interviews.   The interview has been one of the richest sources of data concerning a person's view of himself and other people. Through the interview, the teacher can obtain impressions of the child's level of functioning by helping him to express anything he wants to say. It is also possible to use the interview for obtaining answers to specific questions like those included in the check lists described above, or for studying the child's reactions to certain general topics or structured situations (see Expressive Methods, p. 186). The interview is one of the most useful and flexible of the informal self-report techniques since the teacher can employ interview techniques in daily conversations with the child. Tape recording individual and small group conferences makes them available for later study. While it is one of the major sources of information about the child's view of his world, the interview is extremely difficult to standardize, and therefore subject to many biases in addition to those which characterize other self-report procedures.

Autobiographical Material.   The child's own written account of his feelings, ambitions, or fears can reveal the way he feels about himself and others. The autobiographical technique could be used to obtain a child's account of his entire life. For children below junior high school, however, its major value lies in providing an avenue for relating experiences and personal ambitions or in describing things that are of particular interest or concern. For example, the topic, "Things I Worry

About" might be very useful in giving fourth-graders a method for expressing their doubts or uncertainties. The autobiography is a flexible technique which can involve much or little structure, depending upon the age of the students, the experience of the teacher, and the way the materials will be interpreted.

Evaluation of Self-Report Approaches

Since self-report information comes directly from the child, its validity is heavily dependent upon the child's ability to understand the task and to trust the teacher or psychologist with the information he is asked to provide. In the case of the interview and the autobiography, the child must have a speaking or writing vocabulary adequate to communicate his feelings and experiences.

There are a variety of approaches to interpretation of self-report data. First, one may assume that a child's report about himself is objectively accurate. If he says that he does not have many friends, one can accept that as an accurate account of his acceptance by other children. However, all teachers are familiar with children whose self-descriptions are at wide variance with their behavior, as observed by parents, peers, and other adults. Accepting self-report information as objectively true in the personal, social, and emotional areas of the child's life is therefore somewhat dangerous.

A second interpretive stance is the empirical approach in which the objective truth of the child's self-report is not particularly important. In this technique, what the child says about himself, although objectively inaccurate, predicts other important aspects of his behavior. Take for example the second-grader who announced to his teacher that his father was an astronaut. The teacher knew this was not true. She noted, however, that Mike presented similar exaggerations when approaching unfamiliar tasks. With Mike, then, grandiose tales of his or his father's exploits became a signal for the teacher that the child was unsure of his ability to function adequately in an uncertain situation.

A third approach to interpreting self-report data might be called the inferential approach. Here, the data are studied as the basis for inferring higher-order generalizations or constructs to use as predictors of other kinds of behavior. For example, a child's autobiography could be read with the purpose of forming an impression of whether he has a negative or positive view of himself. If the biography indicates a positive view, in the sense which Combs (1962) has described, effective behavior would then be expected in a variety of situations. Combs and his associates (Combs and Soper, 1963; Courson, 1963; Benton, 1964; Gooding, 1964) have conducted studies involving the use of clinical inferences.

In studying a child, most teachers use a combination of the approaches sketched here. Accepting the child's self-report as objectively true avoids interpretive errors which may occur when the teacher infers and extrapolates from these to other situations; however, it risks accepting inaccurate self-descriptions which result from a variety of perceptual distortions. The empirical approach avoids the need to determine the validity of a student's self-report but does not provide any explanatory concepts for use in predicting behavior in situations different from those observed. The inferential approach is potentially the most fruitful interpretive approach because it generates high-order constructs from which statements about a child's behavior in new situations can be predicted; unfortunately, there is a proportionally greater probability of error in interpretation. Judges or teachers frequently do not agree on a child's standing in a particular dimension; inferences are often based on insufficient or irrelevant samples of self-report data; and the unique demands of the situations within which the child behaves cannot often be defined accurately in advance.

Observations of Behavior

Most of the impressions a teacher uses in assessing a child's psychological health come from direct observation of his behavior during the school day. When observations in important learning, social, and interpersonal situations are carefully made and accurately recorded, they can be valuable in constructing a picture of the child's level and mode of functioning. The validity of the ratings and interpretations derived from these instruments depends upon the competence of the person using them. In most instances, they should not be used independently by a teacher or psychologist until he has given and interpreted them under the supervision of a psychologist qualified in the use of such instruments.

Standardized Instruments.   The following standardized instruments represent procedures which have established reliability and validity for assessing adequacy of psychological functioning.

1. The Haggerty-Olson-Wickman Rating Schedules (1930) were designed to aid in the early detection of children's behavior problems and problem tendencies in nursery school through high school. Schedule *A* provides a record of behavior problems, such as speech difficulties and defiance of discipline. Each of the fifteen problem types is rated on a four-point scale. Schedule *B* permits a rating on thirty-five traits, classified as intellectual, physical, emotional, or

social. Each trait is scored on a five-point scale. The authors report that ratings effectively distinguish between a population of normal school children and a population of psychological clinic referrals of the same age.

2. The Vineland Social Maturity Scale (Doll, 1935–1953), while designed largely as a measure of intelligence, is also distinct in its assessment of the child's social maturity. For use from infancy through 30 years of age, the scale consists of specific tasks listed by age levels, and classified as self-help, self-direction, locomotion, occupation, communication, and socialization. The scale is administered by interviewing a parent or someone closely acquainted with the child. A social age and social quotient (SQ) are obtained from the final score. While the scale correlates highly with measures of general intelligence, it provides specific information about the child's social maturity which can be useful in working with the child and his parents.

3. The Fels Parent Behavior Scales (1937–1949) provide an assessment of the psychological environment of the child's home. Dimensions of the parent-child relationship such as discord in the home, sociability of the family, child-centeredness of family, and rapport with the child are rated by interviewing parents or by observing their interaction with the child in the home. The scales have proven useful in giving a detailed description of the home environment in which the child is developing, and its consequent influence upon his school behavior.

4. The Rating Scale for Pupil Adjustment (Andrews, *et al*, 1950–1953) permits assessment of eleven areas of personality, including over-all emotional adjustment, social maturity, tendency toward depression, tendency toward aggressive behavior, and emotional security. Use of the scale requires considerable psychological sophistication, since rating requires both observation and interpretation of behavior. Intended to facilitate selection and referral of children for clinic treatment, this scale should be used in very close consultation with the school psychologist or school counselor.

Informal Observation of Behavior. Whereas formal observation of child behavior requires precise designation of time and setting for making observations, informal observation can occur at any time and place during the school day. In gathering data from informal observations, it is important to note the conditions under which behavioral incidents occur. It is then possible to interpret much of the variation in the child's behavior in light of the widely differing conditions under which he operates during the school day. Adams (1964, pp. 271-272) points out that there are certain school situations in which the child's behavior is particularly apt to provide evidence of his personal-social effectiveness. These situations include: (1) the informal discussion period (e.g., "Show and Tell"); (2) students' engaging in self-directed activities; (3) the discussion of a controversial issue; (4) social, informal activities away from the classroom; (5) role playing and dramatic presentations; (6) creative art activities; and (7) playground activities.

Observations in Standard Situations. It is much easier to compare one child's level of psychological effectiveness with another's when both have been observed under the same conditions. It is therefore useful to design tasks or situations in which all children participate in order to observe the different modes and levels of effectiveness within a classroom. Teachers are well aware of the widely differing emotions which children display while working on the same assignment. It is not difficult to make a rough assessment of the child's confidence in his ability to handle the task, or of his frustration tolerance when confronted with a task which he cannot successfully complete.

Leaderless group discussions have been used to study adult reactions to situations which lack definite structure and clearly defined leadership. Teachers can use this technique as a standard situation, often in conjunction with a class project, to observe children's interaction in a situation in which the only structure involves the discussion of a certain topic for a given period of time. Under such conditions, some children will emerge as self-confident leaders who effect group organization to facilitate the discussion. Others will attempt to coerce the group into accepting their views; some will withdraw or remain passively uninvolved; and still others will be visibly upset in the absence of firm external guidelines. Since the situational demands are roughly equivalent for all the children, the teacher can place some confidence in the fact that observed differences among children reflect differences in their characteristic views of themselves and others.

Common External Symptoms of Ineffectiveness. In making and recording observations of the child's behavior, it is helpful to keep in mind common behaviors which, if they persist for the child, provide evidence that the child's level of psychological and social functioning is being impaired. Kowitz and Kowitz (1959, pp. 239-255), have listed problems which often warrant special attention by the teacher, counselor, or psychologist. These common problems may each result from different causes, have vastly different personal meanings to the children who manifest them, and require different remedial approaches. Among the reliable indicators of inadequate behavior are:

1. Dishonesty—Lying, cheating, and stealing should alert the teacher that the child who frequently resorts to such devices feels that he cannot compete equally or be accepted on the same basis as other children.

2. Laziness—Laziness is the lay expression for describing the child's unwillingness to perform as he should and could. Use of the term implies that the child could be more active and effective if he were motivated. A more sophisticated view implies that the child's failure to participate represents an immediate inability to engage in the desired activity. For whatever reasons, the lazy child cannot become more involved until his view of himself and the situation is altered. The child may feel, "They will all laugh if I can't read all the words," or "No matter how much I learn, I can't seem to please mother, so I won't try." Until he sees himself and the situation differently, he will be unable to function. The child's failure to exert the effort which is reasonably expected of him should be a signal that all is not well with him.

3. Withdrawal—Chronic failure to interact with other children and the teacher indicates that the child feels unable to cope with the social demands of his life. Because the withdrawn child says little and often causes no disruption in school, it is easy for the teacher to overlook his intense feelings.

4. Fatigue—When a child lacks energy for the demands of the school day, and when no physical basis can be found for his fatigue, he may have fears or conflicts which consume a large proportion of his energy. While the amount of a child's daily activity is related to fatigue, his inability to establish a balance between activity and rest is in itself evidence that he may be functioning at a low level of human effectiveness.

5. Absenteeism—Frequent absences are a reliable sign that the child is not functioning adequately. Health problems are often a cause of absence, and it is difficult to separate emotional problems from physical illness. The child for whom school is a threatening place is prone to develop bona fide illness which allows him to stay at home. Parental attitudes toward school also play a major role in absenteeism. When parents permit the child to be absent for superficial reasons, communicating to him that school is unim-

portant or that he is unfairly treated there, the child will find it difficult to function effectively within the school context.

6. Over-identification with Adults—The only road to mature adulthood passes through childhood. There are no shortcuts. The child who seems to live entirely in an adult world, identifying with adults, preferring them to peers, and appearing to lack the immaturity of childhood, frequently lacks the experiences through which he develops a viable self-identity. The child who over-identifies with adults lacks identity apart from those whom he can emulate and please. Children need the company and love of adults to achieve maturity, but they grow only when they can relate to them as children and not as pseudo-adults.

7. Over-identification with Group—As the child moves through the elementary school years, he is increasingly dependent upon his peer group for many of his personal, social, and emotional needs. This is a developmental stage necessary to acquiring the capacity to relate to others and to function in a world of equals. However, exclusive reliance upon the peer group as a source of satisfaction and security, combined with a general indifference or hostility toward the adult world, is evidence that the child is not functioning at a desirable level of effectiveness.

8. Disrespect for Authority—Chronic defiance of rules and persons in authority suggests that the child feels that authority is unjust, that he is not understood or accepted, and that his only alternative is to protest authority. The teacher should realize that he often represents adult authority, and that the child's defiance of his authority may represent generalized attitudes toward adults which have causes outside the classroom.

9. Disrespect for Property—The defiant attitudes manifested in destruction of property are much the same as those reflected by overt defiance of rules and authority. The major difference is that the child who surreptitiously damages school property is less willing to be openly defiant and less willing to accept the consequences of his behavior. The child who exhibits such behavior is unable to express his feelings, and believes that he is inadequate to cope openly with a world he finds frustrating and unjust.

10. Cruelty—Related to both defiance of authority and destruction of property, the child's cruelty to children or animals represents a rather direct expression of feelings in situations where retalia-

tion or punishment is unlikely. The child who cannot express his feelings to his parents or teacher, or who does not feel adequate to compete with his peers, may behave aggressively with younger or smaller children. The child frequently has parent or adult models who themselves use coercive tactics in relating to others.

These external symptoms represent the coping efforts of children who view themselves as inadequate to meet the challenges and opportunities of their daily lives. A child's particular type of ineffectiveness can be a key to understanding his view of himself and his world, and to helping him function more effectively within the school context.

Evaluation of Observational Approaches

The value of data obtained through observation of the child depends upon several factors: (1) the accuracy with which observations are made and recorded; (2) the extent to which conditions under which observations occur are noted and considered in interpreting observational data; (3) the degree to which observations focus on important aspects of the child's behavior; and (4) the extent to which the child's behavior is not influenced by the observation procedures. When these conditions are met, the teacher has data which can be useful in assessing the child's general level of effectiveness.

Observational data have the advantage of focusing on the child's actions. Observers can agree when a child does not participate in discussions, or when he frequently assaults smaller children. When carefully recorded, observational data can be interpreted in several ways, depending upon the frame of reference of the person studying the child. While the data obtained through observation are helpful in showing the child's typical behavior under given circumstances, they do not indicate why the child behaves as he does. Such data may suggest the child's view of himself, but they in no way assess the world as it appears to the child. Observational data provide little information about why he behaves as he does or how he feels about his behavior. These latter assessments can be based upon the child's own efforts to express his feelings, and upon inferences derived from observational and other data.

Sociometric Techniques

Sociometric techniques are designed to assess the child's classmates' view of him. Sociometric techniques tend to yield a measure of the child's social acceptability to other children. The two most basic approaches are the sociometric test, from which a sociogram describing the social structure of a class is obtained; and the opinion test, or peer nomination technique, which provides peers' estimates of the children who most closely fit certain character or behavioral descriptions. The sociometric test is often used to obtain pupils' choices for seating, work, and play partners, in order to structure the classroom environment for more effective interaction. The opinion test or peer nomination technique can be used to determine which children the group perceives as leaders, as selfish, generous, or popular, or the children who seem to fit behavioral descriptions such as "works quietly," "bothers others," "talks a lot," "is always trying to make people laugh."

The Syracuse Scales of Social Relations (Gardner and Thompson, 1959) is one of the few standardized techniques, with forms available for grades five through twelve. It is based upon the psychological needs described by Murray and his colleagues (1938). At the elementary school level, the Scales are designed to reveal the extent to which a child feels comfortable with and accepted by the group; the extent to which his feelings toward others are consistent with their feelings toward him; and the general social relations within the class.

Evaluation of Sociometric Techniques

Sociometric techniques have been criticized because their use may foster critical attitudes among children; widen existing cleavages within the group; and make more conspicuous the isolation or rejection of individual children. Adams (1964, pp. 291-292) has noted this problem and has suggested that undesirable consequences can be minimized by choosing questions for which pupils' choices can be honored; emphasizing positive choices and behavior; maintaining a casual attitude toward testing procedures; working to minimize questions and discussion of the testing procedures; and using sociometric data when assigning pupils to classroom committees or work groups. The teacher must avoid communicating the attitude that popularity and social acceptance are the most important facets of individual worth.

The reliability and validity of sociometric techniques is high compared to other measurement approaches. Choices and nominations appear to be quite stable over several weeks, particularly when children are of upper-elementary school age and when their responses are based on about five choices for each rating or selection. In contrast to self-report techniques, sociometric techniques are considered to have considerable content validity (Freeman, 1962); that is, the child's choice or nomination is important and useful behavior in itself, since the technique is designed to sample preferences and choices.

Sociometric techniques seem to measure the "environment of opinion" (Freeman, 1962) in which each child is operating. Sociometric data yield evidence of a child's general social acceptance among his peers. Such data however, cannot account for the degree of acceptance. While a high degree of social acceptance is far from the main determinant of human effectiveness, it is clear that children who are consistently rejected, or who are social isolates, lack the capacity to interact constructively. It appears that when questions are carefully designed and administered, sociometric techniques are quite useful in assessing the child's level of social effectiveness.

Expressive Methods

Expressive methods involve opportunities in which the child responds spontaneously, without guidelines to the desired or appropriate behavior. When the child can freely choose his responses, we feel that he is expressing basic needs and feelings. In role-playing, sociodrama, finger painting, drawing, and musical and dance productions, it is assumed that the child's content or style in response indicates his needs and feelings about himself and others. Because of the high degree of inference required and the difficulty one has in making reliable observations, the expressive method is one of the most subjective and least validated approaches to obtaining data on the child's level of functioning.

Role Playing and Sociodrama. These techniques require the child to portray spontaneuosly a feeling or situation. The child assigned to a role may portray himself, or may attempt to behave as he believes someone else would act and feel under the circumstances. Role playing and sociodrama are primarily intended to develop self awareness and understanding of social relations on the part of the child, but can provide the teacher with much information about the child's way of responding and about how he views himself and others in certain situations. Shaftel and Shaftel (1967) have presented a helpful treatment of the use of role playing.

Artistic Productions. When children are given the opportunity to draw, to paint, or to mold any creation of their choice, both the content and style of their productions often reveal their characteristic levels of effectiveness. Drawings of human figures are particularly revealing of the child's concept of himself, his view of others, and his relationship to these people (Machover, 1951). Such interpretations are subjective and based on assumptions of undemonstrated validity. Finger painting, often used as a therapeutic approach, can reveal the child's use of space as well as the nature of his productions.

Evaluation of Expressive Methods

The interpretation of expressive methods is extremely subjective, relying on the teacher's sensitivity and intuition. Because of the great possibility for error in such approaches, she must be cautious in forming impressions, and careful to test impressions against other kinds of information.

CONSIDERATIONS IN INTERPRETING BEHAVIORAL DATA

Assessment of the child's level of human effectiveness must be a continuous process. Teachers do this unconsciously, noting the day-to-day, week-to-week changes in emotions and attitudes of children in their classes. The introduction of more explicit procedures does not suggest that assessment is a quick or permanent evaluation. Children undergo constant change, and new sources of information will continuously modify the teacher's view of the child.

Most of the strategies and procedures described in this chapter require sensitive understanding of children as well as sophistication in forming, from diverse data, a working picture of their modes and levels of functioning. It is in this aspect of assessment that the teacher has the greatest need for frequent consultation with other specialists in child behavior. The teacher's on-going assessment can be facilitated and validated through periodic discussions with the school psychologist, counselor, social worker or visiting teacher, attendance officer, and school nurse or physician. These specialists have access to data which the teacher lacks. Working together, they can build a picture of a child which is more comprehensive and which provides a reliable basis for remediation.

In studying any child, it is helpful for the teacher to ascertain her personal beliefs about the child's problem. She can thus avoid gathering data selectively to confirm her own unstated hypothesis. Since it is virtually impossible to maintain an open mind while interacting daily with a child, it is far better to admit what one believes about him and attempt to study his behavior in ways which minimize the influence of such biases.

Interpretations about the child should be considered in the light of the amount and kind of information gathered about him. A great deal of self-report data may give an excellent picture of the child's view of himself but will tell little about the child's general acceptability to other children. A compromise between depth and breadth of assessment is usually necessary. Certainty in any specific aspect of behavior is seldom obtained.

Levels of Interpretation

Goldman (1961, pp. 143-145) has described the different levels of interpretation and their attendant errors.

Descriptive.   Descriptive interpretations involve a minimum of inference. Descriptive questions can be answered directly from the data. "How often is the child chosen as a work partner?" "How much tolerance for frustration does he have, compared with others in the room?"

Genetic.   Genetic interpretations attempt to provide an explanation for the observed behavior. "How did Susan become so shy?" "Why has Bill suddenly become a bully with younger children?"

Predictive.   Predictive interpretations attempt to state in advance how the child will behave under specified conditions. "Will Tommy make friends at summer camp?" "Would Sara overcome some of her fear of people if she were assigned to work in a booth at the science fair?"

Evaluative.   Evaluative interpretations involve a value judgment about how the child should behave or how he should be treated. "Robert should not be allowed to miss school just because he has a slight headache." "Betty should be given more opportunity to take leadership in the class."

As one moves from descriptive to evaluative interpretations, interpretive statements are based more frequently on inferences drawn from the data (genetic and predictive), and on value judgments about what should be done (evaluative). As Goldman notes (1961, pp. 146-147), the evaluative interpretation does imply prediction. Note the implicit assumption in the statement that Betty should be given leadership opportunity. This is apparently based on the belief that leadership experience will be beneficial to her.

The dilemma arising from this interpretive classification is that the interpretations potentially most useful (genetic, predictive, and evaluative) have the highest probability of interpretive error. The teacher can be accurate in her description of a child's behavior, but description is only a first step. Explaining and predicting are requisite to remediation. Since explanation and prediction require going beyond the data, the risk of interpretative error becomes progressively greater as one tries to develop a useful diagnostic picture of the child. Because of this relationship between interpretive accuracy and diagnostic applicability, more caution and collaborating data are required when making higher-level interpretations.

PROCEDURES FOR INFORMALLY ASSESSING BEHAVIOR

Self-Report Procedures

The Interview.   Factual data about the child are better obtained from other sources; the purpose of the interview is to discover the child's view of himself and his world.

1. Preparation—The teacher should plan the areas of discussion. These areas wil naturally relate to the child's particular difficulty, but his feelings about school, other children, parents, siblings, his outside interests, and his fears or worries, are usually productive areas of exploration. Mental notes are preferable to a case folder, because the teacher is usually more flexible and spontaneous in the absence of notes, and the child is less apt to feel that he is being interviewed.

2. Setting—Interview procedures can be modified for use in any interaction with the child, but the approach is most effective when conducted privately. Other adults and children should not be able to overhear or interrupt the interview. A playroom is preferred for younger children.

3. Teacher Attitudes—It is important to communicate an honest interest in understanding the child and becoming better acquainted with him. Avoid any punitive or disciplinary overtones. It is better to speak first with the child when he is having a "good day" rather than after an upsetting incident or an instance of misbehavior. The teacher's liking for the child, when genuine, should be communicated, and the teacher should be honest with the child. Children are perceptive enough that few assessment interviews can be successfully disguised as "little chats." If the child is curious or concerned, let him know that knowing him better will help the teacher and others assist him in getting along better in school. Enlist the child as a partner in the discussion.

4. Establishing Rapport—Interview rapport refers to the smoothness of interaction and clarity of communication necessary to making the interview productive. Rapport is a product of many factors and is difficult to define precisely. It is a good idea to put the child at ease before proceeding with the discussion, particularly when the child appears reluctant and uncertain. A brief discussion of a nonthreatening topic may be helpful if done in a natural manner. It is generally better, however, to begin talking about the subjects to be discussed, avoiding an uneasy period of superficial chatting, during which the child wonders the real purpose of the discussion. This method also communicates to the child that the teacher is willing to be honest, and will help him talk about things that are hard to express.

5. Questioning—The teacher's questions usually elicit the child's viewpoint more effectively when kept to a minimum; when they are broad questions requiring the child to develop a topic; and when they call for the child's opinion or amplification. To say, "Would you tell me about your family," is more effective than asking a series of specific questions, such as, "What does your father do?", "Does your mother work?", "How many brothers and sisters do you have?", etc. The specific style of questioning yields factual answers readily available in the child's record and prevents an expression of his unique view of his family. Objective facts are important in studying the child, but the interview is not well-suited to obtaining factual data.

6. Recording the Interview—Notes taken during the interview may prove distracting and are best kept to a minimum. If notes are used, they should be made as soon as possible following the interview. In many instances one may tape record such conferences, as an aid to the teacher in developing interview skills, and in obtaining an accurate record of the interaction. Recording interviews is a delicate matter, involving issues of ethics, confidentiality, parental consent, public relations, and interprofessional roles and functions. The teacher must consult with the school administration and personnel specialists concerning the proper procedures.

7. Making the Interview Therapeutic—The diagnostic function of the interview is emphasized here, but we should also consider its therapeutic function. The child can and should grow in self-understanding as the teacher comes to understand him better. The teacher's honest efforts to capture the child's personal and unique view of the world acts as a powerful stimulus to the child in clarifying aspects of his self. To the degree that the child experiences personal acceptance and psycho-

logical security, he is more capable of talking about feelings, events, and ideas that are unpleasant to him. There are many useful sources on interviewing, particularly from the counseling and therapy viewpoint (Axline, 1947; Rogers, 1951; Ginott, 1961), but one of the most outstanding dimensions of the interview is the communication of understanding. Rarely do children and adults encounter others who are capable of accurately grasping their personal meanings. When a child senses that another really knows his world, he is encouraged to explore it further. (See the discussion of emphatic understanding in Truax and Carkhuff, 1967).

Open-Ended Questions. Open-ended questions or incomplete sentences require the child to complete a statement in any way he chooses, thereby revealing his own feelings and attitudes about the topics presented. The following examples illustrate stimuli which may be of particular value:

> What I like most is . . .
> When I get mad . . .
> My mother . . .
> My father . . .
> What I want most is . . .
> I am afraid . . .
> I am happiest when . . .
> My teacher . . .
> Other boys (girls) . . .
> I would like to improve my . . .

Children should be assured that their responses will be treated confidentially. Knowing that their parents or classmates will not see their responses enables children to express themselves honestly.

Questionnaires. Questionnaires can be designed to obtain a wide variety of responses from children regarding their problems, attitudes, and fears. One questionnaire which is easy to administer is the yes–no or true–false variety. Examples of such items would be:

> Do you feel bad when someone criticizes your work?   YES   NO
> I feel bad when someone criticizes my work.   TRUE   FALSE

Other items can be developed to cover areas of common childhood fears; shyness; aggressive feelings; and relations with other children. It is well to include a large number of items which are worded positively, such as "I like school."

Check Lists. This technique is one of the simplest to design and administer to a class. It usually consists of adjectives or descriptive phrases to be checked, underlined, or circled as the child feels they apply to him; for example:

ADJECTIVE CHECK LIST

Directions: Put an X by each word that describes you.

_____ 1. smart	_____ 7. quarrelsome	_____13. bothersome
_____ 2. funny	_____ 8. fidgety	_____14. cranky
_____ 3. tired	_____ 9. energetic	_____15. eager
_____ 4. happy	_____10. friendly	_____16. honest
_____ 5. blue	_____11. shy	_____17. lazy
_____ 6. busy	_____12. sad	_____18. selfish

BEHAVIORAL CHECK LIST

Directions: Put an X by each description that fits you.

_____ 1. makes friends easily	_____ 6. seems to lack confidence
_____ 2. not as smart as most kids	_____ 7. is a good leader
_____ 3. likes to be alone	_____ 8. enjoys school
_____ 4. is fun to be with	_____ 9. feelings are easily hurt
_____ 5. laughs a lot	_____10. daydreams a lot

Such lists can be easily extended. It is critical that the vocabulary level of the adjectives and descriptive phrases be appropriate to the level at which the check lists are used. The technique is perhaps of greatest value for children in the intermediate and upper elementary grades.

Autobiographical Approaches

The Autobiography. The autobiography is simple to administer, and can be logically included within English or social studies assignments. Autobiographies can vary in structure according to the pupils' maturity and the particular emphasis of the assignment. Barr (1958) recommends autobiographies for use above grades three or four. Use in lower grades requires a more highly structured approach, with children asked to respond to specific questions.

Autobiographies are most useful when they are introduced as an exercise in creative self-expression; introduced with a clear statement of who will read them; when clear guidelines are given for writing the autobiography; and when the teacher administering the autobiography has established a high level of rapport with the class. Instructions for an unstructured autobiography assignment might read as follows:

> We have read what some people have written about their lives. It
> might be interesting for you to try to do the same thing. What are
> some of the things you would want to include to let another person
> really know who you are? Include as much or as little as you wish in
> order to describe yourself and how you came to be the way you are.

The following example suggests a more highly structured approach
which the teacher might present after a discussion of the purposes of
autobiography:

> In preparing your autobiography, be sure to include answers to the
> following questions: (a) What are the most important things that hap-
> pened to you when you were very young? (b) Who are the people
> who have made the greatest difference in your life? (c) Since coming
> to school, what are the most important things that have happened to
> you? (d) What things about yourself do you like best; like least;
> or would like to change? (e) Describe yourself as you hope to be at
> some time in the future.

Barr (1958) also describes the family autobiography, a variation on
the autobiography prepared by the student himself. The teacher can
design a set of instructions and questions about family interests, occupa-
tions, travel, and relationships, which will provide a picture of the child's
family, and improve the basis for teacher–parent communication. Barr
recommends that questions emphasize positive aspects of family life, and
that parents omit any questions they do not care to answer. Family autobiographies are of greater value when children participate in developing the questions, and when parents are aware of the purposes of the
information; i.e., better understanding of the child and improved communication with his parents.

Observations of Behavior

Time Sampling.   It is difficult to be systematic or objective about a
child's behavior when observations are made at random or when they are
made only during a period of crisis. The time sampling procedure permits the teacher to observe behavior during certain periods for specified
lengths of time. Everything the child does during this period is noted
and recorded objectively. A comprehensive picture of the child's behavior at one time and place can thus be assembled over a comparatively
short time. A teacher might decide to spend five or ten minutes each
morning observing one child or one small group of children. The record
for one child might look like this:

Pupil: Charles Whitemore   Date: November 10
Teacher: Mrs. Higgins   Time: 9:00-9:05 a.m.
Setting: The classroom during a free study period.

Time Interval	Observation
9:00–9:01	Looked out the window; shuffled feet; opened a reference book, leafed through it, closed it, opened it again and flipped the pages.
9:01–9:02	Opened notebook and started to write; tore out one sheet, crumpled it and stuffed it into desk; started to write again; hesitated, chewed pencil eraser.
9:02–9:03	Looked out window, looked around room, caught Bob Greenwood's attention; made a face at Bob and then pointed out window.
9:03–9:04	Got out of chair and moved to science corner; picked up dry-cell batteries and wires; made an electromagnet and picked up chain of paper clips.
9:04–9:05	Continued to work with electromagnet; was slow to leave science corner when the bell rang.

Situational Tests.   Situational tests can be contrived to yield observations of the behavior of individual children, as well as of the group as a whole. Contrived situations provide standardization for within group comparisons.

Garry (1963) describes a test to determine the degree to which cheating is a problem for individual children and for the class as a whole. A teacher checked her class on the honesty with which they corrected their papers in spelling, arithmetic, and social studies. The teacher had corrected the papers in advance but had marked no errors. Students were given correct answers and instructed to score their own papers. The number of errors overlooked, and original answers changed, provided an overall index of the pressure the class felt to make high grades. In addition, it indicated which children had very great or very little need to falsify their scores. Any generalizations from such tests should be made with caution. Hartshorne and May (1928) administered similar tests of honesty and found that the performance varies greatly from one situational test to another, suggesting little evidence for a general trait of honesty.

Leaderless Groups.   A common situational test is the leaderless discussion group. It has been used in many settings to assess characteristics of cooperation, leadership, and teamwork. Anastasi (1961) reports that factor analytic studies designed to reveal the primary dimensions which persons manifest during leaderless groups, have suggested that three major factors predominate: (1) individual prominence, or efforts to achieve independently personal goals separate from group objectives; (2) group goal facilitation, or efforts to aid the group toward the attainment of its objectives; and (3) group sociability, or efforts toward satisfying and cordial social relationships within the group. The leaderless group can be established for a variety of purposes, the most common of which are: discussion of a topic and reporting on the group concensus; and working toward the solution of an assigned problem.

Observations are most useful when group size is kept between five and eight children each, permitting greater accuracy in recording the activity of each child, and giving each child ample opportunity to participate. The teacher should be able to observe all participants without influencing the group process in any way. One-way observation rooms are preferable because they give privacy to the group and better opportunity for observation. A convenient way to record the interaction is necessary for keeping a record of the child's activity during the group. The record form in Table 14 illustrates a simple tally sheet for use by the observer. Using such forms, the teacher can obtain a frequency count, attempting to classify each child's participation in one of the available categories.

Diaries. Diaries, or logs of daily activities, help provide a picture of the way the child spends his out-of-school time, as well as his feelings

Table 14

Leaderless Group Observation Form

Group Members	Interrupts	Criticizes	Changes subject	Makes suggestions	Helps others express their ideas	Listens attentively	Withdraws	Helps group keep on topic	Helps group make decision to take action	Monopolizes speaking time	Does not listen to others

about such activities. Two important considerations should be noted in using the diary technique: (1) it should be discussed and introduced in such a manner that the child does not consider it just another assignment; and (2) respect for privacy must be shown. Sufficient interest and trust will prompt pupils to discuss their diary entries, but no child should be forced to do so. Make it clear that only the teacher will read the reports, and that the child may or may not discuss the contents of his diary as he wishes.

The teacher may provide the children with forms for recording their activities. The following example represents a highly-structured approach, designed to encourage students to record both factual and subjective data:

Things I Do Out of School

Date and Time	What I did, with whom	How I feel about it: Was it fun? Would I like something else better? Would it be more fun alone or with someone else?

The second example illustrates a more open-ended approach, which gives the child more opportunity to select out-of-school events which have particular significance for him.

Directions: Each day, pick one or two things you do outside of school that are very important to you. Write about it in the spaces below.

Date, Time, Place	What I did and why it seemed important to me.

Wishes. The "Three Wishes" is a clinical technique of long standing among psychologists who work with children. Children find the task interesting, and most have no difficulty in giving three separate wishes. The approach can be used in oral or written form. The oral approach is best-suited to work with an individual child, since children often imitate or are influenced by the wishes of others in a group situation. The following instructions can be used with minor variations:

> Let's play a game. Suppose a Good Fairy gave you three wishes. What would those wishes be? (Note: Some children may wish for an unlimited number of wishes. When this occurs, make note of it, but ask the child to make three separate wishes. It is also important to emphasize three *wishes*. Avoid saying, "What three *things* would you wish for?" Some children, particularly young ones, will ask for things, but others will ask for happiness, friends, to move to another city, to be better in arithmetic, to not have to go to school, etc.)

Fears.   This approach is similar to the wish technique. It can be used in either oral or written form. The following instructions can be given:

> Everyone has a certain number of fears, things that frighten them or that they worry about. What are three of your biggest fears? (Note: Like the wish technique, it is important to emphasize the child's statement of *fears* rather than *things* which frighten him.)

The two approaches can be combined and obtained from a group at the same time.

Teacher Rating Scales.   The standardized instruments described on pp. 176-177 provide good examples of the types of rating approaches which have proven useful in the systematic observation of pupil behavior.

Adams (1964) recommends that the traits selected for rating be (1) independent; (2) definable in terms of observable pupil behavior; (3) related to major goals of the school program; and (4) reasonably unitary in composition. For example, leadership and social acceptance should not be included as separate traits on the same rating schedule because they are so closely related that some of the same behavioral observations could serve as bases for ratings on both traits. If a trait cannot be defined in terms of observable pupil behavior, it should be more precisely defined or replaced by a trait for which behavioral observations can be made. The relationship of traits to school objectives is perhaps more important for ratings of academic performance; however, the social and emotional aspects of pupil behavior cannot be considered in isolation from the broad purposes of the school. A trait of unitary composition is based on a single class of behavioral observations. Honesty, as noted earlier, is apparently a very complex trait and should be rated separately for each of its components, such as cheating, stealing, lying, etc. Even these traits may themselves be quite complex. Children may, for example, be very truthful about all matters except those concerning their home life.

In using teacher rating scales, every pupil should be rated on a given trait before moving to other traits. In this manner, the effect of the rater's overall positive or negative impression of a child will be minimized. Ratings are sometimes used for understanding a child better, but the ratings will usually have greater validity for individuals when they have been made for a large group of children rather than for a single child.

The following examples of rating scales suggest approaches which teachers can use in their own classrooms:

HOW WELL DOES THIS CHILD COOPERATE WITH OTHER CHILDREN?

Very Poorly: Considerably less well than most children his age
Average: About as well as most children his age
Very Well: Considerably better than most children his age

When using a rating scale with three intervals, at least half of the ratings should fall in the middle interval with from 20 to 25 per cent in each of the other intervals.

The effectiveness of scales which use normative terms such as "high," "low," and "average," depends upon the rater's concept of the terms. When two raters use such scales in rating behavior, it is essential that "about as well as most his age" have a common meaning for the type of cooperative behavior as well as for the frequency with which it occurs. The following example has the advantage of specifying (1) the *behavior* considered under cooperation, and (2) the approximate *frequency* of the behavior, providing more useful data for possible remediation:

HOW WELL DOES THIS CHILD COOPERATE WITH OTHER CHILDREN?

Very Poorly	*Average*	*Very Well*
Seldom or never (25% or fewer occasions) suggests ways of cooperating	Occasionally (25% to 75% occasions) suggests way of cooperating	Frequently (75% or more occasions) suggests ways of cooperating
Holds out for his way	Compromises	Compromises
Asks to work alone	Asks to share work	Asks to work with others
Brags about individual accomplishments	Reinforces group efforts	Minimizes own efforts
Plays down group accomplishments		Highlights group accomplishments

Sociometric Techniques

The results of a sociometric test are more valid when they are obtained from a situation in which children are either involved or interested. One advantage of the approach is the development of classroom seating arrangements. Directions such as the following might be given:

> Now that you've had a chance to become acquainted with most of the people in the room, you might want to change your seats, since we often work better and have more fun when we're near the people we like. Put your name on the top of a slip of paper. Then list the names of those people you'd like to be seated near. List your first choice, second choice, third choice, and so on. Make sure you don't overlook a friend who is absent today. No one else will see the names you list. I'll make sure you are seated by at least one of the people you include on your list.

Special care should be taken to be sure that pupils know and can write the names of all class members. All names should be listed on a chalkboard or on a printed list. Children are occasionally asked to indicate others they do not wish to be seated by, thus permitting a measure of rejection to be obtained for some children. However, Adams (1964) notes that teachers are frequently aware of students who are rejected by others, and allowing children to include their negative choices may lead them to believe that the teacher accepts and supports their rejection of some classmates.

After the children indicate their choices, the paper slips can be arranged alphabetically and a tally sheet constructed.

The information needed for the seating arrangement can be obtained from the completed tally sheet. The construction of a sociogram, however, provides a graphic picture of the social structure of the group in a way that is difficult to obtain from the tally sheet alone. The sociogram on p. 201 shows only first and second choices. The inclusion of additional choices usually makes the sociogram highly complex without making it significantly more informative. It is easier to refer to a tally sheet for information on third and fourth choices.

Although this example of a sociogram is based on only eight children, a meaningful pattern does emerge. The expected sex difference characteristic of the intermediate grades, is clearly shown, with mutual selections occurring as intrasex choices, and only two intersex choices appearing.

Dorothy is the least frequently chosen; her only selection was by Barbara. It would be important for the teacher to capitalize on this association. Charles and Edward M. were not chosen on a first- or second-

Table 15

Tally Sheet for Sociometric Analysis

Chooser   Chosen

		Alan	Barbara	Betty	Bob	Charles	Dorothy	Edward M.	Edward S.
Alan	(B)		4		1			3	2
Barbara	(G)	3		2			1		4
Betty	(G)	4	1		2	3			
Bob	(B)	1	4			3			2
Charles	(B)	3			2			4	1
Dorothy	(G)	3	2	1					4
Edward M.	(B)	1			2	3			4
Edward S.	(B)	1	2			4		3	
Choices rec'd First		3	1	1	1	0	1	0	1
Second		0	2	1	3	0	0	0	2
Third		3	0	0	0	3	0	2	0
Fourth		1	2	0	0	1	0	1	3
Total choices rec'd.		7	5	2	4	4	1	3	6

choice basis. Examination of the tally sheet, however, reveals that Charles was the third choice of Betty, Bob, Edward M., and the fourth choice of Edward S. Edward M., on the other hand, received only two third-choice selections and a single fourth choice. It would be important to cultivate these potential relationships, and make it possible for Charles and Edward M. to have some association with the children they chose first and second. Allen, Bob, and Edward S. are frequently chosen and enjoy at least one mutual choice. Since they are apparently valued as associates,

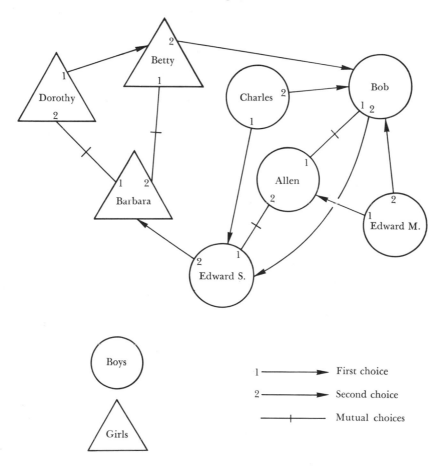

Figure 6

Sociogram

it would be important for Charles and Edward M. to be seated near them.

It should be noted that there is seldom a single seating arrangement in the modern elementary school. Children may have as many as three or four separate seating patterns daily, depending upon the activity in which they are engaged. Using sociometric data, the teacher can maximize the children's chosen associations by seeing to it that every child is seated near a first-choice associate at some time during the school day. The data can also be used to assign work partners and study groupings.

Children in the intermediate and upper elementary grades are capable of choosing associates on bases other than general friendship. Older children are able to choose others as work partners, athletic teammates, and associates for parties, picnics, and other social events. Observing these choices permits the teacher to gather more useful sociometric data. Some children will of course be chosen frequently for every kind of activity, and others will be selectively chosen. The bright but shy child may receive no choices for seating on social activities, but may be selected by several children as a study partner. Capitalizing on recognized acceptance or leadership in one area helps a child to gain confidence and acceptance in other activities.

Peer Nominations

Peer nomination techniques or "guess who" approaches provide an assessment of the social reputation which children hold among their classmates. Children are presented with behavioral descriptions, and asked to name classmates who are best described by the statements. Some approaches include statements describing pupil attitudes: "Someone who feels others don't like him." Such statements require considerably more interpretation than do the behavioral descriptions, and are consequently more appropriate for older children. Directions given in administering peer nomination techniques might be as follows:

> These descriptions may fit some of the children in this class. Some of them may fit you. Read each statement carefully and try to decide who it fits. Sometimes a statement will describe more than one person. Don't forget to include yourself whenever you think a statement fits you. If a statement doesn't fit anyone in our class, leave it blank and go on to the next one.

Sample items for this technique are:

> Here is someone who plays very rough games.
> Here is someone who can get games started.
> Someone who has lots of friends.
> Someone who can sit very quietly in class.

Care should be taken to avoid wording the statements negatively. Enough items should be included to provide a wide range of behavioral descriptions.

When pupils have completed nominations, tally sheets can be constructed to show which persons were selected to fit the various descriptions. Garry (1963) describes two types of tally sheets that might be used in peer nominations. The first style includes pupils' names on the vertical axis and statement numbers on the horizontal axis. Check marks indicate when pupils are selected to fit descriptions; circles indicate self-nominations. The second form includes pupil names on both axes, with statement numbers entered to show how a pupil is seen by others, as well as the ratings given by each pupil. This second form is more complex and permits the teacher to form a number of impressions about the social reputations of children in the class.

Expressive Methods

Role Playing. This approach is valuable in assessing children's problems and feelings, and in helping them achieve more constructive problem solving techniques and interpersonal relationships. The technique is effective with children, who frequently lack the language required to explain their feelings. The child's view of himself and his world often becomes clearer to him and to his teacher through a spontaneous enactment of interpersonal situations.

To be most effective, role playing should be introduced when a child or group of children is unable to solve a particular problem; when conflict exists within a group; when children are trying to explain what happened in some interpersonal experience; or when children are trying to anticipate how new behavior will work in situations which have been causing difficulty. Certain cautions must be observed in utilizing role playing. It is a powerful technique which when misused can upset children by revealing too quickly emotions they may be unable to accept.

Children should not be forced to play a role. Many situations are too threatening for some children to handle even in role playing. When a child seems to fear a situation, he may be able to play a subordinate role in the enactment. If he is still uncomfortable in a subordinate role, he can often gain understanding of his problems by watching others play all of the required roles. He might serve as director of the enactment, choosing characters for the roles and explaining how the characters usually behave.

Role enactments should be brief. Greater success is obtained by repeating several enactments of the same situation and alternating players rather than extending a single enactment for too long a period. This approach allows children to see several solutions to a single problem, and prevents children from becoming so emotionally involved in their roles that they unintentionally reveal more feeling than they are comfortable doing.

Role playing behavior should not be evaluated by the teacher. Evaluation will inhibit spontaneity, and encourage children to try to determine "how it should turn out" instead of working toward a clearer understanding of themselves and the acquisition of new behavior. Discussion should focus on the role, never on the player. Children will portray a role naturally, according to how they feel about themselves and toward the role they are presenting. Three children will usually present three different portrayals of the same role assignment. The teacher must resist the temptation to unmask the player and interpret the role behavior as his own, because children must feel free to be themselves in the roles they portray. The behavior a child exhibits in portraying a given role will be significant to the teacher even though it is discussed with the child as a role portrayal. The following situations lend themselves to the use of role playing in the classroom:

1. *Development of open conflict between children.* Frank and Steve were working together on a project for the science fair when an argument erupted over which one of them would get to install the electric motor in the model. Steve felt that he should do it because he had brought the motor from his father's electrical shop. Frank maintained that the task was his because he had supplied the tools, and because he had done most of the work on the plans for the electrical system.

The teacher could begin by asking for two other boys who had observed the incident to volunteer to re-enact the situation as they perceive it. Next, Frank and Steve could each play his own part with one of the actors after he had observed the way the incident appeared to the other boys. Finally, Frank and Steve could reverse roles, each presenting the viewpoint of the other as he perceives it. Following each enactment, the teacher could lead a discussion about how the participants and observers see the problem. The solution of the problem should remain between Frank and Steve, but by this time they should have gained sufficient understanding of each other's viewpoint that some acceptable solution can be reached.

2. *Child's wish to learn new ways of handling a problem situation.* Barbara reported to her teacher that she wanted very much to make friends with the new girl her age who had moved in across the street, but the girl hadn't asked her over to play. Barbara's teacher knew how timid Barbara was, and how difficult it was for her to initiate friendships.

Under these circumstances, the teacher could suggest a role playing enactment in which two other girls first act out inviting the new girl over to Barbara's house. Next, Barbara could take the part of the new girl. Barbara could finally role play meeting the girl and getting acquainted with her. This enactment could be repeated with different girls playing the new girl, to give Barbara practice in initiating social relationships. Through these enactments Barbara could learn that others, like herself, usually respond to friendly advances; that there are many ways of beginning friendships; and that she can begin to feel comfortable in taking the first step.

3. Teacher's wish to involve children in discussion of common developmental problems.   Miss Randall read to her fourth-grade class the story of Mike, a nine-year-old boy who was having trouble in math. His father warned him that he could not participate in Little League the following summer unless his math improved. Mike's thirteen-year-old brother agreed to help Mike with his math homework. At first he tried to help Mike understand the problems, but when this bogged down, he simply supplied the answers, and Mike wrote them in. Near the end of the term Mike's parents were called by the teacher. She reported that Mike's homework had been excellent, but he had been unable to pass the tests administered at the end of each unit. Mike's parents asked him for an explanation.

At this point, the members of the class are asked how they think Mike will handle his problem.

The teacher could ask that students volunteer to portray Mike and his parents. After discussion, the enactment could be repeated with new role players or with the original players exchanging roles.

There are many possible variations on these examples. Shaftel and Shaftel (1967) have presented an excellent series of stories to serve as stimuli for role playing. Their materials are designed to give children opportunities to learn how to handle a great many problems and conflicts which most children encounter in the normal course of their development. In some instances, the teacher might role play with a single child around a situation which is causing the child difficulty. In leading discussions during role playing, the teacher should be sensitive to the feelings of the participants, to the way observers view problems, and to the feelings which the primary participants experience during the enactments.

Artistic Productions.   As indicated earlier in this chapter, interpretations based on expressive methods of assessment are necessarily subjective, and should be made cautiously, corroborated by other observations. The general rule for using artistic productions as a means of studying the child's view of himself and his world is to grant the child maximum freedom in choosing and executing his creative work. When children understand that their artistic productions will not be evaluated or criticized, their work is likely to reflect their characteristic perceptions.

The following behavior in artistic work can be accepted as tentative evidence that the child does not function at an adequate level of psychological effectiveness:

(1) *Stereotyping*—The child may draw boats for several months, with each successive boat virtually identical to the last one, indicating a need to cling to the familiar.

(2) *Dependency*—When given a free period for drawing, painting, or modeling, some children seem unable to proceed independently, relying upon the teacher or other children to guide them in what they can or should make.

(3) *Over- or under-use of space and material*—Some children seem incapable of filling a sheet of paper with a drawing, or of using more than a small portion of the material allotted to them. Others seem unable to contain their productions within available space, and frequently begin work on such a large scale that they quickly exhaust their materials.

(4) *Deviation from developmental norms*—Lowenfeld (Lowenfeld & Brittain, 1964) has developed a scheme of the natural development of creative expression. Significant discrepancies from the developmental norms should be a basis for studying the child more closely. Lowenfeld's book should be read by every teacher who attempts to better understand children through their artistic productions.

These ideas can be used as general guides in studying all artistic productions. The teacher may also design specific art experiences in order to study children more systematically. The spontaneous drawing of the human figure is believed to provide much evidence of a child's feeling about himself (Machover, 1951). The technique is simple to administer. Children are given a blank sheet of paper and asked to draw a person. When the figure has been completed, the child is asked to draw a second figure of the opposite sex.

Interpretations of human figure drawings can be made from several vantage points. It is generally accepted that the child expresses to some extent his view of himself when drawing a person. Most children draw first a figure of their own sex. When the opposite sex is drawn first, the child often lacks a clear sex identity. The size of the child's drawing can be taken as a rough estimate of his feelings of self-worth, unless the size is grossly exaggerated. Particular omissions or elaborations in the drawing are usually significant. Children with cleft lips and speech problems might forget to draw the mouth more often than normal children. Figures which reflect great attention to facial features or muscular development suggest preoccupation with appearance and physical prowess. These interpretations are guidelines for studying drawings; other evaluative criteria can be developed as corollaries to the basic hypothesis that the human figure is largely the individual's projection of his own wishes, needs, and self-concept.

SUMMARY

From our discussion of personal, social, and emotional development, we can see that assessment of the individual child's level of functioning must be made within the framework of his view of himself and his world. To assess that level of functioning, the teacher has available to her the self-report, observational, sociometric, and expressive techniques, and the additional aid of formal, standardized procedures.

In this area of development, as in the others discussed in this book, we have seen that the interpretation of assessment data is a continuous process in which the teacher must consult with other professionals to assist her and to administer materials for which she is neither qualified nor equipped to handle. She must be aware of the conclusions that have already been formed about the child and realize that the nature of the conclusions depends at all times on the amount and kind of data available for interpretation.

The teacher is always free to elaborate on suggested informal assessment techniques, and to develop techniques which suit the specific needs of her students. As we have stressed throughout this book, the teacher is in an ideal position to assess and make plans to remediate a child's educational problems. Her conscientiousness and interest in her students can help them to live richer lives.

REFERENCES

Adams, G. S., *Measurement in Education, Psychology, and Guidance.* New York: Holt, Rinehart & Winston, Inc., 1964.

American Psychological Association, *Technical Recommendations for Psychological Tests and Diagnostic Techniques.* Washington, D. C.: the Association, 1954.

Anastasi, A., *Psychological Testing.* New York: The Macmillan Co. 1961.

Andrews, G., et al., *Rating Scale for Pupil Adjustment*. Chicago: Science Research Associates, 1950–1953.

Axline, V. M., *Play Therapy*. Boston: Houghton Mifflin Co., 1947.

Barr, J. A., *The Elementary Teacher and Guidance*. New York: Holt, Rinehart & Winston, Inc., 1958.

Benton, J. A., Jr., *Perceptual Characteristics of Episcopal Pastors*. Unpublished doctoral dissertation, University of Florida, 1964.

Blocher, D. H., *Developmental Counseling*. New York: The Roland Press Co., 1966.

Combs, A. W., (ed.), *Perceiving, Behaving, Becoming: A New Focus for Education*. Washington, D. C.: Association for Supervision and Curriculum Development, 1962.

Combs, A. W., and D. W. Soper, "The Perceptual Organization of Effective Counselors," *Journal of Counseling Psychology*, 10 (1963a), 222-226.

Combs, A. W., and D. W. Soper, *The Relationship of Child Perceptions to Achievement and Behavior in the Early School Years*. Cooperative Research Project No. 814, College of Education, University of Florida, (1963b).

Courson, C. C., *The Relationship of Certain Perceptual Factors to Adequacy*. Unpublished doctoral dissertation, University of Florida, 1963.

Doll, E. A., *The Vineland Social Maturity Scale*. Vineland, N. J.: The Training School, 1935-1953.

Fels Institute, *Fels Parent Behavior Scales*. Yellow Springs, Ohio: the Institute, 1937–1949.

Freeman, F. S., *Theory and Practice of Psychological Testing*. New York: Holt, Rinehart & Winston, Inc., 1962.

Gardner, E. F., and G. G. Thompson, *Syracuse Scales of Social Relations*. New York: Harcourt, Brace & World, Inc., 1959.

Garry, R., *Guidance Techniques for Elementary Teachers*. Columbus, Ohio: Charles E. Merrill Publishing Co., 1963.

Ginott, H. G., *Group Psychotherapy with Children: The Theory and Practice of Play Therapy*. New York: McGraw-Hill Book Co., 1961.

Goldman, L., *Using Test in Counseling*. New York: Appleton-Century-Crofts, 1961.

Haggerty-Olson-Wickman Rating Schedules. New York: Harcourt, Brace & World, Inc., 1930.

Hartshorne, H., and M. A. May, *Studies in Deceit*. New York: The Macmillan Co., 1928.

Johoda, Marie, *Current Concepts of Positive Mental Health*. New York: Basic Books, Inc., Publishers, 1958.

Kowitz, G. T., and Norma G. Kowitz, *Guidance in the Elementary Classroom*. New York: McGraw-Hill Book Co., 1959.

Lowenfeld, V., and W. L. Brittain, *Creative and Mental Growth*. New York: The Macmillan Co., 1964.

Machover, Karen, "Drawing of the Human Figure: A Method of Personality Investigation," in *An Introduction to Projective Techniques*, H. H. Anderson and Glayds L. Anderson (eds.), Englewood Cliffs, N. J.: Prentice-Hall, Inc., 1951.

Mooney, R. L. and L. V. Gordon, *Mooney Problem Check List: 1950 Revision*. New York: Psychological Corporation, 1950.

Murray, H. A., *et al.*, *Exploration in Personality*. New York: Oxford University Press, 1938.

Remmers, H. H., and B. Shimberg, *SRA Junior Inventory, Form S*. Chicago: Science Research Associates, 1957.

Rogers, C. R., *Client-centered Therapy*. Boston: Houghton Mifflin Co., 1951.

Shaftel, F. R., and G. Shaftel, *Role Playing for Social Values: Decision Making in the Social Studies*. Englewood Cliffs, N. J.: Prentice- Hall, Inc., 1967.

Thorpe, L. P., W. W. Clark, and E. W. Tiegs, *California Test of Personality, 1953 Revision*. Monterey, Calif.: California Test Bureau, 1953.

Truax, C. B., and R. R. Carkhuff, *Toward Effective Counseling and Psychotherapy*. Chicago: Aldine Publishing Co., 1967.

Chapter 9

RECAPITULATION

Robert M. Smith

There is a decisive need for teachers to deal straight-forwardly with the inevitable nonuniformity that exists in every classroom, regardless of the way youngsters are grouped for administrative purposes. Effective classroom management, and thus, effective teaching and learning will occur only after youngsters' encounters have been governed in an intelligent and informed manner. All components of the instructional program, including methods, curriculum, and materials, must be selected to conform with significant developmental variables. Simple awareness of these factors is not enough. Teachers must become accomplished in developing procedures for judging each child's performance on the multitude of variables that influence achievement. Only when these data are available is it possible to construct an efficient and effective instructional program for each student.

The preceding chapters in this volume have identified samples of evaluative techniques that teachers might use to assess patterns of strengths and weaknesses among students in a variety of important developmental areas. In this chapter, we shall review the common threads that have appeared throughout the book.

INSTRUCTIONAL ADVANTAGES OF INFORMAL DIAGNOSIS

Both experienced and naive teachers who have been placed in an unfamiliar or new instructional setting with students about whom they know little, will recall the periods of frustration and the trial-and-error behavior that often characterize these encounters. In such circumstances questions arise over:

1. What to teach;
2. At what level instruction should be initiated;
3. When instruction should start;
4. The extent to which readiness skills have been accomplished;
5. Under what circumstances instruction should occur;
6. What methods are most appropriate for the students;
7. Which instructional media are preferred (slides, filmstrips, books, programmed instruction, seatwork, etc.) ;
8. The criteria on which to establish instructional groups; and,
9. When to proceed to the next level of instruction.

These and other questions must be answered if the proper instructional program for each child is to be supplied. The answers to these questions will supply vital information about specific weaknesses for which students may need immediate professional attention exceeding the ability of the teacher and other educators.

In instructional situations which are unfamiliar or new to the teacher, the literature suggests that valuable classroom time is often wasted on organizational matters at the beginning of the school year. A certain amount of this inefficiency is the result of teachers' trying and discarding one instructional strategy after another, until one technique "catches on" with a group of students. There is often no firm basis for making decisions concerning instruction in these situations; the fact that a certain program succeeds is often not the result of a systematic study of student behavior. Among the superficial means that teachers use to deal with regular class children who exhibit learning difficulties are: (1) becoming satisfied with minimal expectations of performance and developing an acquiescence to maximum realistic goals; (2) learning to tolerate students; (3) giving youngsters repetitive, busy work; (4) identifying a satisfactory instructional method by chance; (5) retention; (6) transfering a child to another teacher who "understands his problem better;" and (7) socially promoting a youngster.

In fairness to teachers, we must understand that many teacher-training programs in colleges and universities do not include formal instructional experiences designed to help teachers develop skills for systematically studying student behavior. Without the benefits of this important instructional orientation, the random and initially inefficient performance in unfamiliar or dissonant teaching situations is understandable.

In order to respond quickly and effectively on the many occasions when a decision must be made about the educational management of students, the teacher must have specific information about the youngsters. This knowledge provides documentation which allows the teacher to accept or reject various instructional approaches. The teacher faces two important issues in securing this documentation. First, she must know what to look for on which dimensions. Second, the teacher must collect the data systematically by objective and carefully executed observations of characteristic student behavior. Consequently, each teacher must develop a repertoire of informal evaluative techniques in a number of relevant areas. By developing skill in the informal assessment of student behavior the teacher will be able to:

1. Ascertain areas of strength and weakness in pupils and, in many instances, identify the basis for educational difficulties;
2. Gain an understanding of the most efficacious techniques for presenting subject matter to youngsters who exhibit various learning disabilities;
3. Construct curricula in a logical sequence; and
4. Appreciate the degree to which materials should be presented, using one or a combination of pertinent instructional media.

The employment of appropriate diagnostic data allows the teacher to make informed decisions concerning the most suitable educational practices for each youngster. Without these data, valuable time will be lost and instructional efficiency will suffer.

COLLECTING BEHAVIORAL DATA

A number of approaches have been suggested for collecting relevant educational information on students. Data can be gathered from formal standardized instruments, cumulative folders, check sheets, rating scales, case reports, achievement tests, workbook productions, classroom assignments, personal interviews, sociometric devices, and other items. It has been emphasized throughout the book that the teacher should not select evaluative instruments for which special training in administration and interpretation is needed. Certain clinical instruments require a special knowledge that exceeds the knowledge, skill, or experience of even the most well-trained teacher. If the administration of such devices seems warranted, the teacher should refer the youngster to an appropriate specialist to enhance the validity of the data gathered through many individual tests. Teachers should not administer individual intelligence tests, formal speech and language scales, projective tests, certain personality instruments, and social scales, unless properly trained to do so. Erroneous administration and false interpretation are potentially too catastrophic to warrant leniency on this issue. On the other hand, this admonishment should not deter the teacher from generating hypotheses about a child's behavior and checking their validity informally.

Reliability and Validity of Observations

It is important to remember that the value of the information collected depends on how reliably and validly it characterizes the typical, usual behavior of the youngsters under observation. It is the normal behavior that must be of concern to the teacher—the grossly atypical is not an accurate reflection of performance requiring strategies for modification. Constant attention to increasing the reliability and validity of observations will bring necessary changes in youngster's instructional program into clearer focus. If behavioral observations are confounded with erroneous or irrelevant information, the chances for erroneous interpretation is increased and the ability to make specific educational recommendations is seriously hampered.

Reliability of observation can be increased by using more than one method for collecting data; by observing the behavior of students in various settings; and by reassessing behavior at subsequent time periods. The teacher should be cognizant of the various components in each child's dynamic environment which may influence behavior. These variables, which a child may encounter under normal circumstances, must be identified in order to understand better the reasons that a child exhibits certain behavioral weaknesses. Since no one's environment is static, the teacher's job is to identify the relevant variables that influence a child's performance and separate these from irrelevant factors. The continual collection of behavioral data is vital for increasing observational reliability and for gaining a clearer picture of the remedial needs of each child.

Validity can be enhanced by the teacher's careful identification of the specific variables for which observation is desired, and her selection or construction of activities for assessing the child's performance in the areas under consideration. The procedure of offering youngsters a number of evaluative items and attempting to discern the specific areas in which weakness is manifested on an inductive basis should be avoided. The proper procedure is to establish the objective first, develop the evaluative strategies to test the areas included under the objective, and design appropriate remedial strategies on the basis of the child's performance on the test items. This technique is more direct and offers specific documentation for designing appropriate remedial strategies.

Focus on Achievement through Product and Process Analysis

Every evaluation of performance must lead to precise information that is easily translated into instructional strategies. Achievement encompasses many areas; for example, there is often a great contrast between a youngster's verbal production and his non-verbal achievement. The teacher must be sure to pinpoint for evaluation definite factors of performance, instead of attempting diagnostic efforts by way of a broad evaluative approach. Specificity will help to control against generalizing from a child's performance to areas which have not been directly assessed.

The discussion to this point has considered various practices a teacher might use to assess the products of a child's performance. What youngsters are able to produce is indeed important and will help to document areas of special weakness. The astute diagnostician, however, will not be satisfied with the products alone, but will attempt to determine the means by which the child decided, erroneously or properly, to respond to a problem. It is important for the educational diagnostician to observe and evaluate the tactics or processes which individuals use in the solution of problems. This will help to ascertain where certain misunderstandings prevail, and the manner in which each contributes to an incorrect response. An evaluation of the process which a student might use in response to a problem should focus on (1) the degree to which the individual understands the problem; (2) the extent to which the problem is attacked in a systematic way as opposed to random, trial-and-error procedures; (3) how well the student is able to generate a constellation of possible solutions from a series of appropriate alternatives, and evaluate the efficacy of each; and (4) the extent to which the student is able to execute correctly the mechanistic aspects of the process involved in answering the problem.

Although the concept of ability has been mentioned in several chapters of the volume, it may be best for teachers to depend less on the notion of capacity, and instead focus their attention on student attitudes and achievement. To establish, even implicitly, upper and lower limits of ability assumes that one can accurately measure capacity. Professor Neisworth has considered the weaknesses of this assumption in Chapter 2. He points out the inherent dangers in assuming that capacity can be measured, and suggests the concept has limited value for the formulation of instructional programs. Too often the excuse has been given that a child has limited ability, and that this explains why he has not been able to achieve, when in fact the educational program itself has been lacking. The program may, for example, not be structured according to the patterns of strengths and weaknesses manifested by individual children. The appropriate position for teachers should be the study and analysis of the reasons for a child's performing poorly in any of a number of specific dimensions. By analyzing both the child's productions and the process by which he responds to a problem, the teacher will be able to formulate a justifiable remedial program.

Establishing a Profile of Differences

After the observations have been made and the data collected, the teacher should organize the information systematically in order to arrive at rational statements about each child's performance. When formal evaluative techniques are used, it is a simple matter to compare each child's performance to the standardized data, and to make a between-students (inter-individual) comparison. The teacher should compare each student's performance with appropriate normative data, and contrast each child's achievement with that of other youngsters within the class. With this type of analysis the teacher can determine the degree to which each child functions in various subject areas using the performances of his intellectual, social, and physical peers as a contrast.

In addition to these between-student analyses of performance, a comparison of each youngster's achievement should be made with himself as a reference. This contrast can be made with an individual student's performance in different subject areas. A student's performance in arithmetic might be related to his level of achievement in reading, spelling, physical ability, perceptual-motor performance, etc. A youngster's achievement in a certain subject area can be compared to his previous and subsequent performance to determine the extent to which various instructional programs have been effective.

An intra-individual profile analysis uses each child as his own reference point. This technique will help to identify the constellation of areas in which each child is experiencing problems or success, and provides the specific information one needs to structure an instructional program in response to the variety of educational difficulties that appear in many classes. Kirk (1962) and Smith (1968) have discussed this technique of profiling more comprehensively.

FORMULATING REMEDIAL STRATEGIES

Each of the contributors to this volume has emphasized the need for teachers to reduce each subject into its component parts as an aid to precise focus on the basis for each youngster's educational problem. It is too imprecise to say simply that a youngster has an arithmetic or reading problem. This broad categorization does not guide in the formulation of clear remedial measures. Children with similar levels of underachievement in reading may need entirely different remedial programs; thus, every attempt should be made to discern the instructional sequence inherent in each subject area. This effort will allow determination of where, within the instructional sequence, each youngster is faltering.

There are important instructional advantages in properly sequencing subject matter. When the components of a subject are arranged in hierarchy, one can quickly discern where instruction should begin on the basis of each child's performance on the diagnostic activities. The teacher can justifiably assume that the students have mastered the prerequisites contained in satisfactory achievement at the different instructional levels within the sequence.

Finally, teachers can gain an immediate appreciation of the types of remedial activities appropriate for each youngster from the diagnostic activities used to assess his performance. If one uses a digit-repetition task or a sequence of commands to evaluate auditory memory, these activities can be used to help the child develop greater skill in memory. The teacher should keep in mind that the same types of activities employed for diagnosis can be used for remediation.

CONCLUSION

The provision of appropriate educational prescriptions for children who are experiencing trouble in school must be based on certain relevant information about each youngster. These data must be systematically gathered by the teacher and other professional diagnosticians. The teacher should assume the responsibility for a synthesis of the information, and see that proper interpretations are made which will lead to the identification and provision of pertinent instruction. Both formal and informal assessment procedures should be conducted; diagnosis must be viewed as a continual and necessary aspect of proper instruction. The teacher should seek the advice of specialists from various disciplines throughout the process.

Those educators who do not subscribe to the belief that teachers must develop skill in educational diagnosis, and provide remediation accordingly, are implicitly suggesting that either individual variation does not exist in classes, or that, if variability is present, it is irrelevant to the instructional program. These assumptions are not supported by the evidence, and are antithetical to the conviction that every component of the educational system must strive to help children achieve their absolute best. Perhaps it is fortunate that youngsters' "absolute best" cannot be measured, thus eliminating a potentially dangerous mechanism that might be used to justify a sub-par performance on the part of teachers and their students.

REFERENCES

Kirk, S. A., *Educating Exceptional Children*. Boston: Houghton Mifflin Co., 1962.

Smith, R. M., *Clinical Teaching: Methods of Instruction for the Retarded*. New York: McGraw-Hill Book Co., 1968.

Index

Index